WRITING AT THE STATE U

WRITING AT THE STATE U

*Instruction and Administration at
106 Comprehensive Universities*

EMILY J. ISAACS

UTAH STATE UNIVERSITY PRESS
Logan

© 2018 by University Press of Colorado

Published by Utah State University Press
An imprint of University Press of Colorado
245 Century Circle, Suite 202
Louisville, Colorado 80027

The University Press of Colorado is a proud member
of the Association of University Presses.

The University Press of Colorado is a cooperative publishing enterprise supported,
in part, by Adams State University, Colorado State University, Fort Lewis College,
Metropolitan State University of Denver, Regis University, University of Colorado,
University of Northern Colorado, Utah State University, and Western State Colorado
University.

∞ This paper meets the requirements of the ANSI/NISO Z39.48-1992 (Permanence of
Paper)

ISBN: 978-1-60732-638-0 (paperback)
ISBN: 978-1-60732-639-7 (ebook)
DOI: https://doi.org/10.7330/9781607326397

Library of Congress Cataloging-in-Publication Data

Names: Isaacs, Emily J. (Emily James), author.
Title: Writing at the state U : instruction and administration at 106 comprehensive uni-
    versities / Emily J. Isaacs.
Description: Logan : Utah State University Press, [2017] | Includes bibliographical refer-
    ences and index.
Identifiers: LCCN 2017007228| ISBN 9781607326380 (pbk.) | ISBN 9781607326397
    (ebook)
Subjects: LCSH: Academic writing—Study and teaching (Higher)—United States. | State
    universities and colleges—United States.
Classification: LCC P301.5.A27 I83 2017 | DDC 808/.0420711—dc23
LC record available at https://lccn.loc.gov/2017007228

CONTENTS

FIGURES

TABLES

FOREWORD

Anne Herrington

As will be apparent to careful readers of this book, I don't write as a disinterested person. I've known Emily Isaacs since her time as a graduate student at UMass and have followed her work since then. Still, I am confident that readers will agree with my judgment that *Writing at the State U: Instruction and Administration at 106 Comprehensive Universities* demonstrates just how much can be learned from a bird's-eye view when the research is as thorough and well contextualized as Isaacs's. I use "bird's-eye view" as that is how Isaacs depicts her study, acknowledging that while it does not provide an in-depth view of any one institution, it does give a broad, multifaceted view of the state of writing programs across these institutions, ranging from staffing and curricula in first-year composition and basic writing to WAC and writing majors, from placement testing to writing centers. And it is much needed. As Isaacs notes, there have been no large-scale studies of writing programs in the past twenty years and no studies of state comprehensive colleges and universities (SCUs) although they grant baccalaureate degrees to half the students enrolled in public four-year colleges and universities in the United States.

The research study on which the book is based is impressive—well designed and comprehensive. Isaacs draws on a huge amount of data she has gleaned from public sources, instead of relying on surveys as many previous studies have done. Indeed, Isaacs is critical of survey-based studies because of sampling bias and the sometimes questionable accuracy of the data obtained. Acknowledging that she loves the hunt for information, Isaacs goes beyond information available on writing-program websites to search other institutional sites (e.g., official catalogues, registrars' offices, institutional research offices), complementing the institutional data and policies with data from such sources as NCTE, CCC, WPA, the American Association of State Colleges and Universities and State Higher Education Executive Officers Association. She also draws on a survey of WPAs at the 106 institutions, using this data as a secondary source. She further contextualizes her data in relation to

DOI: 10.7330/9781607326397.c000

previous empirical studies of writing programs—beginning with a 1927 study!—and other relevant current scholarship.

The study stands out amongst current scholarly work for its empirical nature, but Isaacs is no positivist. Indeed, she readily recognizes her interests, particularly as a former WPA at an SCU and as a person committed to equity in education. She characterizes her approach as more "reportorial" than "rhetorical," critiquing many previous studies—including Kitzhaber—that she views as overly rhetorical, putting forth claims that are often unfounded. Her aim is to be as descriptive as possible in coding and interpretation, using descriptive and inferential statistics where appropriate to analyze possible associations and correlations. Thus, the book is filled with data, ranging from class sizes to percentages of faculty and part-time instructors for first-year composition (FYC), from the percent of schools having WPAs to the percentage having writing majors, and from the percent referencing process, skills, or grammar approaches in their FYC syllabi to the percent using various forms of placement into basic writing. Isaacs comments, "I certainly fear I bore readers," but she does not. Her own interpretations of the data are evident—clearly marked to distinguish them from the "reporting"—and I appreciate the way she brings us into her thinking as she ponders the meaning of certain findings, particularly when they are counter to her expectations. I also appreciate the thorough explanation of her methods in the book, including in an appendix for those of us who are research nerds or who just want to know the research decisions that led to a certain finding. This is research transparency at its best.

Before launching into the findings about writing programs, Isaacs presents a valuable overview of the larger context of funding for public higher education, making a persuasive case that WPAs need to attend to this. She shows that while public funding has declined, institutions have made up for that decline by raising tuitions—something any of us at state institutions know all too well. But what is too rarely considered is that while schools have thereby kept a relatively stable per-student revenue stream, the percentage of expenditures for instruction have *decreased*. It is this shift in allocation of institutional dollars that helps explain staffing shifts, particularly the substantial growth in the use of part-time faculty Isaacs documents from her research. That is, she finds that for 35.8 percent of institutions, most first-year composition courses are taught by adjuncts, while for only 27.4 percent, most are taught by tenure-line faculty. Recognizing that funding patterns vary widely by state, Isaacs urges

WPAs to inform themselves of the funding statistics for their states and institutions as they work to make cases for their programs.

Looking at what she calls the "writing infrastructure" at SCUs, Isaacs sees few signs of the more radical program changes recommended by some scholars. For instance, instead of being housed in independent writing departments, 85.7 percent of FYC programs are housed in English or similar departments; 7.6 percent are found in independent writing departments. She also finds little evidence of the writing requirement's being abolished. Indeed, 67.9 percent of institutions require two courses of FYC, another 31.1 percent require one course. Isaacs also considers writing programming beyond FYC, including writing across the curriculum. Here she reports conflicting data: while survey respondents at approximately two-thirds of the schools report having WAC programs, Isaacs's review of syllabi and other institutional documents indicates just one-third have programs. She speculates that some may be informal and thus not visible in public documents and that costs may preclude formal programs at some schools.

Regarding writing-program leadership, Isaacs reports that 71.4 percent have WPAs and shows that the presence of a WPA is positively associated with greater presence of process writing methodologies and rhetorical instruction in first-year writing as well as the presence of training in writing instruction for first-year writing. As a former WPA, Isaacs considers some form of required faculty development or training essential for a coherent writing program, a view I share. Thus it is discouraging to see that only 44.9 percent of the programs in her study require some kind of faculty development or training for FYC instructors. And, while the presence of a WPA is associated with having a faculty-development or training program, only 56.7 percent of the institutions with WPAs *require* it (compared to 44.9 percent across the full sample). Isaacs points to this as an area requiring additional research to explore the reasons, including cost, contractual restrictions, and/or perceived lack of value of such programming.

Considering class size for FYC, the average is 23.3 but ranges from a low of 15 to a high of 30!—just another reminder of how conditions vary by institution. Further, the average is higher for historically black state colleges and universities (HBSU) and Hispanic-serving institutions than for institutions without these designations: 25.54 and 25.3, respectively. Isaacs acknowledges a small sample size for HBSUs (ten) and Hispanic-serving institutions (twelve). Still, she points to these differences as "unwelcome."

In terms of schools that offer basic writing, 82.3 percent use some form of standardized test for placement decisions: ACT, SAT, Accuplacer, or a state "objective" (multiple-choice) test. Acknowledging that some of these schools also supplement these tests with other methods, Isaacs finds this "outsourced solution" worrisome, particularly given recent research on the differential impact of these tests by race/ethnicity. Given the importance of testing, Isaacs urges WPAs to become more involved in local research and advocacy for "meaningful assessments that not only place students adequately but also support strong practices in teaching and learning" (78–79).

Isaacs's recommendation to WPAs is all the more important given the current attention to assessment of learning outcomes and the rush of testing companies to enter this market. While she does not report data on outcomes assessment, it is useful that she does examine the presence of outcomes statements. Drawing on institutional documents and the survey, she finds that only 22.6 percent of institutions have adopted or adapted the WPA Outcomes for their FYC courses. She also explores the question more broadly, finding that 76.4 percent have program or departmental outcomes statements, 62.3 percent of the schools have either college or university-wide outcomes statements, and 9.4 percent have statewide outcomes statements. As Isaacs points out, here's an area for future research, one important certainly for all public institutions: to consider how writing programs negotiate among these various levels of outcomes statements and, even more important, how they relate to assessment policies and practices.

To determine the instructional emphasis in FYC, Isaacs relied on course descriptions, outcomes and goals statements, and survey responses. Isaacs acknowledges that while these are limited sources for a nuanced picture, they still serve to indicate trends. Isaacs concludes that process and rhetorical approaches dominate, which is probably not surprising, although she reports an increase in the prevalence of process approaches from what Richard Larson found in 1994 (Larson 1994). A focus on skills or grammar was found at fewer than one quarter of the schools. Interestingly, process-writing features were more likely to occur in materials from research universities than from BA-granting institutions. Much to her surprise and disappointment, Isaacs also found little evidence of expressivist approaches, speculating that "the dominance of argumentation suggests that the expressive period is, indeed, on the wane." She concludes, "Perhaps today, across the country, writing teachers still place priority on and hold time for expressive writing, but it is a shame that this work that clearly people who write have always valued has been relegated to the unofficial, unarticulated landscape" (123).

Isaacs concludes with the chapter "Next Steps," which includes suggestions for those at the local level and the national level. Some of the national-level suggestions may be controversial, such as advocating for disciplinary accreditation since accrediting agencies—for example, for engineering—are able to exert pressure on institutions for change. Less controversial, she suggests that the WPA or CCCC organize a grant competition for "WPA Consultant-Evaluator Services" to aid programs that are struggling. Her focus, though, as it is throughout the book, is on WPAs and others at SCUs. Her next-step suggestions include, for example, instituting training programs for FYC if they are not already in place, attending more to placement testing, and, most important, engaging in regular self-assessments, "defining both areas of greatest pride and also areas of great concern, using the latter to create a bucket list of areas to address" (164). More than anything, this book is written for those WPAs and colleagues, and it is an invaluable resource, providing a broader context from which to view their own programs and ideas and data from which to advocate for change.

Besides the specific suggestions in the closing chapter, the book is valuable to any of us in writing studies who wish to understand trends at a large set of public institutions. Further, it points to the kind of data useful for understanding programs at our local institutions, public and private, two and four year, and it provides a model for future large-scale studies. Finally, through her research and this book, Emily Isaacs models traits of a good writing program administrator—pragmatic, practical, principled, and forward thinking. She closes thusly,

> I hope I have contributed usefully both to a discipline and to people at a class of institutions that have always exhibited an impressive practical bent and a can-do spirit. In the face of "no money," we devise work-arounds. In the face of "not interested," we do it any way. In the midst of it all, we teach writing day in and day out, reading drafts and responding to student writing, a powerful experience that makes students remember their teachers forever and makes teachers truly know where students are and what they need. (168)

It is this spirit, those principles, that drive this book.

ACKNOWLEDGMENTS

Writing at the State U is an idea that became a reality through the help of many people at my university, Montclair State University, and beyond it as well. I thank and acknowledge my faculty and staff colleagues in the English Department, three deans, and the provost, all of whom supported my wish to be an administrator *and* active teacher-researcher by granting me a sabbatical, two research grants, and support through the assignment of graduate assistants. These colleagues also supported me by allowing me time to hibernate from the push of administrative needs so I could read, write, and crunch data. Graduate assistants who worked on collecting and coding data, editing and creating charts, and many other tasks, are Janine Butler, Vera Lentini, and Joe DeGuzman. Being an administrator who is also active in research is only possible when those around us are willing to make accommodations for such research, as has been my case. For this support I especially thank Phyllis Brooks, Holly DenBleyker, Rob Friedman, Willard Gingerich, Kim Harrison, Luis Montesinos, Marietta Morrissey, and Minnie Parker.

My research community of scholars who have helped me think about my project begins with Melinda Knight, who is responsible for first getting me on the trail of pursuing questions of the state of the field through collecting publicly available information, but it does not end there. I owe much to the 2011 Dartmouth Summer Seminar for Writing Research, organized by researcher-administrator par excellence, Christiane Donoghue, and led by Christiane and also Chris Anson, Charles Bazerman, Cheryl Geisler, Chris Haas, Neal Lerner, and Les Perelman. Special thanks to my coding and research partner, Julie Bleakney. At Montclair State University, colleagues Caroline Dadas and Jessica Restaino have rooted for me all along the way, attending more 4Cs presentations than they could possibly have been interested in; Andrew McDougall from the university's math department for originally selecting my sample for statistical significance; and Emily Dow, instructor in the Department of Psychology, provided invaluable support through her statistical prowess and also as an unexpected but valuable reader of drafts of the manuscript. Of extreme help were individuals at state comprehensive universities who completed surveys, and special thanks to

Sarah Arroyo, Teresa Burns, Jackie Cason, Alan P. Church, John Gooch, Brenda Helmbrecht, Aviva Taubenfeld, and Amy Woodworth, all of whom participated with me on a CCCCs panel sponsored by this project. Finally, I have had many advisers, including two anonymous reviewers, the supremely sympathetic and focusing Michael Spooner at Utah State University Press, and my forever readers-mentors-cheerleaders, Norbert Elliot and Anne Herrington. Family, with their capacity to focus on the bottom line (Is it done yet?) as well as their total faith in my intellectual capacity and indefatigable nature, have been crucial, from Toby, Joshy, and Jamie Modiano, to my spouse Paul Modiano, and my role model, my mother, Nancy Bixler Isaacs.

WRITING AT THE STATE U

1
TEACHING, ADMINISTERING, AND SUPPORTING WRITING AT THE STATE COMPREHENSIVE UNIVERSITY

Writing at the State U: Instruction and Administration at 106 Comprehensive Universities[1] presents a detailed, contextualized, and empirical analysis of the state of writing programming at four-year state comprehensive universities, a broad classification that includes research universities, MA-granting universities, and BA-granting colleges. The idea of this book began with an idea for another book: I wanted to write about the challenges but also possibilities for great writing instruction and support at US state comprehensive universities (SCUs),[2] as this was a subject with which I was deeply, and personally, familiar. I believed I had figured out how to be an effective writing program administrator (WPA) at my school, Montclair State University in New Jersey, although it had taken close to a decade of hard work to create, organize, and support writing curricula, programming, and approaches to staffing and faculty development of which I could be proud. Along the journey I had often felt apart—and sometimes excluded—from the scholarly conversation on writing program administration, as it was so often set within the context of the research university or, less frequently, the small college. I received invaluable support from the WPA listserv and from conference conversations where WPAs from SCUs abound. But my long and often lonely journey to develop a strong and well-regarded writing program at an SCU made me want to reach out and provide support to writing faculty and WPAs in similar situations and also to graduate faculty at research universities whose preparation of these faculty is limited by their own research-university contexts. From my conversations with WPAs and writing faculty at SCUs, I know many wonder how they can shape a good program without what the doctoral programs they had graduated from had been equipped with: graduate students to teach the majority of the classes (and who could be required to take a graduate class in writing studies); a staff of directors, coordinators,

DOI: 10.7330/9781607326397.c001

and secretaries; and a cohort of writing studies colleagues to work with, among other assets. The book I thought I'd write was inspired by my wish to show what could be done. (In fact, a lot can be done, and many departures from what is possible at a research university actually amount to a superior writing experience for the undergraduates we are pledged to serve because comprehensive universities, like BA-granting institutions, are typically less beholden to research and doctoral-education imperatives that can deemphasize undergraduate education).

However, I soon realized that what I really knew was what I had done at Montclair State University. I had a great case study. But I didn't know much about what was happening in other writing programs at other SCUs that weren't specifically represented in the scholarship or run by personal friends. With experience working with my colleague Melinda Knight on a study that used publicly available information to study writing at 101 top universities, I believed publicly available information would allow me to sample and explore a large number of SCUs so as to draw a much fuller, albeit bird's-eye, portrait. With Melinda, I had found that much can be discovered about how an institution teaches and administers writing by combing carefully and systematically through publicly available information. With these goals and primary method established, I developed these research questions:

1. To what extent have established principles and practices of writing instruction and administration been implemented at state comprehensive universities?

2. In what ways is writing instruction at state comprehensive institutions, as a class, different from writing instruction at other classes of institutions, and from writing instruction at different historical time periods?

3. How are the major scholarly debates in FYC instruction and WP administration reflected—or not—at state comprehensive universities?

My strategy for investigating these questions was to collect existing data that would reasonably be available at all institutions in a large sample, from catalogs and other publicly available data, to get a robust, bird's-eye view. But first I had to select a sample, thus raising the question, what is a state comprehensive university?

STATE COMPREHENSIVE COLLEGES AND UNIVERSITIES: HOW THEY FIT IN THE HIGHER EDUCATION LANDSCAPE

The category of SCUs, also called *regional public universities*, is fairly broad, including selective state institutions (e.g., James Madison

University in Virginia), large research universities (e.g., Texas A&M, Northern Arizona University), and even very small institutions (e.g., University of Maine at Presque Isle and Mayville State in North Dakota). As an institutional class, the SCU is subject to less scholarly attention than is the flagship state university, yet according to the association that represents SCUs, the American Association for State Colleges and Universities, collectively, SCUs enroll 3.8 million students, occupying a kind of middle ground within the public-education landscape between the most elite research university and the small private college or the community college. Informally, the SCU is well known in higher education and to the public; there are approximately 420 such institutions nationwide (American Association of State Colleges and Universities 2010).[3] Thus, greater understanding of writing programming at SCUs is valuable not only to the institutions that fall under this classification but also to higher education and writing researchers who wish to understand the state of college writing in the country today. Surprisingly, to date, in the robust and expanding body of scholarship devoted to writing program administration, no writing scholar has specifically attended to SCUs as a class, even though these institutions grant baccalaureate degrees to half[4] the students enrolled in public US four-year colleges and universities and 28 percent of all students attending private or public four-year colleges or universities (American Association of State Colleges and Universities 2014, 11).

STUDY DESIGN

Institutional class selected, I designed my methods for investigation. Following Richard Haswell's (2005) call for empirically based scholarship and bolstered by Dan Melzer's (2009, 2014) work analyzing writing assignments through an Internet-based search process, among others, I sought a method that would enable me to speak broadly about national trends. Although researchers in writing studies have historically developed samples by sending out invitations to participate in a survey, for this study I chose to select a representative sample and gather most of my data independent of these participants. In choosing a master list of institutions to sample from, I selected the membership list of the American Association of State Colleges and Universities (AASCU), as I wanted a list that would provide a cross-section of colleges and universities that represent a broad and diverse range of public four-year institutions. AASCU schools range from student enrollments of 845 to 58,000, with an average enrollment of 10,430; collectively, they are responsible for educating 51 percent of all minority students and 48 percent of students who enroll in public four-year institutions (American Association of State Colleges and Universities 2014, 9–11),[5] facilitating my goals of discovering what is happening in the vast middle of public, four-year higher education. The 106-institution sample was pulled from the AASCU list randomly after stratification by region and size.[6] (I aimed for a sample of about 100 and ended up with 106, as this was the number that allowed for statistical representation of the sample in respect to region and size). Building on previous researchers' methodologies (Burhans 1983; Sideris 2004), during the fall of 2011, I collected all catalogs or bulletins and searched institutional websites to find documents that provided answers to the variable list I had identified, drawing on the methodologies developed with Melinda Knight for the "top university study." Thus, for each institution I have a host of assessment reports, captured websites, and schedule snapshots along with official catalogs or bulletins. Data were located in similar places: catalogs first and foremost but also Institutional Research reports, department and program websites, assessment units' publications, and registrar documents and reports. This primary data set was then amplified by a survey distributed to identified and confirmed leaders at each of the schools; this method provided some additional data and allowed for triangulation through cross-checking.

Preliminary data gathered, to develop specific questions and a first draft of categories to use for sorting data pertaining to these questions, I drew on previous state-of-the-field studies, of which there are many, beginning with Warner Taylor in 1929 (see table 2.1 for a comprehensive list of studies). For some areas of inquiry, scholarship within the field prompted me to develop additional categories (e.g., prominent discussion of the writing-about-writing movement led me to include this category). These initial drafts of variables and associated categories (or values), developed prior to data collection, were expanded and revised significantly as I collected and reviewed the data (e.g., I added categories in placement methods, such as the international baccalaureate, as the data taught me about possibilities that previous researchers hadn't discussed.) Thus, like many other writing studies researchers (e.g., Barton and Donahue 2009; Brandt 2014; Dadas 2013; Gladstein and Regaignon 2012; Purcell-Gates, Perry, and Briseno 2011), I was guided by a grounded-theory approach (Birks and Mills 2015; Glaser and Strauss 1967). Through a process of moving back and forth from research on other data sets to reviewing data I had collected, I created a list of 148 variables to guide my further data collection. The variable list is too lengthy for inclusion here, so it can be found in appendix D.

I have arranged the variable list with notations that explain my sources for each variable, notations about my sources, and notations about how conflicts were resolved when conflicts existed between two sources (e.g., between the catalog and the survey response).

In the presentation of my study discoveries, I compare my findings to those presented by previous researchers (e.g., Burhans 1983; Gere 2009; Kitzhaber 1962, 1963; Larson 1994; Moghtader, Cotch, and Hague 2001; Smith 1974; Taylor 1929; Wilcox 1968, 1969, 1972, 1973; Witte, Cherry, and Meyer 1982; Witte et al. 1981; Witte, Meyer, and Miller 1982). In my selection of data, I have sought out a range of evidentiary points that help build multifaceted, measurable constructs for understanding FYC instruction in the sample, similar to the construct-representation work undergone to develop *The Frameworks for Success in Postsecondary Writing Instruction* (O'Neill et al. 2012), which constructs writing success as gained from the development of necessary "habits of mind" and also from experiences with a variety of "writing, reading, and critical analysis experiences" (O'Neill et al. 2012).

Variable types include the following range:

Quantitative variables—for example, how many courses in FYC are required?

Categorical-descriptive—for example, what is the title of the WPA's position?

Categorical-dichotomous—for example, is there a WAC requirement? (yes or no)

Categorical-nominal variables—for example, what instruments or methods are used for placement decisions?

Categorical-ordinal variables (variables that can be ranked)—for example, what level of autonomy do faculty have in designing syllabi?

Data collected, I worked systematically, alone or with a research assistant, to code the data. Many of the data were quantitative or of a categorical nature that required little interpretation. However, where interpretation was required, I worked with a research assistant, blind double coding and then discussing the cases we disagreed on. More details about the data collection and coding methods are provided in the appendices (see apps. A and C), though I'll make two other points. First, my effort in data gathering was to lean toward the simplest, most reliable data points by asking questions for which the responses were indisputable—numeric or categorical. Second, I ventured into interpretative areas with care and some ground rules: when I made judgments regarding the emphases of courses and programs as determined by reading course descriptions and outcomes-related documents, I coded this data with a second coder with coding sheets that were pretested for high interrater reliability.

Data coded, I conducted my analysis through both quantitative and qualitative means. The quantitative analyses begin with reporting frequencies but also with identifying and reporting associations among variables, allowing readers to see when conditions converge. Thus, through the help of basic descriptive and inferential statistics, I was able to conduct association, correlation, and cross-tabulation analyses to provide indicators of the variables that typically were present when practices were consonant with those advocated for in the literature and by our national organizations, and to show when they were not. For example, the presence of a tenure-track WPA is positively associated with smaller class size, an emphasis on rhetorical instruction, and professional training of writing teachers. Along with presenting correlations and associations within the data and against data pulled from the Carnegie Classification database (Carnegie Foundation 2011), in my analysis I compare my findings to relevant studies on the state of the field, along with findings from a 2010 study (data-collection date) I conducted (Isaacs and Knight 2012, 2014). In this study, which I will refer to as the *top university study*, Knight and I collected data on 101 four-year colleges and universities, across institutional type, based on a selection derived from the annual rankings published by *US News and World Report*.

THE VALUE AND LIMITATIONS OF THE BIRD'S-EYE VIEW

In the last decade, the discipline has embraced empirical methodologies, both close, careful studies by researchers such as writing center scholars Isabelle Thompson and Jo Mackiewicz (Mackiewicz and Thompson 2013, 2014; Thompson 2006, 2009; Thompson and Mackiewicz 2013; Thompson et al. 2009) and what I call a bird's-eye view by WAC researchers like Thaiss and Porter (2010) and Melzer (2014) and by the team of researchers working on the ongoing WPA/WCD (writing center director) study (Fralix et al. 2015). Bird's-eye studies in our field typically use surveys and self-reporting as their primary means for data collection. Mass survey was quite possibly the best option for many years, and there has been so much published research based on voluntary survey that the method is seldom questioned. Yet, this method relies on information provided by interested, willing parties. Does the investment of these individuals matter? Does this investment skew the results? These are the questions I asked when I designed this study. SCUs tend to include many colleges and universities that will not be represented on these surveys because they do not have WPAs or other faculty and staff who partici- pate on the WPA and similar listservs and who are willing to answer the many surveys distributed through these listservs. I think any real under- standing of the impact of our field requires that we gather and report on what is happening at institutions that are not part of our community as defined by membership in one of our field's organizations. Thus, to avoid the problem of the self-selection skew, essential to my study were two decisions: to random sample and to gather data through publicly available information.

Thus this study is most similar to those conducted by Witte and col- leagues, and also by Ron Smith, studies at least twenty years old (Larson 1994; Smith 1974; Witte et al. 1981; Witte, Cherry, and Meyer 1982; Witte, Meyer, and Miller 1982). I was interested to see any evidence of recent changes to the higher education landscape, such as the increase in reliance on contingent faculty; the rise in assessment and accountabil- ity; the development of extensive university and college websites; and the 2008 reauthorization of the Higher Education Act that requires col- leges and universities to publicly (via the Internet) report course sched- ules, transfer policies, and other relevant information (Tromble 2008). We are more public with our practices and processes, as the interest in accountability has risen with concerns over debt and graduation rates, giving rise to increased federal investigation and oversight and require- ments for increasingly public reporting by colleges and universities (White, Elliot, and Peckham 2015, 12).

There are drawbacks to the bird's-eye approach as well. First and foremost, the approach precludes a close view, so texture, details, and, most of all, explanations for choices made are not provided. This study does not tell you *why* phenomena have occurred; it simply tells you *what* has occurred. For textured close studies of the challenges of practical implementation of best practices in the field, we are fortunate to have many and varied case studies and multi-institutional studies to review. Second, the analyses, and the conclusions I draw, are based on what can be found through public-document and website review. Some of these conclusions are more subject to debate than others based on the nature of the inquiry. Thus, for example, class size based on the numbers I gath- ered from looking at actual course schedules strikes me as pretty close to indisputable, with the caveat that the data are tied to one specific semes- ter. However, I also report on such matters as emphasis on rhetorical instruction and argumentation in FYC, relying on course descriptions from official catalogs and outcomes-type statements found in the cata- log, in reports, and on university and college websites. I imagine faculty might quarrel with the findings here, noting that these public documents are either out of date, political, or simply do not tell the whole story. These are reasonable points to make, so readers should remain aware that the story here is based on the *public* record. Quite simply, the quality and quantity of data provided in reliable public sources shaped my study greatly.

This study does not benefit from the kind of insider and deep knowledge that an interview or review of a range of syllabi would present. However, as Clinton Burhans asserted thirty years ago, from this kind of information (today electronically mined, in his day sent by post mail) we can find "an informative and reasonably indicative body of data" (Burhans 1983, 640). I have read and coded hundreds of these institutional documents, with support from a second coder when data required any interpretation or judgment. Through this process I have come to value the powerful signaling that phrases such as these indicate: *writing as a process*; *rhetorical awareness* and *purpose and audience* on the one hand and *effective written products, fundamentals of writing,* and *grammar, usage, and mechanics* on the other. All these phrases, and ones like it, were found throughout the data, again and again, contributing to readers' sense of the construct of writing each institution is presenting. As explained by Edward White, Norbert Elliot, and Irvin Peckham, "[A] writing construct is that stated conceptualization of writing that informs a writing program and its assessment" (White, Elliot, and Peckham 2015), though it is also clear that institutions articulate writing constructs repeatedly, and while my methodology captured several of those articulated constructs, it only captured those that are part of the public record.

Representatives at SCUs have also reminded me of the varying degrees to which outcomes for their courses are made public via their websites, suggesting another limitation (that is lessened by the survey). As another prime example of a limitation, originally I planned much greater investigation of writing centers, but little material about writing centers is consistently available in institutional catalogs or in other public documents. Whereas one institution would present a writing center's mission and approach, another one would only inform external readers of its services. In my discussion of data points, I have described the sources of my data in an effort to invite readers to consider the limitations of the findings. Nonetheless, I think there is value in what I have found, for in this age of readily available information via the Internet, and of public and government pressure on higher education to be transparent and accountable, what can be gleaned about writing instruction through public, official, and available documents is increasingly extensive and important.

Beyond limitations due to methodology, this research is limited by my own point of view, as is always the case with human research. A brief discussion of my own standpoint and the biases, assumptions, and gaps these generate is necessary, particularly because I come to this project with an argument about the collective skew of previous studies toward writing studies' "insiders" and therefore weighted against SCUs. First, I have worked at New Jersey's Montclair State University, an SCU, for twenty years. I am one of those academics who has never intellectually strayed too far from her graduate-school roots. I was trained at the University of Massachusetts Amherst, where I studied with Anne Herrington, Charles Moran, Peter Elbow, and Marcia Curtis, who taught from a strong commitment to basic writing, first-year composition, process writing, WAC, humanistic assessment, and a belief that writing is always personally and individually inflected. As Herrington and Curtis wrote in *Persons and Process*, their study of four students' experiences with college writing, "Students . . . use the drafting process as much to configure their identities in relation to their various subjects as to master the forms, genres, and language in which these subjects were conveyed" (Herrington and Curtis 2000, 383). I suspect that my principle ideas about what effective writing instruction and administration look like have been deeply informed by those experiences: thus I am positively inclined toward FYC, process writing, and WAC, and I am suspicious of and disinclined toward assessment methodologies and writing instruction that removes the subjectivity of the writer from writing. Beyond formal schooling, the people I have always been around—at home in suburban Boston, and then at UMass and Montclair, have taught me the (not exclusively) northeastern values of irony, skepticism, moral responsibility, the Western intellectual tradition, and—hard to admit—perhaps intellectual superiority. I work against the latter especially, but it really is in the drinking water I've been sipping for fifty years. More personally, I am a middle-class, middle-aged, straight white woman with three sons still some years from college. Over the years I think I have become more conservative in some ways (for which I blame parenthood principally), but both personally and professionally, I haven't changed at all in respect to my deep, practically instinctive interest in working to advance the possibilities of those who, by the luck of birth, face a more difficult road in terms of education and economic and social possibilities. Finally, in the five years I have worked on this project, I have gone from WPA to English department chair to associate dean. I hope the move up the administrative ladder has served to make me more familiar with the context in which decisions about teaching and administering writing programs are made, though I am aware that there are readers who believe little is gained and much is lost when an individual moves from teacher to administrator. I think my standpoint, which I have surely not adequately explored, shaped the questions I asked in this study in large and small ways: from the sample selection and focus on SCUs to my deep attention to FYC and my decision to look for—although I did not find it—evidence of expressionism in these schools' approaches to FYC.

In summary, while this study is in the vein of many earlier studies, perhaps Witte and colleagues' most of all (Witte, Cherry, and Meyer 1982; Witte, Meyer, and Miller 1982; Witte et al. 1981), *Writing at the State U* provides historical context while capitalizing on publicly available data and fairly simple statistical analyses that have not often been used by researchers who have conducted "status" research of this nature.

CHAPTER OVERVIEW

I have often been asked to characterize my findings along the lines of this question: is the news for SCUs good or bad? Judgment—good or bad—depends on what your priorities are. For example, do you care most about class size or instructional approach? Assessment methodologies or the extent of faculty training? The presence of WPAs or reliance on adjunct faculty? An increase in writing majors or the presence of any kind of vertical writing programming? Further, even within a single area of inquiry, whether or not you perceive the findings as good or bad depends on your level of optimism or pessimism about the practical possibilities of implementation of best practices in the contemporary landscape of public higher education, which is, as always, limited by either budgetary priorities or budgets themselves and a culture that historically hasn't focused on writing instruction, much less seen writing studies as a discipline. If you come to this book as an optimist, you'll read much herein that will disappointment you; but, if you are more pessimistic, I think you'll find much that pleasantly surprises. I myself vacillate between these attitudes: on the one hand, I went into this study worried that the majority of SCUs had been largely left out of the writing revolution of the last half century (not the case!), and on the other hand, based on my own experience, I was aware that radical change was possible. So look to the findings of this study with an awareness of your own dispositional instincts and also, perhaps, of your subjective position as determined by what kind of institution you have worked in, as likely those local experiences deeply affect what you expect to be possible elsewhere. A brief story to illustrate that point: recently I had the opportunity to spend time with faculty at an Ivy, and when the discussion turned to graduation rates for undergraduates at US colleges and universities, otherwise well-informed faculty from this institution could not believe me that national six-year graduation rates were about 60 percent. From their vantage point, anything less than 90 percent for *four-year graduation* was unacceptable, and also unfathomable.

In the chapters that follow, I present my findings not only in the context of the historical record and previous studies, detailed in chapter 2, but also within the often-heated theoretical debates that surround the data. Thus, within discussions of the major findings, I provide a snapshot history of the debates that surround the major findings, which I think will provide valuable understanding to readers. Two examples should be useful: the question of the role of literature in first-year composition and the question of independence for the discipline of writing studies. Some readers might think that the issue of literature in composition is a dead one, resolved long ago, but the issue will simply not be put to rest, as evidenced by the presence of literature in composition courses (see chapter 3) and also the currency of the question in the scholarly research (just published in the last decade include Anderson and Farris 2007; Bergmann and Baker 2006; Foley and Huber 2009; Isaacs 2009; Raymond 2010). For readers who have not had first-hand experience with a comp-lit war, some sense of the history of this debate is useful in understanding its importance and why it remains an issue. Similarly, the issue of writing studies independence has been the subject of journal discussion since at least 1975 (Tade, Tate, and Corder 1975), and the question has generated reams of scholarship (see, for example, Balzhiser and McLeod 2010; Carpini 2007; Cushman 2003; Estrem 2007; Farris 2013; Giberson and Moriarty 2010; Howard 2007; Lowe 2007; Mendenhall 2013; National Council of Teachers of English 2009; O'Neill, Crow, and Burton 2002; Schumaker 1982; Scott 2007; Shamoon and Martin 2007; Taylor 2007; Weisser and Grobman 2012). Yet, as is made clear in chapter 5, scholarly discussion (fulsome and promising) and practice (not much happening) can be far apart.

Readers who, understandably, simply need answers are welcome to skim through the book for figures and tables (listed after the table of contents) or to simply turn to the chapter-end summary boxes of statistics I think are most likely to be useful on a practical level. The chapters are written as stories of what has happened all around the data—the issues and the other studies—but there are times when an administrator simply needs the bottom-line statistics.

In chapter 2, "Assessments of Writing Studies' Practices: 1927 to the Present Study," I give a historical review of many of the studies that precede this one, tracing the development of questions and concerns that have occupied scholars. These include questions about FYC course focus, approach, and staffing, the status of the faculty and administrators who support FYC, and such issues as placement and course substitutions, as well as institutional issues such as the placement of writing studies within a college or university. Throughout these studies are references to fiscal support and the great challenge of finding appropriate funding for teaching and supporting writing. It's a recurring theme: anticipating, surviving, or recovering from budget crises. This theme gives rise to the final substantive section of the historical review—understanding the last twenty-five years of funding for public higher education. While writing studies scholars typically do not go beyond the popular press or the *Chronicle of Higher Education* to understand public higher education funding, my review of National Center for Education Statistics (NCES) and State Higher Education Executive Officers (SHEEO) research studies as well as analyses by higher education economists suggest to me that we are missing part of the picture: while support for public higher education has undoubtedly decreased, tuition increases have quite ably enabled institutions to maintain the same relative per-student dollars for spending, deeply discounting claims that the "current" state of affairs for funding writing studies staffing is merely the effect of budget cuts. I urge readers to wade into the perhaps unfamiliar waters of NCES and SHEEO reports and the *Journal of Higher Education* or, at the very least, to pay attention to this review in chapter 2. We must understand and broadcast that this state of affairs of, most pointedly, relying increasingly on adjuncts is not merely a case of decreased dollars but is rather the effect of priorities.

In chapter 3, "The Back End of First-Year Composition: Institutional Support through Infrastructure and Policies," I report on the institutional structures that undergird what colleges and universities are able to do with FYC. Faculty may have little or no influence in the matters of class size, administrative release for writing program administration, options for staffing, and the ability to offer students credit-bearing basic writing instruction, despite the importance to these matters of teaching writing well. These structures and policies are typically decided upon at college, university, or even state levels and not at the programmatic or departmental level, though they deeply affect what faculty are able to do in terms of writing instruction. I report on infrastructure and support provided for FYC through discussion of FYC program location, WPA administrator status, and course staffing, looking at these findings in comparison to previous studies, other populations, and in respect to institutional type. In the area of assessment, I look at placement and exemption provisions at these schools, finding that there are many more options than I believe many of us realize—these agreements and arrangements being made at a high institutional or state level. In this chapter, significant differences are shown to be associated with institutional size and institutional selectivity, with FYC students in nonselective colleges and universities most likely to be taught by a tenure-track professor.

In chapter 4, "What Are We Doing in First-Year Composition?," I examine the impact the field has on general education writing instruction at SCUs. To report on the contents of first-year composition courses, I relied on catalogs, websites, and official institutional documents and also on representatives' reports of practices gathered through the survey, as discussed in appendix A. I report on SCUs' FYC requirement: its presence and absence, as well as instructional emphases, number of courses, and use of outcomes statements or other articulations of student-learning expectations. I report on what these SCUs are doing in respect to research instruction and the study of literature and describe and categorize the foci of these courses. SCUs' emphasis on process writing methodologies and skills instruction is also explored. In reporting on these findings, I have identified characteristics significantly associated with institutional characteristics, such as school size (pulled from the Carnegie Classification's system), region, salient instructional practices, characteristics of the faculty, and administrative structures. My research reveals FYC as deeply embedded in SCUs, with course content often paradoxically at once in and out of sync with the field's recommendations for best practices.

In chapter 5, "Beyond First-Year Composition," I discuss writing in the disciplines, general education writing, writing centers, and vertical writing programming to offer a view of how public colleges and universities are addressing writing beyond the first-year composition requirement. In this section I look at the scholarship on vertical writing programming from WAC to the development of minors and majors in writing studies, and I compare what I observed at SCUs to what is reported by other researchers. In addition, I report on the presence of writing centers and their locations, considering these findings against other studies, as well as on the debate over writing center fiscal and administrative location.

In chapter 6, "Writing at the State Comprehensive U," I summarize major findings of the study and address the future of writing instruction, administration, and support at SCUs. I offer strategies and suggestions for improving writing instruction and support at state comprehensive colleges and universities, identifying those areas most under faculty control. In addition, I speculate on some roles national leaders and organizations such as NCTE might take on to think and act as a discipline, not as faculty at individual institutions.

In appendix A, I provide a more detailed description of the methods used to conduct this study and analysis. I provide a narrative of my method and share some of the dilemmas I addressed during the course of designing and implementing the study. Data collection is pinned to the fall 2011 semester. With very few exceptions, all catalogs and bulletins cover that time period, and other publicly available documents from university and college websites were pulled during the period from September 1, 2011, to December 31, 2011. In addition, the survey was sent out and completed during that same time period. Drawing on both the experiences of other researchers who have shared their methods and my own experiences, I attempted to fashion a method that would get me a full bird's-eye view: distanced, but wide. Not surprisingly, my methodological choices resulted in many drawbacks or limitations, which I outline more fully in appendix A. Appendix B is a reproduction of the online survey completed by representatives at ninety-two of the institutions in the sample. In appendix C, readers will find the coding sheets I developed and relied upon. The final two appendices are lists: appendix D presents the variables as I had them organized in SPSS (software for analyzing data), and appendix E lists all the institutions in the study.

I hope that *Writing at the State U* will provide a baseline for other researchers who advocate for particular writing-programming approaches and analyze trends in the field. I especially hope this book will also be useful to writing faculty at state comprehensive universities who wish to understand better the trends and possibilities at institutions like their own for practical, local consideration and action. I imagine two different types of readers. First, writing program faculty and administrators who are in the midst of a crisis (a common state of affairs) and need information quickly should review the table of contents or index to find the section where such information is discussed and also consult the end-of-chapter statistical-summary boxes. Second, readers who are concerned about and interested in writing at the state comprehensive university will find in *Writing at the State U* a story about writing studies others who have surveyed the field have not yet told. In sum, readers will learn that while there are pockets of deep concern at SCUs, the evidence suggests that the practice of writing instruction and support has advanced significantly in concert with the field's maturation. The state comprehensive university is a major part of the four-year higher education landscape and thus should be as well understood as the research university and the small liberal arts college.

Notes

1. Project approved by the Montclair State University Internal Review Board.
2. The term *state comprehensive university*, and its acronym SCU, was selected over *public regional university*, which is also used frequently, in deference to Bruce B. Henderson of Western Carolina University, who has published extensively on SCUs and who founded a journal by this name (Henderson 2007).
3. The exact number depends on source data and definition; for example, the Carnegie Classification system and the AASCU have different numbers.
4. Enrollment paints a similar picture: the National Center for Educational Statistics reports that 7,709,197 students were enrolled in four-year public institutions in the fall of 2009; AASCU reports that 3,800,000 students were enrolled in their member institutions (AASCU 2010)
5. The National Center for Education Statistics, in a 2009 report, reports that 7,709,197 students were enrolled in four-year state institutions; the American Association of State Colleges and Universities claims 3.8 million students at their member institutions. AASCU is open to all state institutions, whereas the Association of Public and Land-Grant Universities (APLU) caters to public research universities only.
6. In statistics, stratification is a method of sampling designed to improve representativeness of a sample. More specifically, it refers to a method of sampling wherein subgroups are created (in this case, by region and by size) and sampled first prior to randomly sampling the entire population.

2

ASSESSMENTS OF WRITING STUDIES' PRACTICES
1927 to the Present Study

Central to the analysis in *Writing at the State U* is comparison: of the findings of this study with historical and contemporary studies of similar and dissimilar data sets that focus on questions similar to my own and against the scholarly, theoretical discussions I present as a backdrop to the investigation. While the study presented in this book is unique in method and in its focus on SCUs, it follows many others in pursuing the question of the state of higher education writing instruction in the United States. Throughout this book, readers will find references to these other data sets and the conclusions made by these researchers. Empirical studies in writing studies take many forms: the "scene of writing" has expanded since our early investigation, as noted by Roozen and Lunsford (2012), and so too have our methods. I emphasize the historical record of this strand of empirical research—focused on our methods for teaching, administering, and supporting postsecondary writing—as I have observed that writing studies scholars in the past and today tend to perceive their current (bad) conditions as extraordinary and atypical when in fact, more often than not, they are neither. Situating quantitative findings amidst the historical story follows the call for "research in context" put forth by Cindy Johanek, who observes that "narratives and numbers often coexist in some fashion in most research contexts," though too much research relies too exclusively on one or the other (Johanek 2000, 114). Ultimately, in this presentation of research in historical and comparative context, readers can see the ways in which my hypothesis that SCUs are a unique class is correct, and where it is not.

DOI: 10.7330/9781607326397.c002

1927: WARNER TAYLOR ESTABLISHES SURVEY METHODOLOGY AND MAJOR QUESTIONS

To begin this historical review, we have been asking questions about the state of our practice since at least 1927 when Warner Taylor sought to understand the state of "Freshman English" by sending questionnaires (77.3 percent returned) to representatives at 232 colleges and universities that addressed such issues as patterns in textbook selection, curricular emphasis (including such issues as presence of literature and emphasis on particular genres), and approaches to placement and exemption. Taylor's findings are discussed throughout this book, which I have organized by area of inquiry and topic, detailed in the table of contents and later in this chapter. However, what comes through in this early study by Taylor, and in several subsequent studies, is the sense that the researcher believes we are at the edge of a significant change: "There is unquestionably, if not a spirit of unrest over Freshman English through the country, at least a spirit of inquiry" (Taylor 1929, 3). For Taylor, there is an inconsistency between the "disquietude" expressed at Modern Language Association (MLA) meetings and the practices revealed through his study. Thus, he finds unrest has yet to take shape into action, noting that "the course stands fundamentally as it was a decade or more ago. More colleges are using placement tests for sectionizing students today, fewer are using standard rhetorics; but at bottom traditional practices persevere" (3).

Another trend that reoccurs across these studies, starting with Taylor, is evidence of the difficulty of staffing first-year composition, with researchers expressing concern for both teachers who are undervalued and underpaid and students who are taught by faculty who are poorly prepared. Taylor reports that few faculty of "professional" rank teach freshman English, expressing dim hope for improvement: "In some future Eden, perhaps, Freshmen will be taught by the oldest and wisest members of a department" (17).

1955: EMERSON SHUCK ADVANCES METHODOLOGIES AND BEGINS STUDY OF WRITING PROGRAM ADMINISTRATION

Emerson Shuck, writing in 1955, was one of the first researchers[1] on the state of FYC to publish his research in *College Composition and Communication*, which had its inaugural issue in 1950 and was designed to serve college teachers of composition and communication by providing a "systematic way of exchanging views and information quickly" and for "developing a coordinated research program" (Gerber 1950).

Shuck, from Bowling Green State University, reported on two question-naire surveys he administered: one in 1953 that was sent to thirty-five midwestern institutions, "selected to give a representative cross-section of types and sizes" (Shuck 1955, 205), with a return rate of 74 percent; and a second in 1954 that was sent to 83 "multi-purpose" US institutions, with enrollments between twenty-five hundred and seven thousand (effectively eliminating both very small and very large institutions), with a return rate of 84 percent. Shuck was unusual in his interest in regional differences and in the effects of institutional size, enabling him to pro-vide evidence for the importance of these variables. Thus, for example, Shuck finds a relationship between school size and class size, noting that schools with 1,000 or more students in freshman English have an average class size of 24.7 students per section compared to a class size of 23.8 at institutions with 500–999 students and 22.1 at institutions with 300–499 students. While he doesn't report on statistical significance for these differences, his methodology represents an important step in coming to understand the factors—both within and outside our con-trol—that affect the conditions of first-year composition instruction. Shuck, following Earl Sasser (1952) and Taylor (1929), also focuses on placement and exemption, looking to see how colleges and universi-ties identify and provide for their strongest and weakest writers. These researchers' concerns were prompted by rising enrollments, fears about poor preparation, and particular interest in the "superior student" who, Shuck finds, is typically provided for through placement in advanced or "fast" sections (207). Shuck's final section is devoted to "Administrative structure" (208), signaling the first of many efforts to understand how departments (at this point, almost always English departments) manage FYC, addressing issues that remain today: from whether or not a WPA is needed—61 percent of Shuck's respondents thought so (209)—to the kinds of tasks and decisions appropriately managed by a director, chair, or committee or left to individual faculty discretion.

1960S: RESEARCHERS VARY IN METHODOLOGY BUT UNITE IN LEVELING SHARP CRITICISM

The 1960s saw several studies published on the state of FYC: by Albert Kitzhaber (1962, 1963), Thomas Wilcox (1968, 1969, 1972, 1973), and Bonnie Nelson (1968),[2] with the most frequently referenced being Kitzhaber's study, ultimately published as *Themes, Theories, and Therapy: The Teaching of Writing in College*, sponsored by the Carnegie Foundation. The methods for Kitzhaber's study are not entirely clear: he writes that he collected syllabi from ninety-five four-year colleges and universities he describes as a "fairly representative cross section of American institutions of higher education" (Kitzhaber 1963, 9). We don't know how he determined that the sample was a cross-section, how he selected schools, or how many, if any, of the selected institutions didn't participate. Kitzhaber also unevenly expanded his sample data by informally selecting and then visiting eighteen institutions. I suspect Kitzhaber's study is a kind of touchstone because of his prominence and centrality to the field (president of NCTE, author *Rhetoric in American Colleges, 1850–1900* and dozens of articles and reports, keynote speaker at the 1966 Dartmouth Seminar and the Anglo-American Conference on the Teaching and Learning of English) and because he writes so well and persuasively and is not shy about making grand claims. His methods, however, do not lend confidence to his findings. Whereas Sasser and Shuck stay close to the ground, focusing on reporting and limiting their editorial comments, Kitzhaber uses data to support a series of critiques that read as though they were developed prior to data collection. In the excerpt below, we can see Kitzhaber's writing style as well as his principal research conclusions.

> Anyone reading this many syllabuses or visiting this many freshman English programs—or even a fraction of the number—would almost certainly be struck by at least three main weaknesses of the course as it is now constituted. First, he would be impressed by the confusion exhibited in the course—a widespread uncertainly about aims, a bewildering variety of content, a frequent lack of progression within the course. Second, he would notice a variety of administrative adjustments and precautions that indicate little confidence in the expertness of those who teach it. And finally, he would notice that the textbooks for this course are for the most part less rigorous and less scholarly than those for other college freshman courses. (Kitzhaber 1963, 10)

The entire manuscript of *Themes, Theories, and Therapy* is similar if not sharper in tone as Kitzhaber reviews syllabi and his notes from course visits, using data and quotations from faculty and course material to drive his indictments home. Indeed, he is compelling, and unequivocal, as these few of many potential quotes demonstrate:

- The only constant in all varieties of the course is some provision for supervised practice in writing, but, ironically, most of the confusion in freshman English stems from different notions of how writing ought to be taught. (10)
- It is seldom a course that most teachers—even most graduate students—look forward to teaching, but instead one that they merely endure and too often do not give their best efforts to. (15)

- Freshman textbooks in many fields could stand considerable improving, but those for freshman English courses—in particular, the handbooks and the books of readings—are, as a class, likely to be among the poorest, the least scholarly, that the student will encounter. (15)

Kitzhaber published two versions of his report on his research: one as a chapter in the book (quoted above) and an earlier, more reportorial version that was published in *College English*. In the *CE* article, he presents findings in support of the decline of basic writing and grammatical instruction, the abandonment of writing clinics and laboratories and proficiency exams, and an increase in honors opportunities.

Thomas Wilcox's study follows up on Kitzhaber's and has some similarities in tone, but it is decidedly more specific and intentional in methodology. He too has a dismal view, though Wilcox reports out numerically and with more measure and caution. Wilcox's study was published by the University of Wisconsin's *Bureau of Educational Research Bulletin* and includes some discussion of the English department at the University of Wisconsin, as is frequently the case with these types of studies (e.g., Albert Kitzhaber situates his research within the context of his school, Dartmouth). Wilcox also took an interest in exploring regional differences, frequently referring to practices in "the East," an approach also taken by the other midwestern researcher, Emerson Shuck. Wilcox worked with the Modern Language Association and the Association of Departments of English (ADE) in the development of his survey which, sent to three hundred randomly selected English departments from a comprehensive list of 1,320 institutions, was returned at a rate of 95 percent. Wilcox also visited sixty institutions that were nominated as having an undergraduate English program that was of "unusually high quality, unusually effective, or unusually promising" (Wilcox 1968, 442). From this sample, which leans toward the most promising schools for writing instruction, Wilcox reports out on the details of the presence of the FYC requirement, course content, use of textbooks, class size, and some characteristics of the faculty who teach FYC. Despite the inclusion of sixty recommended programs, he concludes with a nod to Kitzhaber.

> The "enormous variety" which Kitzhaber found when he surveyed freshman English in 1961 is still apparent, and it does not seem that any single concept of the course or any one policy on freshman English will soon prevail. The ideal program which teachers and administrators (and textbook publishers) have sought for 50 years has not yet emerged, and the debate over freshman English continues much as before. (Wilcox 1972, 686)

The 1960s and early 1970s, as Anne Herrington notes in her review of the first twenty years of *Research in the Teaching of English*, was dominated by both an effort toward quantitative, scientific methods and a faith in clear determination of best practices through these methods. Writing in 1969, James Hoetker observed that "the only hope for rational settlement of disputes about curricula and methods lies in the presentation of objective evidence scientifically obtained" (quoted in Herrington 1989, 119).

1974: RON SMITH ENLARGES THE SAMPLE BUT REMAINS A BLEAK PROGNOSTICATOR

Ron Smith is more similar to Kitzhaber than to the careful Wilcox, and thus he is bold, if not accurate, in his predictions of the disappearance of freshman composition and, more generally, a bleak future for higher education. Driven by the desire "to discover generally what had happened, if anything, to the composition requirement and Freshman English during the last few years" (1974, 138), Smith modeled his survey after Wilcox's, with some changes: he increased the sample to seven hundred randomly selected institutions, which may explain the lower return rate of 70 percent (138). Highlights of Smith's findings include that many fewer schools require FYC (76 percent compared to Wilcox's 93.2 percent) and that there has been an increase in possibilities for exemption, with 95 percent of schools providing pathways to bypass freshman English. He sees these developments as evidence that the opponents of freshman English are "succeeding rather than dying, retiring, or languishing" (146). Smith notes that freshman English has been attacked nationally and locally, and he therefore predicts its demise: "All signs point to more schools dropping the composition requirement, more diminishing the one that exists, and more taking advantage of what will probably soon be better equivalency examinations" (148). Smith tracks differences in practices at public and private schools, and at larger and smaller schools, concluding that freshman English has more endurance at public colleges and universities. Smith refers repeatedly to the battle between proponents and opponents of freshman English and paints a picture of higher education in turmoil, though he does so without providing much specification on these points. He writes of increased pressure on "the economies of higher education" and of programs' inability to prove their value "in this age of computers—or of men who think that way" (148), citing assessment mandates, budgetary constraints, and priority changes particularly. Believing that higher education and writing instruction was caught in a maelstrom, Smith saw a bleak future.

1980S: WITTE AND PETERSON HIGHLIGHT WPA ISSUES AND OPPORTUNITIES, AND BURHANS BEMOANS LACK OF PEDAGOGICAL ADVANCEMENT

The 1980s was a period of much activity, including publication of a series of reports by Stephen Witte, Paul Meyer, Thomas Miller, Roger Cherry, and Lester Faigley, a catalog review by Clinton Burhans, and the first dedicated WPA-status-and-working-conditions report by Linda Peterson. Supported by a grant from the Fund for the Improvement of Postsecondary Education (U S Department of Education), Witte, Meyer, Miller, and Faigley's survey of writing program directors targeted the 550+ individuals who were on the Council of Writing Program Administrators' mailing list; from these 550, 23.1 percent ($n = 127$) completed the *three-hour* survey (Witte et al. 1981, 10–11). Notably, in their study design, the authors rejected the hypothesis-testing approach, opting instead for a descriptive approach, arguing that "hypothesis-testing assumes a level of background knowledge and theory which we believe does not exist for writing programs" (1). Witte et al. did not publish their findings in journals but instead distributed their report through ERIC as an educational document. The authors reported on all aspects of the survey, frequently breaking down by region and institutional type the descriptive statistics they had calculated. Notably, the authors present findings on what writing programs directors believed were the most and least successful aspects of their programs. With one major exception, these lists will strike readers as all too familiar, despite the passage of some thirty-plus years, underscoring that the history makes clear that most of our current crises are perennial.

Most frequently identified successful aspects of writing programs:

- writing labs/workshops
- teaching students to write in clear, efficient prose
- teacher training programs
- peer tutoring or collaborative learning
- and placement procedures (96)

Most frequently identified "least successful" aspects of writing programs:

- the commitment of tenured faculty
- support of the English faculty
- inefficient writing program administration (104)

Today I seldom hear complaints of inefficiency in writing program administration, likely and hopefully because of the professionalization of writing program administration and colleges' and universities' decisions to hire these professionals, as I discuss in chapter 3.

As is made clear in the details of Witte and colleagues' report, the writing programs they surveyed had many differences, leading them to conclude, "If there is to be drawn a major conclusion from the examination of the writing programs we surveyed, it is that they are generally very different from one another, that they are each designed primarily to serve the local needs of the institution, the department, and the student body" (Witte et al, 1981,120). Note the difference in editorial tone in Witte and colleagues' commentary on this issue of diversity of programming as compared to Kitzhaber and Wilcox, who preceded them, and Clinton Burhans, who followed.

But first there was the appearance of Linda Peterson's article "The WPA's Progress" (1987), drawn from a small survey of WPAs via the WPA mailing list, the first of several that sought to understand and document the challenges and successes of writing program administrators and writing program administration as a field (see also Balester and McDonald 2001; Charlton and Rose 2009; Hartzog 1986a; Healy 1995; Olson and Ashton-Jones 1988; Peterson 1987; Skeffington, Borrowman, and Enos 2008). These studies, the majority of which were (finally) authored or coauthored by women, relied on mailing lists, and later listservs, and were motivated by the challenges WPAs face, typically focusing on status, opportunities for advancement, workloads, and working conditions. As discussed in chapter 3, since Peterson's study, there have been clear signs of improvement for those who pursue administrative work. In the 1980s, however, Peterson's study, published in the newly formed journal, *WPA: Writing Program Administration*, must have provided a mix of comfort and distress as it documented that WPAs across the country were confident that their workloads were unreasonably greater than those of other faculty, even though most of the WPAs in Peterson's study ultimately received tenure.

Another scholar from the predictor-of-doom camp, Clinton Burhans (1983), focused on the endurance of "current-traditionalism" and exhibited a markedly different approach and style than did Witte and his colleagues, who were following a social scientific or educational research methodology, whereas Burhans, who published extensively on American literature, followed a humanities research model. Whereas Witte and colleagues were cautious, detailed, methodical, and almost seemed to avoid generalizations, Burhans draws major conclusions from fewer points of data; for example, he writes, "The Figures in the first two tables [detailing types of courses] offer little evidence of any real or stronger commitment to teaching writing . . . and little likelihood that what commitment there is will produce any improvement over the past" (646). His study is composed of 263 institutions selected by Burhans, in ways that are not detailed, to comprise what he describes as a "representative and statistically significant" (640) sample "weighted with schools from which we customarily expect the highest level of professionalism in theory, research, and application" (641). Burhans relies on data collected from university and college catalogs, asking eight questions that aim to discover what college English teachers are "thinking and doing" (640) in their classes and programs and to what extent teachers and program are influenced by "two decades of new information and knowledge about composition and writing" (640). In particular, Burhans sets out to understand the staying power of current-traditional methodologies compared to contemporary methodologies, drawing on Richard Young (1978) to define the former and Maxine Hairston (1982) to define the latter. Burhans's essay is full of disappointment: for him, his study confirms that the twenty-five- to thirty-five-year "knowledge gap" between theory and practice hypothesized by Sara Lundsteen et al. (1976) had not yet been bridged. Presenting many dismal statistics and unimpressive language from catalogs, Burhans concludes, "Myths die hard, and the current-traditional myths are no exception. In the perspective of this study the gleaming visions of a neat paradigm shift should give way to the sobering realization that the imperative of change will be longer and harder than many of us have hoped, that Lundsteen's gap, at least in the study, conception, and teaching of writing, is far wider than even she had speculated" (652).

In addition to these landmark studies, the 1980s is also marked by an expansion and shift in research methodologies in the field beyond the social scientific, highly quantitative method of Witte and colleagues and Burhans's humanities, rhetorical method. Peter Smagorinsky cites the mid-1980s as "when all hell broke loose in terms of methodological pluralism" (Smagorinsky 2008, 390). Anne Herrington describes the early period of *Research in the Teaching of English (RTE)*, the 1960s and 1970s, as dominated by those who followed and supported founding editor Richard Braddock's view that "only research employing 'scientific methods,' like controlled experimentation and textual analysis" (quoted in Herrington 1989, 119), should be included. Herrington asserts that quantitative, experimental research had dominated the field, but by the 1980s, *RTE* had published much more qualitative research drawn from various theoretical perspectives" (119). Kevin Roozen and Karen Lunsford, reviewing one hundred years of scholarship across NCTE journals for a 2012 *RTE* article, reported on the increasing variety of empirical research approaches evident (Roozen and Lunsford 2012, 196) in the 80s and beyond, suggesting that the "scene of writing" had expanded.

In the area of writing program administration, we see the publication of studies that draw on case study and teacher-researcher methodologies (see, for example, Bishop 1997; Bloom 1998; Enos, Borrowman, and Skeffington 2008; George 1999; Rose and Weiser 1999).

1994: LARSON FOCUSES ON LACK OF CONSENSUS AND ASSESSMENT

In the 1990s another leader in the field, Richard Larson, sought to provide a broad status report on the state of writing instruction. Like Wilcox, Kitzhaber, and Burhans before him, Larson drew a negative conclusion from his empirical study of the state of writing instruction in the United States. Commissioned by the Ford Foundation, Larson distributed a survey to 575 institutions, a sample selected by a mix of random sampling and selection (institutions recommended by Larson and all historically black colleges and universities [HBCUs]), resulting in 240 usable surveys (a 41.7 percent return rate). The survey was followed by visits to seven campuses deemed "distinctive or unusual" (1994, 10). Following the data analysis, and in a tone of exasperation, Larson summarized his view of the state of the first-year composition requirement: "It would seem as if there are as many writing programs abroad in this land as there are institutions offering such programs, almost as many as there are teachers of writing. Furthermore, there is no consensus at all about the possible directions that might be taken in efforts to make changes in such programs—in what they seek to do, in what they teach, in the way they view writing" (40). Although Larson is able to cite a few exceptional examples of successful first-year composition programs, for him, hope lies in teaching writing in the disciplines (34–39). Further, in a report full of recommendations for the Ford Foundation and, presumably, other readers, Larson anticipates the assessment movement, emphasizing the need for stringent expectations of university and college writing programs to provide evidence of student writing improvement: "One of the most troubling findings from the study was the almost complete *absence* in most institutions of any effort to determine *whether the First Year writing program is achieving its purposes*" (46–47).

TWENTY-FIRST CENTURY: LISTSERV SURVEYS OF WPA AND WRITING FACULTY EXPERIENCES AND PERCEPTIONS

The first two decades of the twenty-first century have seen publication of several new studies, including status studies previously mentioned

(Balester and McDonald 2001; Charlton and Rose 2009; Skeffington, Borrowman, and Enos 2008). Also published has been a follow-up to Ron Smith's 1974 study (Moghtader, Cotch, and Hague 2001), a large survey of the members of the Conference on College Composition and Communication (CCCC) that focuses on the experience of the membership community (Gere 2009), and a study focused on a previously underrepresented group, small liberal arts colleges (Gladstein and Regaignon 2012). These studies are expansions or updates of previous studies, and all rely on surveys, with various rates of return. It appears as though the listserv survey had cemented itself as the means for gathering data, despite the difficulty of receiving strong response rates and concerns around self-reporting. An interesting method of addressing the sample problem is being pursued by the authors of the WPA Census, still underway, which, as of January 2015, has received data from 734 four-year colleges and universities and is pursuing two-year college data at the time of this book's publication. These authors' strategy is to increase the size of the sample by putting the survey online and by advertising it frequently on listservs and conferences.

Many of these twenty-first-century studies focus on issues of status, and therefore their authors work deliberately to observe whether changes have occurred in the profession by replicating significant parts of earlier studies. For example, in 2001 Valerie Balester and James McDonald compared the status of types of WPAs (writing center directors and writing program directors), seeking to discover whether writing center directors' status had improved since an earlier study (Olson and Ashton-Jones 1988). Concerned especially with the on-campus relationships forged between these two types of writing leaders, the researchers found that relationships *had* improved since Gary Olson and Evelyn Ashton-Jones's survey but that leaders of writing programs "enjoy[ed] a more privileged place in institutional structures" (77) than did writing center directors. In 2009 Jonikka Charlton and Shirley Rose followed up on Linda Peterson's 1986 study focused on the characteristics and working conditions of WPAs. Charlton and Rose reported that twenty years had brought improvements in WPA work and working conditions, with women increasingly present and an increasing percentage of WPAs coming out of graduate programs in rhetoric and composition (137).

Other empirical researchers have documented practices in postsecondary writing instruction through surveying faculty, but also students, and reviewing student writing and documents as well. For example, Joanne Addison and Sharon McGee published their study of a several high schools and colleges, looking especially to see differences between faculty and student reports. In summary, they reported, "We believe that the data suggest that faculty are assigning and students are completing writing assignments, that some deep learning is taking place and that students and faculty view writing as important beyond school" (Addison and McGee 2010, 168–69). Research on WAC practices have also been notable, as discussed closely in chapter 5, with most attention paid to the WAC/WID mapping project (Thaiss and Porter 2010) and Dan Melzer's study of WAC through examining course assignments (Melzer 2009, 2014).

Notably, beyond these status studies is historical review scholarship that has sought to understand and explain significant aspects of the field's methods and growth in such areas as assessment.

At the close of this chapter is a table that lists and details the essential methods (sample characteristics and method of development) of those studies most frequently referred to as points of comparison to the state comprehensive university data. This page is a good page to bookmark and refer back to while going through chapters 3, 4, and 5. Considering a study's sample size and characteristics (e.g., institutional types included) as well as its method for data collection and response rates is valuable when weighing comparisons.

SOCIAL SCIENCE VERSUS HUMANITIES: THE REPORT VERSUS THE ARGUMENT

With this brief history of the field's investigation of the state of writing instruction in the United States, I hope I have at once established the arc that precedes this study and the tension that exists across these studies concerning a choice between a reportorial approach (evidenced especially by Gere, Shuck, and Witte) and a rhetorical approach (evidenced especially by Kitzhaber, Burhans, and Larson). The advantages of the rhetorical approach are clear to me as a reader: these texts are engaging, as writers make the case for a viewpoint, using their study data to support their theses. They are lively and fairly irresistible to quote. However, and this is part of the reason they are so quotable, the pull toward having a conclusion or making an argument pushes researchers into statements the data simply don't support. As one among many examples, Ron Smith used fairly scant data to predict the end of the first-year composition requirement, a prediction that has proven entirely incorrect. The reportorial approach I have chosen to adopt throughout the bulk of this book is less engaging than I would like it to be, and I certainly fear I bore readers! It seemed like Witte and his colleagues were describing my own manuscript when they wrote,

When we began our study, we realized that our report might seem to be presenting statistics on the average height, weight, and age of people in Switzerland when photographs of the Jungfrau, Lake Geneva, and the Rhone River might be of more interest . . . Too often in the past, single examples have been held up as "typical" while far more numerous examples have been ignored. We did not quantify because of our love for numbers nor to level out differences across institutions. Indeed, we chose to do a national survey because we did not want to elevate a few programs as ideal while ignoring what the great majority of colleges and universities in this country actually do. (Witte et al. 1981, 1)

Feeling precisely the same way, I only hope readers accustomed to rhetorical approaches will have patience with, and see value in, this reportorial approach.

NONEMPIRICAL ASSESSMENTS OF THE FIELD FROM SCHOLARS AT LEADING INSTITUTIONS

Assessments of the field have not been reserved for those among us who have a propensity for collecting reams of data, surveying, and coding. Indeed, it is my view that assessments of the field have been dominated by theoreticians and rhetoricians who use other means to assess where we are. Often these assessments are bound by writers' local conditions, the major debates in the field as played out in publication and at conferences, and wider reading about literacy and higher education. What they provide is a vision for where we should attempt to go next, and what they lack is much grounding in data. Jaime Armin Mejia, writing a response to Richard Fulkerson's (2005) *College Composition and Communication* article bemoaning the state of composition and the influence of critical and cultural studies in particular, offers this critique of Fulkerson: "This open question about how widespread the influence of CCS [critical and cultural studies] casts a rather long shadow over the findings Fulkerson presents, especially if we are to take his observations as realistically reflecting 'the composition landscape.' What the journals and books, both professional studies and textbooks, say—or don't say—about our practices within composition classrooms, in my view, doesn't exactly reflect what's actually going on in many composition classrooms" (Mejia 2006, 744). Mejia points out that his perspective as a Chicano teaching mostly "Texas Anglos" (739) gives him a quite different perspective than Fulkerson's. Notably, at the time of his essay, Mejia was at Southwest Texas State University (now Texas State University), then and now a state comprehensive university. Mejia wasn't seeing himself, a Chicano teacher at an SCU, represented in the scholarly discussion. Mejia's critique is based on his observation that Fulkerson's assertions about the state of the field are not drawn from "what's actually going on," an observation that can apply to most of the studies I review in this section.

These assessments and statements, like Fulkerson's, which I'll discuss below, are sometimes part of keynote speeches made at our annual Conference on College Composition and Communication (and later published in *College Composition and Communication*, or *CCC*) or distributed through NCTE or CCCC position and other statements. They are important to understanding our perceptions of the field and may often prove to be catalysts and support for new initiatives. For example, Kathleen Blake Yancey (2004), in the *CCC* article drawn from her CCCC address (which as of mid-2016, Google Scholar tells us, has been cited 347 times), argues for an expanded definition of writing, greater attention to genre, and the development of writing majors, effectively supporting much scholarship and praxis in digital and multimedia writing as well as in vertical writing programming. In the interior chapters of this book, I draw attention to this influential theoretical scholarship, but I'll make a few general observations here. First, in these often influential state-of-the-field texts, on the one side we have those inclined toward a dark view, who pronounce the field—or some aspect of it—as chaotic and insufficiently unified (e.g., Fulkerson, Haswell, and the editorial comments of survey writers already discussed); on the other side we see hopeful announcements of recently arrived-at unity, often connected to a popular idea or movement from within the active scholarly community, as exemplified by strands of scholarship on the WPA Outcomes Statement, (Behm et al. 2012; Harrington et al. 2005), directed self-placement (Royer and Gilles 1998, 2003), and an FYC curriculum focused on writing about writing (Downs and Wardle 2007; Wardle and Downs 2010).

Finally, there are those who embrace the diversity of our approaches, arguing against the value of "unity," or as Greg Colomb puts it, that there is danger in the unity of a "franchise": "Consider, for example, the effects of the proliferating official statements of what we (all) should be doing: outcome statements, best practices, certificates of excellence, position statements, model assessment galleries, model frameworks for communications and so on . . . [T]he more of such convergences we create, the fewer degrees of freedom each of us might have" (Colomb 2010, 26; see also CCCC addresses by Bartholomae [1989], Glenn [2008], and Hesse [2005]). I review these influential state-of-the-field essays that are rhetorical in nature as a backdrop to the empirical view. In the chapters that follow, I draw on these and many other scholars' contributions to further contextualize my findings in the ongoing conversation about the state of the field, which includes varying perspectives on the issues of unity and consensus—their presence and value.

FULKERSON AND HASWELL: REGRET FOR THE FIELD'S LACK OF UNITY

"Composition at the Turn of the Century" by Richard Fulkerson (2005) and "Hieroglyphic World" by Richard Haswell (2010) are two significant review essays written by prominent figures in the field. Written after the authors had enjoyed many years of leadership and scholarship, these essays are exemplary in representing the view that the field lacks unity and is at peril in its practice of teaching writing as a result. Fulkerson and Haswell offer their critiques of the field via reviews of book collections that aim to introduce new teachers and scholars to the field. While they are similar in their method and in their criticism of the discipline for lacking unity, their hopes for the discipline are different: whereas Fulkerson calls for a theoretical unity, Haswell wishes for unity via research grounded in empirical studies, such as many that have emerged in recent years (e.g., see Addison and McGee 2010; Dryer 2013; Elliot, Briller, and Joshi 2007; Kelly-Riley and Elliot 2014; Melzer 2014; Thompson and Mackiewicz 2013; White, Elliot, and Peckham 2015). In his frequently cited essay, Fulkerson compares two book collections written twenty years apart and references sales data of several textbooks as support for his analysis of the state of FYC, which is that FYC instruction has divided into three diverging approaches. Fulkerson finds each of these approaches problematic in theory or in practice, though he is most disturbed by critical and cultural studies composition pedagogies; to his mind, "The 'social turn' in composition, the importation of cultural studies from the social sciences and literary theory, has made a writing teacher's role deeply problematic" (655). Fulkerson asserts that this move reflects "content envy on the part of writing teachers" (663) and runs the risk of turning composition courses into courses of "indoctrination" (665). What comes through most clearly is Fulkerson's (2001) clear dismay with the evolution of the field. Since the process revolution, which he views positively, Fulkerson sees the field as having fallen into a wide range of different approaches to teaching writing, the most popular of which he finds deeply problematic.

Haswell, in his more recent review of five popular composition anthologies, critiques the field for lacking cohesion, for focusing overly on historicizing and "meta-talk" (114). He is disturbed by the poor representation of empirical studies, writing assessment, the lack of commonality of authors or texts across collections, and, most of all, an insufficient focus on practice: "As a field we decamped literary studies and its captivation with heady theory and yet have become enraptured with our own theory, which still attracts editors, foments discussion, and (it seems) sells anthologies. Theory is primary, practice is tacked on" (106). Arguments against the specific points of these two authors' summary essays are readily made (and found) in scholarship, but it remains the case that Fulkerson's and Haswell's view that the field lacks needed unity strikes an oft-repeated refrain.

Increasingly, it is assessment scholars who similarly if implicitly critique the field for lacking unity when they call for unity around specific processes or language. For example, see Linda Adler-Kassner in her "no vampires" exhortation to teach writing about writing (and not about other "content") (Adler-Kassner 2012, 132–34); look also to Howard Tinburg and Patrick Sullivan in their call for a shared understanding of "college writing" (Tinberg and Sullivan 2006) and White, Elliot, and Peckham, who encourage writing program administrators to approach assessment through their design-for-assessment (DFA) model. This model follows Brian Huot (Huot 1996) in its localism, which they posit as "conceptual glue that holds writing assessment together" (White, Elliot, and Peckham 2015, 143). With its emphasis on consequential validity, which they define using Messick—"'the degree to which empirical evidence and theoretical rationales support the *adequacy* and *appropriateness* of *inferences* and *actions* based on test scores or other modes of assessment'" (quoted in White, Elliot, and Peckham 153–54)—DFA is, to date, the latest effort by assessment theorists to unify the field through a theory of writing program assessment. Assessment scholars, like these mentioned, are striving to unify the field not so much by arguing for a teaching method or "subject" but by prescribing a set of processes for assessing writing, writing instruction, and writing programs that makes data collection, measurement (in various forms), reflection, and attention to intended and unintended consequences essential components in college and university writing programs.

Often in concert with these assessment scholars, the field's major professional organizations—NCTE, WPA, and CCCC[3]—have sought to create a unified understanding of or approach to the discipline by publishing and disseminating frameworks, standards, or calls for a particular focus. Professional-organization documents that aim to provide unity to our approach to teaching writing include NCTE's "Teaching Composition: A Position Statement" (National Council of Teachers of

English 1985) and "Beliefs about the Teaching of Writing" (National Council of Teachers of English 2016), the Council of Writing Program Administrator's "WPA Outcomes Statement for First-Year Composition" (Council of Writing Program Administrators 2014; originally published in 1999, rev. in 2008 and 2014), and CCCC's "Principles for the Postsecondary Teaching of Writing," (Conference on College Composition and Communication 2015; original publication 1989; revised in 2013). Currently, "Principles for the Postsecondary Teaching of Writing" best summarizes and includes NCTE's earlier documents. These documents, as well as others not listed here, are the result of discussion and negotiation and were written collaboratively and in an effort to shape and reflect the discipline, with one eye on respecting reasonable differences of opinion and another on coalescing on central areas of agreement as established by research.

Alongside these organizational efforts, on the individual level we see many efforts to persuade the field to adopt particular approaches toward some aspect of writing. From an assessment and political strategic stance, Linda Adler-Kassner in *The Activist WPA* (Adler-Kassner 2008), and with Peggy O'Neill in *Reframing Writing Assessment* (Adler-Kassner and O'Neill 2010), encourages writing faculty toward the adoption of shared language and common practices. One example of a movement currently being advocated is WOW, an argument for approaching first-year composition as a "writing about writing course" (Downs and Wardle 2007; Wardle 2009; Wardle and Downs 2010). WOW is at once both an idea about how to teach first-year composition and a reflection of the ever-growing desire to establish the discipline more firmly, through laying claim to foundational research and principles that can be taught at the undergraduate level. While the success of this particular movement is as yet not established, it is an example of an effort to unify the field, born from a critique of what is seen as weaknesses in current practices.

Throughout *Writing at the State U*, I refer to both the theoretical and empirical scholarship that has inspired the data I have collected and reported on. Table 2.1 provides an accounting of the empirical research I have reviewed here or included in the chapter discussions. As I hope is clear, I believe research findings on such topics as class size or institutional home is best understood in the context of the methodologies researchers employ. Of particular importance are sampling plans (target populations), methods for collecting information, and, when surveys are completed, response rates. As readers work through the individual chapters, this table will provide a useful reference for recalling these important details.

Table 2.1. Major studies of the state of writing programs, instruction, and administration

Author(s), short title	Data collection date; publication date(s)	Sample size; target population	Method details
Warner Taylor— "Freshman English"	1927; 1929	232 colleges and universities; English departments	Survey by postal mail; return rate of 77.3%; sample—not detailed but "located in all parts of the country and representatives of all types"
Earl Sasser –"Some Aspects of Freshman English"	1951; 1952	123 of 189 (65%); English departments	Survey by postal mail; sample—"selected colleges and universities"
Emerson Shuck— midwestern universities	1953; 1955	26 of 35 (74%); English departments	Survey by postal mail; return rate of 74%; sample—focused on midwestern institutions
Emerson Shuck— multipurpose universities	1954; 1955	70 of 83 (84%); English departments	Survey by postal mail; return rate of 84%; sample—institutions with enrollments between 2,500 and 7,000
Albert Kitzhaber—"Freshman English"	1960–61; 1962 and 1963	95 English departments	Document review (syllabi) and selected visits to campuses; sample—not detailed but described as "fairly representative cross section"
Bonnie Nelson for ADE, MLA and ERIC—"College Programs in Freshman Composition"	1968; 1968	66 of 200 (33%); English departments	Document review: syllabi and course descriptions; sample—"fairly representative cross-section"
Thomas Wilcox— study of undergraduate English programs	1968–70; 1968, 1969, and 1971	285 of 300 (95%); English departments	Survey by postal mail; sample—selected randomly from list of 1,320 "high quality" English programs; visited 63 "promising" schools
Ron Smith—current status of freshman English	1973; 1974	491 of 700 (70%); English departments	Survey by postal mail to sample selected from 700; sample—random sampling
Linda Peterson— "WPA's Progress"	1985; 1987	59 of 100 (59%); writing program directors	Survey by postal mail; sample—100 randomly selected CWPA members; also passed out at conferences
Stephen Witte, Paul Meyer, Thomas Miller, and Lester Faigley— national survey of WP directors (Report #2)	1981; 1981	127 of 550 (31%); writing program directors	Survey by postal mail; sample—all 550+ individuals on CWPA mailing list

continued on next page

Table 2.1.—*continued*

Author(s), short title	Data collection date; publication date(s)	Sample size; target population	Method details
Stephen Witte, Roger Cherry, and Paul Meyer—"Goals of Freshman Writing Programs" (Report #5)	1981; 1982	45 of 104 WP directors (43.5%); 76 of 134 writing teachers (56.5%)	Survey consisting of a series of open-ended questions, sent by postal mail; sample—all 550+ individuals on CWPA mailing list
Christopher Burhans,—four-year college and university catalogs	1982 and 1983; 1983	263 four-year colleges and universities	Document review: catalogs; sample—not detailed but "representative and statistically significant" yet tilted up, toward those expected to be of the "highest level"
Richard Larson—Ford Foundation report on college writing programs	1986; 1994	240 of 575; 41.7%; humanities and English chairs	Survey and data request for documents (syllabi and other material) sent by postal mail; sample—random sampling of MLA mailing list and selection of recommended institutions; follow-up visit at 7 institutions.
David Chapman, Jeanette Harris, and Christine Hult—writing concentrations within English departments	1992; 1995	360 of 1543 (23.3%); representing 316 schools	Survey by postal mail; sample— individuals and programs; 3 mailing lists (ATTW, AWP, and CWPA)
Valerie Balester and James McDonald—"WPA status and working conditions"	1997 and 1998; 2001	176 of 850 (20.7%); writing program and writing center directors	Postal mail survey, posting on listservs (WPA-L and WCENTER), and conference (CCCC and NWCA) distribution; sample—"biased in favor of WPAs active in professional associations"
Michael Moghtader, Alanna Cotch, and Kristen Hague—"First-year Composition Requirement"	1998; 2001	233 of 700 (33%); writing program administrators	Postal mail survey; sample—representative sample from Barron's Profiles of American Colleges (1,670 institutions)
Dan Melzer—"Assignments across the Curriculum"	2002–2006; 2009 and 2014	100 institutions (2,100 writing assignments)	Review of institutional websites
Jonikka Charlton and Shirley Rose—"Twenty More Years in WPA's Progress"	2007; 2009	226 of 413 (55%); writing program directors	Electronic survey; sample—CWPA members only

continued on next page

Table 2.1.—*continued*

Author(s), short title	Data collection date; publication date(s)	Sample size; target population	Method details
Jillian Skeffington, Shane Borrowman, and Theresa Enos—"Profiling the WPA Administrator"	2008	82 (unknown WPA list participants percentage)	Electronic survey; sample—WPA Listserv
Anne Ruggles Gere—CCCC membership survey	2008; 2009	643 of 103 (62%); college composition teachers and administrators	Electronic survey: sample—CCCC members
Chris Thaiss and Tara Porter—"State of WAC/WID"	2006–2008; 2010	1,338 of 2,617 (51%); WPAs, department chairs, and writing leaders	Electronic survey; distribution on listservs and by solicitation e-mails
Jill Gladstein and Dara Regaignon—*Writing Program Administration at Small LA Colleges*	2009; 2012	109 of 130 (80%); writing leaders	Electronic survey and follow-up e-mail/phone interview; sample—small liberal arts colleges that are members of the Annapolis Group
Emily Isaacs and Melinda Knight—top university study	2009; 2012 and 2014	101 colleges and universities; institutional websites	Public document review: data available on websites; sample—institutions on various "top lists" from *US News & World Report*

THE CONTEMPORARY CONTEXT: PUBLIC HIGHER EDUCATION UNDER SIEGE?

An understanding of the contemporary economic climate of public higher education is important to thinking about what we're doing with writing studies at state universities, as the effects of both budgetary priorities and budgets themselves profoundly challenge our best practices. Many readers may think they already understand the economic climate—"bad, and it's getting worse!"—but I urge more careful attention to this issue as my research suggests that public higher education has largely retained its revenue stream while changing its priorities, moving increasingly away from dollars spent on instruction.

My choice to focus on public higher education was in part prompted by concern about the steady decline in government support for public higher education. Every year, it seems, campus leaders announce decreased or "level" funding, which, they explain, really means a decrease due to cost increases for pensions, healthcare, and other personnel costs. For WPAs at public colleges and universities, the three budgetary elements we need to pay particular attention to are these:

- the big picture of state support, which helps us gauge the value held for public higher education by the public and/or our representatives
- per-student spending, which not only suggests the university's available resources for supporting writing studies but is also closely tied to tuition and thus has an impact on the student body—who can attend our institutions and also the kind of financial pressures those who do attend are under
- the types of faculty hired at our institutions (full time, by type, and part time, by type), in what proportions, and how these proportions have changed over time

Data on these budgetary elements are typically presented on a national or state level and thus do not reveal what I suspect are varying experiences at individual institutions. Although some research (Weerts and Ronca 2012) suggests that states' funding of different classes of public higher educational institutions remains proportional even as overall funding fluctuates, our own experiences make clear that research universities, comprehensive universities, and community colleges are treated differently and that even within these classes, political or other forces can bear down in ways to create substantial disparities. Thus, as we look at the national and state data, we must keep in mind that institutions can receive dramatically different levels of support.

To begin, the contemporary picture of state support for public higher education is dismal, but not equally so across the states. To get beyond the headlines, we can look to analyses of state higher education funding conducted by the nonprofit State Higher Education Executive Officers Association (SHEEO),[4] which reviews financing of public higher education at the state and national level. On the national level, state support for public higher education has indeed declined in terms of what public colleges and universities receive but also in terms of the proportion of total state-tax revenue available (McLendon, Hearn, and Mokher 2009, 686). Most recently, during the period between 2009 and 2013, state appropriations decreased 23.0 percent nationwide (SHEEO 2014, 25). Looking back further, Peter Mortensen examines *Grapevine* data to conclude that funding for public higher education decreased by 42 percent from 1980 to 2011 (Mortensen 2012, 27).[5] Mortensen casts his analysis wider by reviewing National Income and Product Accounts (NIPA) to find *total* dollars spent on higher education; with this approach, he finds that state and local support peaked in 1975, with state and local entities contributing 60.3 percent of the total dollars spent on higher education compared to 34.1 percent contributed to higher education in 2010 (27). AASCU researchers looked at changes over twenty-five years from 1987 to 2012, noting that state appropriations per full-time equivalent student

declined 30 percent, from $8,497 to $5,906, in dollars adjusted for infla-
tion (Hurley, Harnisch, and Nassirian 2014, 2). Any way you look at it,
state support for public higher education has been in decline since 1975.

A complicating note to this dismal story is that there is tremendous
variety among the states in terms of funding public higher education.
For example, drawing again on the SHEEO/*Grapevine* data, although all
but two states (Alaska and Wyoming) saw a reduction in state support to
public higher education between FY08 and FY14, the nationwide average cut of 23 percent includes Arizona, which cut funding 48.3 percent,
and New York, which cut funding 11.1 percent (Mitchell, Palacios, and
Leachman 2014, 3–4), verifying earlier findings of variability among the
states (Barbett and Korb 1997, x). Simply put, we're not all in the same
boat. Some efforts have been made to understand the factors that might
explain these differences in state support. Researchers David Weerts and
Justin Ronca, examining changes from 1984 to 2006, find that, not surprisingly, state appropriations decrease most in states with higher percentages of unemployment: "For a 1% point increase in unemployment,
there is a 7% decrease in funding for higher education" (Weerts and
Ronca 2012, 167), confirming previous findings by McLendon, Hearn,
and Mokher(2009, 705). Further, the impact of state expenditure on
corrections (prisons) makes the top of the list of competing priorities
that drive down funding to public higher education: "For every $10,000
per capita increase in funding on corrections, there is a 12% decrease
in funding for higher education" (Weerts and Ronca 2012, 167). In summary, Weerts and Ronca find that there is great variation across states
and that research universities, followed by comprehensive universities,
have experienced the greatest fluctuations since 1984, whereas community colleges have experienced the least change (167–68).

Most of us would agree that the most damaging result of the withdrawal of state support for public higher education has been the
increase in costs to students in tuition and fees, an observation the
data support. Tuition has increased annually by over 5 percent between
2009 and 2013 (State Higher Education Executive Officers 2014), with
students' tuition dollars comprising 47.5 percent of total education
revenue for public universities in 2013 (SHEEO 2014, 10). In comparison, SHEEO's analysis of funding indicates that twenty-five years earlier,
in 1988, tuition accounted for only 23.8 percent of total educational
revenue (21). The College Board reports that the average published
price of tuition and fees at public four-year colleges and universities
increased 50 percent over ten years, from fall 2003 to fall 2013 (College
Board 2013, 15).

However, important to note is that public colleges and universities have been *very* effective at using tuition increases to maintain a reasonably stable per-student revenue stream. Looking closer, in the five-year period between 2009 and 2013, after tuition increased, public higher education was faced with a net loss of only 5.9 percent in FTE "constant dollar" funding (SHEEO 2014, 10). This relatively low revenue decrease is the result of higher education funding moving increasingly from the public to students and their families. If we look further back, comparing constant dollar FTE expenditure from 1988 ($11,264) to 2013 ($11,580), we see a very slight increase in spending of 2.8 percent over these twenty-five years (SHEEO 2014, 10). In summary then, tuition and fee increases have generally made up for decreases in state support, with public colleges and universities—on average—experiencing level per-student revenue.

Despite this revenue leveling through tuition increases, there have been significant changes in how colleges and universities spend their money. I'll focus just on what NCES reports four-year public colleges and universities have spent in the area of instruction (65 percent to 70 percent of which goes to salaries and wages) over the almost twenty-year period from 1992–93 to 2011–12 (National Center for Education Statistics 2013).[6] Analysis of NCES reports reveals that over this period, four-year public colleges and universities decreased relative expenditure in the category of instruction by 9.9 percent, from 29.4 percent in 1992–93 (National Center for Education Statistics 1993) to 24.75 percent in 2011–12 (National Center for Education Statistics 2013). Looking over as long a period as NCES allows paints an even more dire picture: for 1976–77, NCES data indicate that 46.4 percent of expenditures at public four-year institutions were for the purpose of instruction (National Center for Education Statistics 1995), compared to 24.75 percent in 2011–2012 (National Center for Education Statistics 2013). Money spent on instructional costs has halved over twenty years! Is this steady decrease in spending for the purpose of instruction the key to the rise in reliance on contingent labor in public higher education? I don't know—likely the explanation is much more complicated, and the responsibilities charged to public four-year universities and colleges appears to have expanded greatly since 1976—but this radical decrease in expenditures on instruction would clearly limit the money available for hiring tenure-line or other full-time faculty to teach FYC, among other disciplines.

My next question hopefully imagines yours as well: to what extent are higher education dollars spent on nonfaculty versus faculty, and of the latter group, how have the proportions of full- to part-time faculty changed? The answer is not entirely expected: colleges are spending a greater proportion of revenue on faculty than on nonfaculty than was the case twenty years ago, but they are nonetheless hiring proportionally fewer full-time faculty than part-time faculty. A 2012 NCES report on public higher education's proportional full-time-equivalent (FTE) faculty and staff breaks down along five categories: administrators (executive, administrative, or managerial professionals), faculty, graduate assistants, other professionals, and nonprofessional staff. In a comparison of proportional spending in these categories over the twenty-year period from 1991 to 2011, NCES reports an *increase* in spending on faculty (from 32.6 percent in 1991 to 38.4 percent in 2011), graduate assistants (from 9.7 percent to 11.5 percent), and other professionals (from 16.5 percent in 1991 to 20.7 percent in 2011), made possible by a significant *decrease* in nonprofessional staff (from 36.5 percent in 1991 to 24.9 percent in 2011) (National Center for Education Statistics 2012b) and a small decrease in executive, administrative, or managerial professionals (4.7 percent in 1991 to 4.5 percent in 2011). However, when NCES examines hiring increases by instructional type, these dismal changes are observed: compared to a 19 percent increase in full-time staff (faculty and nonfaculty), hiring of part-time faculty has increased 54 percent (across all sectors—public, private, and for profit) over ten years from 2001 to 2011, and hiring of graduate students has increased 36 percent (National Center for Education Statistics 2012a). Another means to view this change is to note that the proportion of tenured faculty at public four-year institutions has also decreased over about twenty years, comprising 56.3 percent of the full-time faculty population from 1993–94 and 48.0 percent in 2011–12 (National Center for Education Statistics 2012a). Recognizing that there has been substantial growth in the number of part-time faculty and slight growth in the number of non-tenure-track full-time faculty, is important to understanding what is possible for writing studies in the public higher education landscape.

In summary, the last twenty years have witnessed dramatic decreases in public support and proportional dollars spent for the purpose of instruction alongside equally dramatic increases in costs to students and in employment of part-time faculty, all while per-student revenue has remained essentially stable. More to the focus on writing studies, providing first-year composition students with full-time faculty, tenure-line or not, is a goal with which writing program administrations struggle. This is, however, no new struggle, as is clear from studying historical documents of writing program administration and reading again and again of the "current" crisis in funding. Thus I enter into the discussion of the state of public higher education in the second decade of the twenty-first century gingerly. I know I can provide little more than a brief, contextualizing review of contemporary opinion, mindful that commentators have argued many times before that *now* higher education is indeed in the most truly desperate fiscal and political situation. I suspect it always *feels* like we're in the worst of times, yet because that can't always be the case, I suggest caution to those tempted to make such proclamations.

The next chapter, "The Back End of First-Year Composition," gives a view of the policies and institutional support state comprehensive universities are providing to enable writing instruction and support to their students. The way faculty develop and teach general education writing is clearly influenced by organization and material conditions, from where the writing courses are located disciplinarily to the status and training of the faculty who actually teach these courses. In this chapter I detail these material conditions that enable—or disable—our best efforts at writing instruction.

Notes

1.   In 1952, *College Composition and Communication* published Earl Sasser's report on responses to a questionnaire entitled "Some Aspects of Freshman English" (Sasser 1952). Sent to 189 colleges and universities, the report does not explain how the sample was collected, and it is fairly brief.

2.   Least referenced of the three 1960s researchers on the state of the field is one of notably few women, Bonnie Nelson. Appearing in the MLA's *ADE Bulletin* in 1968, Nelson reports on an analysis of syllabi and course descriptions sent in from sixty-six schools from a selected sample of two hundred. Nelson's (1968) report, under the aegis of the MLA, is designed as a comparison to Kitzhaber's, which was completed four years earlier. Nelson's report tends towards description of individual programs, emphasizing the range of approaches and innovations among the colleges and universities whose documents she has reviewed.

3.   NCTE: National Conference for Teachers of English; WPA: Council of Writing Program Administrators; CCCC: Conference on College Composition and Communication.

4.   SHEEO has in recent years joined with Illinois State University's fifty-year-old *Grapevine*, which has been providing data on state tax support for higher education since 1960.

5.   From this report, Mortensen also establishes that public support for higher education peaked in 1975–1976. From *Grapevine*, he finds that in 1976, states peaked at $10.58 per $1,000 of state dollars spent on public higher education, compared to $6.30 in 2011. From NIPA (National Income and Product Accounts), he looks at total spending on higher education (including private), finding that the public share—federal, state, and local—of these costs was 60.3 percent in 1975, down to 34.1 percent in 2010 (Mortensen 2012, 27).

6. For readers who are interested in NCES's breakdown of costs for four-year public higher education, here it is for 2011–12, the latest data available: 24.75 percent on instruction (two-thirds of which, for a total of 16.44 percent, toward salary and wages), 11.78 percent on research, 4.45 percent on public support, 6.62 percent on academic support, 3.83 percent on student services, 6.93 percent on institutional support, 5.85 percent on operations and maintenance of plant, 5.61 percent on depreciation, 3.87 percent on scholarships and fellowships, 7.88 percent on auxiliary enterprises, 12.29 percent on hospitals, .48 percent on independent operations, 1.90 percent on interest, 3.76 percent on other.

3

THE BACK END OF FIRST-YEAR COMPOSITION
Institutional Support through Infrastructure and Policies

For WPAs and faculty responsible for writing instruction, often the greatest source of frustration comes from running into the brick walls represented by one's institution's seeming inability or unwillingness to provide the structures necessary for strong first-year composition instruction. While there is much a WPA and the faculty can do to improve course design or criteria for hiring and faculty retention, for example, matters of class size, administrative release for writing program administration, full-time lines, and credit for a basic writing course are among the many areas typically beyond faculty control. As a writer of more unsuccessful proposals requesting improvements in these areas than I care to count, I am intimately familiar with these frustrations: administrations that can't or won't reduce reliance on adjunct faculty, fund the administrative release I believe I need, give me control of basic writing placement, or provide financial support for training contingent faculty.

Yet, despite the limited role faculty often have in creating the necessary infrastructure and university policies for a successful writing program, the infrastructure and relevant university-wide policies have much bearing on the quality and direction of the courses and programs we provide for students. Increasingly, state universities and colleges are not independent actors; rather, they are locked into articulation agreements and subject to state-wide higher education councils, often highly political entities, that have an impact on such decisions as general education requirements and assessment criteria for placement and exemption. Thus, examining programs' support and constrictions via policies, and what often amounts to a measure of a university's commitment to writing instruction and general education more broadly, is crucial to evaluating and understanding the state of writing instruction in higher education.

DOI: 10.7330/9781607326397.c003

BROAD VIEW OF WRITING INFRASTRUCTURE AT SCUS

State comprehensive universities appear to see first-year composition as part of what English-department faculty should be responsible for, but they are also happy to support FYC with dedicated administrators (WPAs). Thus, FYC programs (or courses) are most frequently located in English departments, and WPAs are present at the majority of schools in the sample. Further, the data provide little evidence of significant differences in approaches to writing instruction and programming at those schools that have staff rather than faculty WPAs. This question of the impact of faculty versus staff writing-program-administration leadership was pursued by looking for differences in other variables from the study. The only significant difference found was that schools that have faculty WPAs have greater participation at the conference sponsored by NCTE, the Conference on College Composition and Communication (CCCC), which may partially reflect colleges' and universities' decisions to fund research more regularly for faculty than for staff. Participation at CCCC over a two-year period was selected as a proxy—albeit an imperfect one undoubtedly, for engagement with the field—for two primary reasons: first, because CCCC is our field's major conference, participation at it struck me as a reasonable proxy for engagement; second, it was data I was able to obtain from an independent source (NCTE), avoiding the problems of skew related to participation with self-reporting. In terms of faculty teaching FYC, large schools are most likely to have FYC taught by graduate students. Training in writing instruction—required or optional—is provided inconsistently at the SCUs in the sample, and the presence of training is, surprisingly, not well associated with the presence of WPAs. Class sizes range from fifteen to thirty, with significantly larger ranges found at Hispanic-serving and historically black state colleges and universities (HBCUs). Basic writing is highly present at 80.2 percent of the sample, though most students are placed through a variety of external assessments administered by the College Board, ACT, or other independent entities. What we see in these discoveries is that the institutional infrastructure for general education writing instruction varies widely, and often unpredictably.

INSTITUTIONAL HOME FOR FIRST-YEAR
COMPOSITION: ENGLISH DOMINATES

To start with what I suspect is a charged issue, the departmental placement of FYC courses, I found that the majority of FYC courses were taught under the aegis of English departments—fully 77.1 percent were

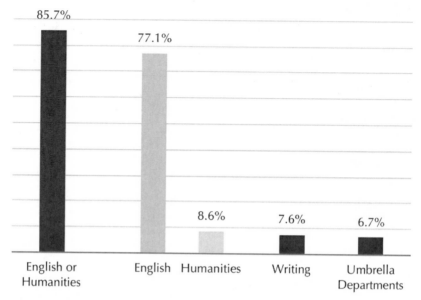

Figure 3.1. Institutional home for first-year composition

so located, with an additional 8.6 percent in humanities or other academic departments, for a total of 85.7 percent housed in English or similar units. Writing departments provided an institutional home for just 7.6 percent of the FYC courses, raising the question of what happened to the remaining 6.7 percent.

These writing programs (or sometimes just courses) were placed in what I call *academic umbrella departments*: either an interdisciplinary department (e.g., the writing program at California State University, Northridge is in the College of University Studies and Programs) or a general education program, as is the case with The College of New Jersey. This finding that first-year composition is predominantly placed in English or humanities departments suggests that, outside a few notable exceptions, the dream of writing-department independence has not been realized at state comprehensive universities.

Following *Coming of Age: The Advanced Writing Curriculum* (Shamoon et al. 2000), a collection whose authors argue for advanced curriculum more explicitly than for breaking away from English, *A Field of Dreams: Independent Writing Programs and the Future of Composition Studies* (O'Neill, Crow, and Burton 2002, 45) directly took up Maxine Hairston's famous 1985 call for compositionists to "break bonds" with English departments and "leav[e] the house in which we grew up" (Hairston 1985, 282). Over a decade old, *A Field of Dreams* provides readers with a variety of experiences with "independence" at various institutions, programs that have enjoyed varying levels of success. The book is widely cited along with other endorsements of disciplinary independence for the field (e.g., Howard 1993; McLeod 2006), and interest in writing independence continues, as evidenced by overflowing sessions on the topic at conferences and excited conversation on listservs. Enthusiasm for breaking bonds appears far from abating. Melissa Ianetta, who strikes a cautionary note in the face of this enthusiasm, suggests that the impulse for writing program independence is based primarily on the *disciplinary needs* of the people who are in tenure lines in composition and rhetoric. Although advocates of independence often cite English departments' reliance on adjuncts to teach FYC, Ianetta notes that there is little evidence or theoretical rationale to suggest that independence will result in better labor conditions for writing teachers. Improving working conditions for adjuncts, which was at the heart of Sharon Crowley's oft-cited argument for abolishing the FYW requirement (Crowley 1998, 241), is also frequently referenced as a rationale by the writers of *Field of Dreams*, as Ianetta details. Ianetta cautions that suggesting independence as "emancipation" may result in "internal satisfaction and external prestige" (Ianetta 2010, 642) without necessarily improving labor conditions, decreasing reliance on adjunct faculty, or increasing participation of tenure-track (TT) faculty.

In support of Ianetta's prediction, I found that 91.5 percent of the FYC programs located in English or humanities departments reported that (at least some) tenure-line faculty taught in their programs, whereas 73.3 percent of FYC programs located in writing departments reported that (at least some) tenure-line faculty taught in the program. In other words, a quarter of the FYC programs located in independent writing departments were taught entirely by non-tenure-track faculty, indicating that a significant minority of independent writing departments either have no tenure-line faculty or that they do have these faculty, but these faculty don't teach FYC. What we don't know from this study is *why* tenure-line-faculty participation in teaching FYC is lower in independent writing departments and programs, though the finding suggests some concern for FYC in independent writing programs is warranted.

That there are not more independent writing departments or programs providing an institutional home for FYC in the sample seems rooted in an observation made throughout this book: what is a trend in the literature and conversation at conferences is often revealed not to be the case when we look systematically at practices at state comprehensive universities. Thus, at conferences and in journals, enthusiasm for independent departments of writing, perhaps developed more for the purpose of majors and programs than for FYC instruction, is clear. In reviewing the published scholarship on the subject, there is very little evidence of faculty arguing for the placement of FYC in English or similar departments. As Ianetta notes, CCCC, and I would say leaders in the field more generally, "seem[s] to be tacitly authorizing the move away from the department of English by forwarding a singular historical narrative" (Ianetta 2010, 54). It is rare to find a defense of FYC's placement in English departments, and when a defense is launched, it is often almost apologetic, as is found in Lennie Irvin's description of the FYW program at Eastern Michigan (a sample school): "The FYWP remains within the English Department rather than its own separate department due in part to the unique set up of the EMU English Department"; more specifically, he notes that the "strong presence of other writing programs and writing faculty helps this first-year writing program reside comfortably within the English Department" (Irwin 2009).

It seems that despite the enthusiasm of those like Susan McLeod (UCSC writing program) and Rebecca Howard (Syracuse Department of Writing), both of whom work at noncomprehensive universities and have documented the realization of the independence dream (Howard 1993; McLeod 2006), FYC is predominantly found within English or other nonwriting academic departments. This is not to say there hasn't been some increase in independence: Chapman, Harris, and Hult (1995) found that only 3.8 percent of the four-year institutions they surveyed had independent writing programs. Explanation for the modesty of the impact of the independence movement and whether it reflects the judgment of the writing faculty at these institutions or simply upper-administrative priorities, perhaps born from economic interests, tradition, or even the insistence of literature faculty, is clearly beyond the scope of this research project, though it would be an interesting question to have answered. Notably, and as will be discussed in chapter 5, the call for writing majors, minors, and other programs has been taken up much more widely than the call for departmental independence, though these programs have most frequently found a home in English or in other academic departments rather than in writing departments.

The question of institutional location for writing programs has not been pursued frequently in "status" studies, but I will briefly reference and compare findings in studies by Gere (2009) and Skeffington, Borrowman, and Enos (2008). The authors of the latter study, with eighty-two participants, found that 92 percent of respondents reported that their programs were located in English departments, and just 6 percent were in separate rhetoric or writing departments (Skeffington, Borrowman, and Enos 2008, 11). Reflecting a greater diversity of schools, Anne Ruggles Gere's much larger survey of CCCC's members found that 68.94 percent of respondents reported that their writing programs were located in English departments, compared to 4.6 percent in humanities and 19.88 percent in "Other" (Gere 2009). In Gere's study, just 4.35 percent reported locations in rhetoric or composition departments, and another 2.17 percent identified a writing center as their institutional home. As a cautionary note, these studies differ from this state comprehensive university study in that they asked questions of individuals, not institutions; thus, they are studies that tell us what the majority of the *people* in their samples reported about the institutional locations of the writing programs they work in. Nonetheless, these reports also provide little evidence of widespread development of independent writing departments.

Comparison with the top university study (Isaacs and Knight 2014) provides further evidence that FYC is seldom institutionally located in independent writing departments, as detailed in figure 3.2 below. As one of the authors of the top university study, with Melinda Knight, I can comment further: we found that 12 percent of the FYC programs were administered centrally, located in the provost's office (e.g., at Middlebury College) or in Academic Support Services (e.g., at Carleton College). For this study, we defined *department* as an academic unit that provided a degree (major or minor) and coursework, a coding strategy that I followed for this second study. In the top university study, which consists of 101 institutions, 58 percent of which are private and many of which are elite, English has a less tight grip on FYC, with a sizable minority of programs finding homes outside typical departmental units.

What we see often in elite, private schools is more independent programs, but the independence can come at the cost of affiliation with an academic department that offers a major or at least a minor. These independent writing programs, such as at Harvard or Duke, and also at such small schools as Haverford and Wellesley, have been discussed fairly frequently in the literature and are characterized by their primary devotion to the work of teaching FYC.

DRILLING DOWN: THE CONDITIONS THAT CORRELATE WITH INSTITUTIONAL LOCATION

What factors are associated with institutional location? In this study, significant relationships for the location of FYC were found along two variables:

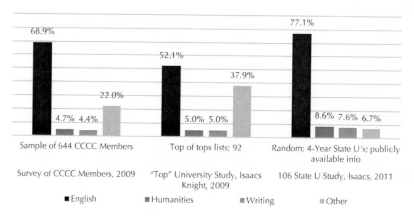

Figure 3.2. FYC location by department

basic Carnegie Classification and institutional size.[1] As might be expected, an institution's size and Carnegie Classification are themselves closely aligned. Institutional size and FYC location, which are detailed in figure 3.3 below, can be simplified as follows: as universities get larger, they are more likely to situate FYC outside English or humanities departments.

Beyond size relationship, I also found that PhD-granting institutions are slightly more likely than MA- or BA-granting institutions to have FYC located in an independent writing department: 10.3 percent of doctorate-granting institutions had FYC programs in independent writing departments, compared to 9.5 percent of MA-granting institutions and 0.0 percent of BA-granting institutions. Further, BA and MA institutions are most likely to have writing programs located outside academic departments—that is, in central administration, general education, or consortium programs (at 7.9 percent of MA-granting and 7.7 percent of BA-granting institutions) as compared to doctorate-granting institutions. Finally, BA-granting institutions are most likely to have FYC programs located in English or humanities departments (92.3 percent, compared to 86.2 percent and 82.5 percent for doctorate and BA granting, respectively), a finding that will come as no surprise. Thus, size and institutional type are important parts of the story of first-year composition administrative location.

In summary, nearly fifty years since William Riley Parker provided readers with a brief history of the origins of English departments, including their acquisition of responsibility for teaching writing, and questioned "whether or not the nineteenth-century union of literature and composition was a true marriage or merely a marriage of convenience" (Parker 1967, 11), we can at least attest that the union has lasted.

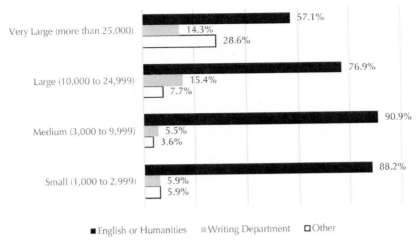

Figure 3.3. Institutional size and FYC location

THE RISE OF THE WPA?

The workshop report of the first Conference on College Composition and Communication in 1949 (Sams et al. 1950), printed in the second issue of the journal of the same name, is a useful starting point to review the history of printed arguments (or pleas) for a dedicated writing program administrator.[2] In this 1949 report the workshop attendees call for a "chairman," whose seven areas of responsibilities will ring familiar in contemporary ears (excluding gendered language), as exemplified by these two excerpts:

> (2) He should try to find means by which these people can grow in their profession and by which more and better teachers may be trained to replace them and himself . . .

> (4) He should fight for a fair share of professional recognition for the members of his [freshman English] staff, for their salaries, housing, teaching loads, research leaves, vacations, and promotions. For the chairman of a composition course, this is an uphill fight.

From this position statement on the duties of what we have come to call the WPA, I will flash forward past many public calls in the inaugural issue of *WPA: Writing Program Administration* (Bruffee 1978) and in the MLA's *Profession* (Steinmann 1978) and *College English* (Jordan 1965, cited in Heckathorn 2004), to the Portland Resolution of 1992, which constituted a major effort toward professionalizing writing programs through professionalizing those who organize and deliver FYC courses and programs. Originally called for by then-*WPA* editor Christine Hult

(McLeod 2007, 75), and endorsed by a committee and ultimately the CCCC, the Portland Resolution aimed to do for WPAs what the Wyoming Resolution of 1987 had done for the teaching of writing more broadly. Effectively, the resolution, which aimed to articulate "prerequisites for effective administration of writing programs as well as equitable treatment of WPAs" (Hult et al. 1992, 88), is an argument for the necessity of WPAs at four-year institutions at least. Thus, although I can find within *College Composition and Communication* or *WPA* no position statement or resolution declaring that all colleges and universities *should* have a designated writing program administrator who is distinct from the chair, this seems to be a tacit and reasonable expectation outside small departments wherein the chair essentially functions as the WPA or where a committee structure functions effectively (see Calhoon-Dillahunt 2011, for example, for an argument for a committee structure at a community college). Further, from the standpoint of the MLA, and as documented by Amy Heckathorn, position advertisements for WPAs grew rapidly from the inception of the MLA's *Job Information List (JIL)* in the 1970s through to the present, providing further evidence of the rise in and acceptance of the WPA as an important, if not essential, position in the contemporary college or university.

Within this sample I found a widespread but far from universal presence of writing program administrators, with WPAs serving at most of the large and/or doctoral schools and significantly fewer present at MA- and BA-granting schools. In total, 71.4 percent of FYC-requiring institutions had writing program administrators. There was a relationship between the presence of a WPA and size of institution (χ^2 (df = 3, n = 105) = 19.17, $p < 0.05$), so that as a school gets bigger, it is more likely to have a WPA. In fact, 97 percent of the large and very large institutions had WPAs, compared to 60 percent at the medium and small institutions. For doctoral institutions, 75.9 percent had WPAs, whereas 73.0 percent of MA-granting institutions had WPAs, and 53.8 percent of BA-granting institutions had WPAs. I will emphasize that this low percentage of WPAs at BA-granting institutions may not be a cause for dismay. As noted by many who have written about teaching writing in a small-college environment (Amorose 2000; Gladstein, Lebduska, and Regaignon 2009; Hanstedt and Amorose 2004; Hebb 2005; Taylor 2004), the cultures and needs of small colleges are such that strong writing instruction and programming may well occur without a designated WPA; as Jill Gladstein, Lisa Lebduska and Dara Regaignon explain, "Small colleges typically eschew complex administrative structures; often there is a great deal of pride in a relatively flattened hierarchy . . . Additionally, at a small school, many of the responsibilities associated with the work of a WPA may be shared among several individuals, rendering the work itself less visible and more difficult to codify than work that is formalized under a named position" (Gladstein, Lebduska, and Regaignon 2009, 17).

How does this current finding compare to earlier data? Studies on the presence of WPAs are difficult to find; most studies of WPAs, including excellent work on preparation, status, and conditions by Peterson (1987), Hartzog (1986b), and Charlton and Rose (2009), target WPAs themselves and thus do not capture information about institutions that *do not* have WPAs. Curiously, the 2009 CCCC survey (Gere 2009) does not ask this question, though it does ask about WPA salary, rank, and other characteristics. Similarly, in Gladstein and Regaignon's study of small liberal arts colleges (Gladstein and Regaignon 2012), institutions without some kind of writing program or director were not included. I had to go back to Emerson Shuck (1955) to find reports of a 1954 survey of seventy US "multi-purpose institutions," selected for range in size and type, to find an investigation of this question. Shuck found that 24 percent reported duties for "freshman English" as falling to the chair, 61 percent as falling to a "designated director" (209), and the remaining managing the work through a committee or other arrangement. In Shuck's study, the presence of WPAs was also found more frequently in larger schools. Notably, there was only a small increase (61 percent to 71 percent) in the presence of WPAs in the sixty years that passed between these studies, though the samples are different. In reviewing the lack of more recent discussion of this subject, it appears that researchers have not been focused on finding out how much the WPA model has been put into practice or perhaps that research methodologies haven't allowed for reporting on this area.

DO WPAS MATTER?

For those of us invested in the discipline, there is likely little debate about the value of WPAs. We believe their presence makes for better curricula, teaching, and more opportunities for students, within the world of FYC and even beyond, through their influence in the development of writing programs and other writing initiatives. And we hope the presence of WPAs has a positive impact on the work lives of faculty, both materially through the creation of better positions and job conditions, and intellectually, through the teaching communities that they help develop. This study has limited data to draw upon to answer this essential question, yet when I compared institutions in the sample that

had WPAs with those that did not, I was able to uncover several significant associations that provide evidence for the benefits of a WPA. More
specifically, the data revealed positive associations with the presence of
WPAs, particularly tenure-line faculty WPAs, and the following variables,
all of which, I believe, are widely held to be desirable:

- greater presence of training in writing instruction for FYC faculty (discussed below)
- greater presence of programmatic or department-level outcomes or
  equivalent types of statements (discussed below)
- greater presence of evidence of process writing methodologies, rhetorical instruction, and argumentation in FYC courses (see chapter 2)
- less evidence of emphasis on skills instruction in FYC courses (see
  chapter 2)
- on average, a lower class size (discussed below)

Of course, the slight *negative* association of the presence of a WPA
with tenure-track-faculty teaching FYC is not a point to be missed.
This finding is evidence in support of David Bartholomae's specula-
tion about this unintended consequence of the rise in the discipline
of composition.

> A skeptic might argue that there is a link between the growth of composi-
> tion as a field and the increased reliance on part-time, non-tenure-stream
> instructors, that the English profession's response to the felt pressure
> to *do* something about composition was to do the predictable, to create
> and endorse a research agenda and field expertise. This isolated the
> problem and made it easier for faculty members in general to say that
> they were not prepared to teach or take responsibility for composition.
> (Bartholomae 2000, 1954)

While certainly unintended, this data begs for further, serious conversation about the consequences of professionalization: has professionalization of composition led to less teaching of composition by tenure-
line faculty? Or are these coincidences of timing, as we have increasingly
entered an era in which, in total, fewer courses are taught by tenure-line
faculty across the disciplines?

STAFF OR FACULTY? RANK? DOES STATUS MATTER?

This issue of WPA status is of professional interest, of course; it functions as one of the shorthand records of the progress we have made in
establishing the discipline and the effort to increase the reward structures for the people who have expertise in writing program administration. In addition, we should ask about the effects of status: are the

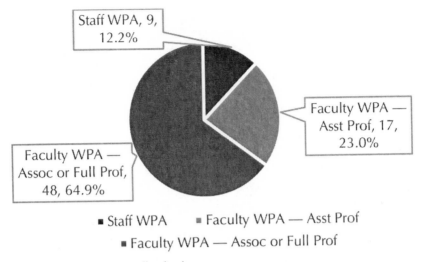

Staff WPA, 9, 12.2%

Faculty WPA — Asst Prof, 17, 23.0%

Faculty WPA — Assoc or Full Prof, 48, 64.9%

■ Staff WPA   ■ Faculty WPA — Asst Prof
■ Faculty WPA — Assoc or Full Prof

Figure 3.4. WPA position: staff or faculty

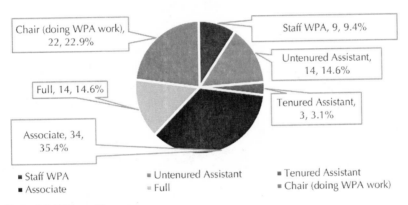

Chair (doing WPA work), 22, 22.9%

Staff WPA, 9, 9.4%

Untenured Assistant, 14, 14.6%

Full, 14, 14.6%

Tenured Assistant, 3, 3.1%

Associate, 34, 35.4%

■ Staff WPA   ■ Untenured Assistant   ■ Tenured Assistant
■ Associate   ■ Full   ■ Chair (doing WPA work)

Figure 3.5. WPA position range

writing programs run by tenure-track faculty different than those run by staff? Are there any distinguishing characteristics of programs run by faculty with higher rank? These probing questions are not easily answered, and much is unclear; nonetheless, from this sample I provide the data (what percentage were in what position) and identify significant relationships, as discussed below. To begin, just one institution reported that a committee of faculty accomplished the WPA work, and 22 percent relied on a chair or equivalent to run their writing program. Among those institutions that had WPAs ($n = 75$),[3] they broke down as represented in figures 3.4 and 3.5.

Beyond these pie charts are some interesting details: about one-fifth of the assistant professors are also tenured, with a total of 78.5 percent of the WPAs with faculty status having tenure (excluding chairs who do the work of WPAs in the absence of a dedicated WPA). How do we view the information that there are still untenured assistant professors (14.6 percent) serving as WPAs? Or that 22.9 percent of the sample do not have WPAs? The data do not, of course, provide any answers to the questions that these findings raise. However, when we look at these findings in total, for four-year state comprehensive universities, the Portland Resolution goal of job security—the "WPA should be a regular, full-time, tenured faculty member or a full-time administrator" (Hult et al. 1992, 90)—has been significantly but not fully realized. Further, faculty presence in WPA positions in this state comprehensive university study was slightly favorable to what was found in the top university study, where 22.2 percent of the programs with WPA positions were led by staff and 77.7 percent were led by faculty, 24.5 percent of whom were untenured.

Few Disadvantages with Staff WPAs

Reviewing the institutions led by staff rather than faculty WPAs reveals few distinctive characteristics, and in fact, the only two relevant hypotheses that were born out were CCCC participation and class size, the latter of which I discuss later in the chapter. In respect to CCCC participation, as expected, schools with WPAs who were tenure-track faculty were more likely to be represented at CCCC over a two-year period than was the case for schools with WPAs in staff positions. That said, the differences weren't dramatic: 69 percent of institutions with tenure-line faculty had a CCCC presentation presence compared to 50 percent of institutions with staff WPAs. Perhaps even more interesting than these positive associations are all my hypotheses that were *not* supported. I found no significant relationship between staff versus faculty status with the following variables: FYC institutional home; adaption/adoption of WPA Outcomes; emphasis on skills, argumentation, or rhetoric; or even such hot issues as use of Accuplacer, Compass, or directed self-placement for placement of students into FYC courses. The limitations of this study as a bird's-eye rather than a close view may provide partial understanding for why so few correlations were found. I hypothesize that closer research would yield significant and valuable differences, though that's conjecture on my part. Nonetheless, the null finding on these hypotheses is important to observe and consider as preliminary evidence that tenure-line status for WPAs may have less impact than many of us have imagined.

Table 3.1. WPA status: comparison across studies

Study (date of data)	Full Prof	Associate Prof	Non-Tenure-Track/Not Yet Tenured	Tenured (of those in TT positions)
"Progress," Peterson, 1986	20.0%	44.0%	30.0%	82.0%
		64.0%		
"20 More Years," Charlton and Rose, 2007	20.0%	28.0%	44.0%	68.0%
		48.0%		
Top university study, Isaacs and Knight, 2009		57.0%	22.0%	Not available
State comprehensive university study, Isaacs, 2011	18.7%	45.3%	32.0%	68.0%
		64%		

To compare the WPA-status findings of this research with other studies, I rely on Charlton and Rose's comprehensive study and summary of previous research, along with findings from the top university study to present table 3.1.

Despite differences in methodology, of note is the persistence across these studies of about one-fifth of WPAs in full-professor ranks. In other respects, we see some variation—the current study suggests that individuals at four-year state comprehensive universities are slightly more able to achieve tenure and associate professor status than those in Charlton and Rose's CWPA-membership sample, a finding I find more significant when I hypothesize that CWPA membership is likely to lean toward those who have academic positions in the first place. In light of these details, the data suggests that, on average, state comprehensive universities tend more greatly toward enabling faculty status and advancement than do private universities.

GRADUATE-STUDENT AND ADJUNCT WPAS

The scholarly discourse on status and treatment of WPAs is rich, with much discussion of the difficult and unreasonable expectations institutions have of these administrators. Most of us have our tales of woe, and a great many of us have written them down and tried to make meaning of them, myself included. The data here don't allow for understanding of the experiences of these WPAs—whether they find themselves adequately compensated, appropriately released from teaching, or able to pursue their academic goals. A few findings, however, are significant in their absence. First and foremost, I did not find any graduate-student or part-time WPAs, although in the survey and document-review process, I looked specifically for these categories. This finding is significant and good news, particularly given the scholarship on adjunct/part-time faculty and graduate students serving in WPA positions (Brown 2002; Desser and Payne 2002; Fontaine 1998; Helmbrecht and Kendall 2007; Jakuri and Williamson 1999; Long, Holberg, and Taylor 1996; Vaughn 2004) and Helmbrecht's critique: "I challenge WPAs, gWPAs, and English departments to (re)examine the institutional and professional forces that hail graduate students in rhetoric and composition into administration" (185).

To conclude this section on the WPA, I offer a brief discussion of titles. Under the category of job security, the Portland Resolution called for "a recognizable title that delineates the scope of the position (e.g., Director of Writing, Coordinator of Composition, Division or Department Chair" (Hult et al. 1992, 90). In the survey, and through confirmation through the public-document review, I collected title information, finding that titles vary broadly but that 68.9 percent included the term *director* and 28.4 percent included the term *coordinator*. Further, in their WPA titles, 48.6 percent included the word *composition*, 36.5 percent included *writing*, and just one institution, the University of Dallas, included *rhetoric*.

WHO TEACHES FYC?

Who teaches first-year composition is crucial to most of us for two different reasons: who teaches FYC speaks to the quality of our instruction and also to the quality of the life provided for the people who select this work as their profession. The profile of college and university teaching faculty is ever changing but always, it seems, in the same dismal direction: each new report, at least to this date, indicates that more of our instructional staff are part time and fewer are on tenure-track lines. Researchers from within our field have documented this trend (over the last twenty-five years, see for example Bousquet 2008; Crowley 1998; Harris 2000; Horner 2009; Lamos 2011; Schell and Stock 2001; Scott 2009), as have many organizations (AAUP 2013; ADE 2009; Coalition on the Academic Workforce 2012) and the federal government (National Center for Education Statistics 2012a). Reports vary, though none announce good news. Within the field, Tony Scott reports, "At medium-to-large universities, contingent labor teaches as many as 93% of FYC classes" (Scott 2009, 46). Somewhat more optimistically, and from a broader higher education perspective, the Association for American

Who Teaches FYC?*
- 88.8% report that tenure-track faculty teach FYC
- 59.2% report that renewable lecturer faculty teach FYC
- 53.1% report that limited term lecturer faculty teach FYC
- 94.9% report that adjunct faculty teach FYC
- 38.8% report that graduate students teach FYC

Who Teaches FYC Most?
- 27.4% report that the majority of FYC courses are taught by tenure-line faculty
- 18.9% report that the majority of FYC courses are taught by indefinitely renewable lecturer faculty
- 8.4% report that the majority of FYC courses are taught by full-time lecturer faculty on limited terms
- 35.8% report that the majority of FYC courses are taught by adjunct faculty
- 8.4% report that the majority of FYC courses are taught by graduate students

* For this area of inquiry, I have a sample size of 95, and I rely on representative reporting through the survey. Although I examined websites and catalogs, reviewing faculty lists to amplify or verify survey data, I determined that relying on the survey data, for this area, was most consistent and appropriate.

Figure 3.6. Who teaches FYC

University Professors (AAUP) reports that 70.2 percent of the labor force is contingent, with 19.1 percent in full-time non-tenure-track faculty positions, 51.1 percent in part-time positions, and just 29.8 percent on tenure lines (with 20.7 percent in tenured positions and the remaining 9.1 percent untenured) (AAUP 2013, 4).

To get a handle on practices around staffing in the sample, I focused not on specific numbers but on two data points I could reliably collect: first, the full range of types of faculty who taught FYC at these institutions, and second, the types of faculty (tenure-track, non-tenure-track renewable lecturer, non-tenure-track limited-term lecturer, graduate student, adjunct) who taught *most* sections of FYC at their schools. For the first data point, I was able to gather information through both the survey and institutional websites, and for the second point I relied primarily on the survey. To begin this discussion, the following two lists summarize the findings from the sample.

Tenure-Line Faculty Are Most Likely to Teach FYC at
BA-Granting, Small, and Open-Admissions Institutions

Behind these sample-wide descriptive statistics are significant differences among institutions that will not surprise those who work in higher education but would be news to those people who attend and/or pay for others to attend our institutions. Prominently, I found significant relationships between types of faculty who taught FYC most and condensed Carnegie Classification (χ^2 ($df = 8$, $n = 94$) = 23.98, $p < 0.05$),

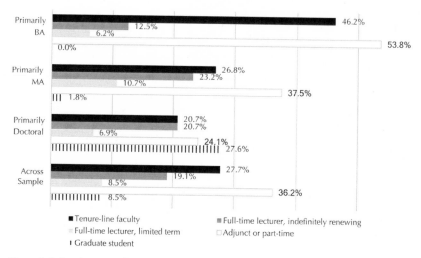

Figure 3.7. Faculty type who taught FYC most, by Carnegie Classification

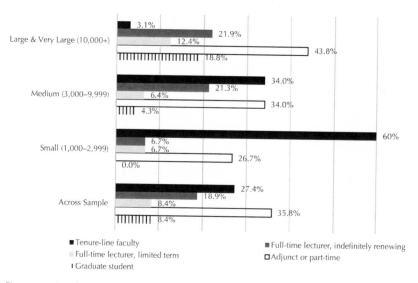

Figure 3.8. Faculty type who taught FYC most, by institutional size

size (χ^2 (df = 12, n = 94) = 24.71, p < 0.05), and, marginally, institutional selectivity (χ^2 (df = 8, n = 87) = 14.46, p < 0.10), as detailed in figures 3.7, 3.8, and 3.9. For each figure I have reproduced the sample wide (across sample) breakdown for ease of comparison.

From the data presented in these figures, I observe both expected and unexpected findings. In the expected category, we see that small and

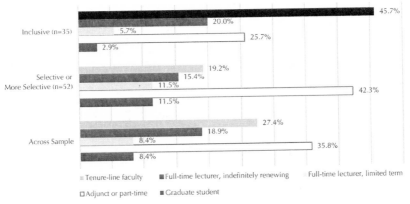

Figure 3.9. Faculty type who taught FYC most, by admissions selectivity

BA-granting institutions are most likely to employ tenure-line faculty for the work of teaching FYC. In respect to type of institution, 43.8 percent of the BA-granting institutions had tenure-line faculty teaching most FYC courses, compared to 31.5 percent at the MA-granting institutions and just 6.3 percent at the doctorate-granting institutions. In respect to size of the institution, 60.0 percent of the small institutions had tenure-line faculty teaching most FYC courses, compared to 9.0 percent at the medium-sized institutions, 4.0 percent at the large institutions, and none at the very large institutions. These findings of greater instruction by tenure-track faculty at smaller institutions are consistent with Smith's 1974 study and also with findings from Moghtader, Cotch, and Hague (2001), who replicated Smith's research. These findings are not surprising, but they are noteworthy. Another predictable finding is that doctoral institutions are relying most heavily on graduate assistants, and MA and BA institutions are relying more heavily on adjunct and non-tenure-track faculty.

In the category of unexpected findings, I want to highlight the relatively high occurrence of tenure-line faculty as majority staff (at 27.7 percent of the institutions), the relatively few graduate students (at 8.5 percent of the institutions) in this category, and the generally better staffing situation at inclusive, over selective, or more selective institutions. Given the dismal reports about the decreasing presence of tenure-line faculty across higher education, how do we account for nearly a quarter of these institutions reporting that tenure-line faculty teach the majority of FYC sections? A likely explanation might be found in what Ianetta describes, in respect to another misperception, as the field's tendency to focus heavily on "certain institutional vantage points—namely R1 institutions" (Ianetta 2010, 54). A practical explanation is related to the effect smaller institutions have on the national portrait of tenure-track-faculty teaching provided by national studies such as the 2004 National Study of Postsecondary Faculty report, which finds tenure-line faculty representing 34 percent of the nation's faculty, or the Association of Departments of English survey (2008), which reports that TT faculty represent 35 percent of the total (Bartholomae 2011, 14), down from 40 percent in 1996–97 (ADE Ad Hoc Committee on Staffing 2008). From my finding, which presents a more positive view than I expected, it might seem that we are not so far away from Kitzhaber's exhortation: "No matter how large the university or how many advanced-degree candidates it has who need subsidizing, no English department should use only graduate students and junior instructors to teach the freshman course" (Kitzhaber 1962, 133).

This discovery of significant full-time faculty participation in FYC instruction is made more significant if we total tenure-line faculty and full-time non-tenure-track lecturer faculty in continuing lines. As argued for by Bartholomae (2011), Joseph Harris (2006), Kelly Kinney (2009), Michael Murphy (2000) and the MLA/ADE (ADE Ad Hoc Committee on Staffing 2008), non-tenure-track lecturer full-time lines may allow for positions advantageous to both students and teachers, a point of view that has been argued against by the likes of Marc Bousquet (2002), Cheryl Glenn (2000), and James Sledd (2001). In this sample, when I count both tenure-line faculty and non-tenure-line full-time continuing positions, I find that most FYC courses are taught by tenure and non-tenure continuing faculty at 46.8 percent of the relevant sample. Another way to see this picture is by looking at size: the majority of small institutions had FYC taught primarily by full-time faculty, whereas at the medium, large, and extra-large institutions, this was not the case, though for medium-sized institutions, the addition of limited-term-lecturer faculty to tenured faculty brings the total to 55.3 percent. It should be noted that the total effect of these large institutions on student experiences is much greater, given the numbers of students they educate. Related, if we look at non-tenure-track full-time faculty presence, it appears that many colleges and universities have taken seriously the trend toward non-tenure-track full-time hiring advocated by the MLA. As Bartholomae (2011) notes, here is a case in which the interests of administrators and tenured faculty appear to have found common ground: "Tenure-track faculty in English, those who argued for and reaped the rewards of increased support for research, participated in the redefinition of the humanities workforce. It was not just done to them (or to us). In a sense, our interests and the interests of the institution lined up perfectly" (26). It is hard to feel entirely comfortable with this result, though I agree with Bartholomae's assertion that those of us who have argued for and received reductions in teaching responsibilities in exchange for research or administration are complicit, even if we have managed to persuade ourselves otherwise.

Further, in comparison to Smith's 1974 findings on faculty teaching FYC, I observe fewer distinctions than expected: Smith and colleagues observed that 40 percent of four-year state universities reported that required comp classes were taught by regular, full-time staff only (140), which I compare to 46.3 percent for this study. A more significant difference is in the use of part-time faculty: Smith reported that 50 percent had some TAs teaching FYC, and 53 percent had some part timers teaching comp (140), whereas from this study, we see 94.9 percent of institutions employed part-time faculty, though only 38.8 percent employed graduate students. The latter number is likely a reflection of sample differences because, compared to my study, Smith's survey methodology resulted in more institutions with graduate programs.

The two unexpected findings from this study on graduate-student instructors deserve brief discussion. That only 8.4 percent of the institutions relied primarily on graduate students for staffing of FYC is yet another reminder that higher education practices do not mirror conference and even journal discussions which, in respect to labor issues, have magnified the role of graduate instructors as contingent laborers. The finding that inclusive institutions relied less on contingent instructors of any kind, much less than competitive or very competitive ones did, came to me as a surprise, and I cannot find scholarly discussion of this phenomenon. We can all posit the same guess: perhaps inclusive institutions especially emphasize teaching. Faculty at these institutions might also have higher teaching loads, and thus the difference between per-course cost for tenure-line versus other faculty teaching may be smaller, making per-course costs for tenure-line faculty less expensive for these institutions than for schools whose faculty have smaller teaching loads. Clearly more research in this area, both theoretical and empirical, is needed.

FYC FACULTY DEVELOPMENT AND TRAINING: UNEVEN AND UNPREDICTABLE

While faculty development and training is typically initiated by faculty leaders and WPAs, I include this discussion in this chapter because faculty development often requires compensation, which must be provided by higher administration. My decision to investigate the faculty-development and training approaches of universities and colleges in the sample reflects my assumption that instruction in FYC benefits from regular and well-planned training and continued development. This belief is likely shared by many in the scholarly community, evidenced by the fact that there was a statistically high association between an institution answering affirmatively to the question "Are instructors who teach FYC specifically trained for teaching writing?" and participation at CCCC ($t(93) = 3.05$, $p < 0.05$). Institutions that did not train faculty to teach FYC had a mean number of presentations of 2.25 ($SD = 4.08$), and those that did train faculty to teach FYC had a mean of 5.88 ($SD = 7.52$). Nonetheless, I recognize some problems with the position that FYC faculty necessarily need explicit training in FYC from the employing university, as I can well imagine the argument that training and faculty development around FYC instruction should be no more necessary (or present) than in any other field, as such preparation should be reliably occurring through graduate instruction, prior to point of hire. (And indeed it often is, but my entering assumption was that still, too frequently, faculty hired to teach FYC do not actually have sufficient training in the field.) At smaller institutions particularly, formalized training may be replaced by the excellent informal "training" that occurs when close office proximity of senior faculty and junior faculty allows for an apprentice model of daily and informal faculty development. I make these qualifications before noting that there was a significant correlation between institutions whose representatives indicated the presence of FYC faculty development and Carnegie size, with all the small institutions in this study reporting that they did *not* provide required or optional faculty-development activities.

Thus, while 33.7 percent of the total sample responded affirmatively to the question about faculty training, if we remove small institutions, the percentage increases to 40.0 percent. Beyond this specific question about whether institutions provided any FYC training, institutional representatives were presented with a "check-all-that-apply" question that listed a range of different development or training activities that were either required or offered; when these numbers are totaled, we see greater involvement with professional training and development: 49.3 percent of the medium-sized and larger institutions *required* some kind of activity (from the list below) for training or development; 79.5 percent reported that they *invited* their faculty to participate in these opportunities. As schools get larger, faculty are more likely to be trained in writing (χ^2 ($df = 3$, $n = 95$) = 12.91, $p < 0.05$), a discovery that few will find surprising. Figure 3.10 below indicates the range of activities

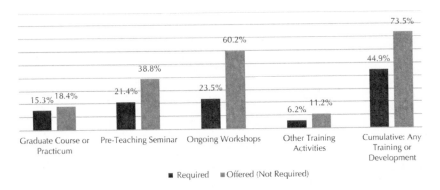

Figure 3.10. Training and development activities: required and offered

reported as being provided at the seventy-eight institutions that had enrollments of three thousand or more students and for which usable data was available.[4]

In these findings we can see evidence of uneven preparation and alignment of teaching in FYC at four-year state comprehensive universities. While scholarship in the field on what kind of professional training or development is best varies widely, the plethora of scholarship on FYC faculty preparation,[5] most especially on graduate-assistant training (see, for example, Estrem and Reid 2012 for a useful history of the focus on graduate-student training in the scholarship), speaks to the widespread consensus on the value of such programming. There is no evidence of debate among scholars about the importance of such programming, but implementation is, evidently, a greater challenge than I had realized. This data suggests that Heidi Estrem and Shelley Reid's call for a WPA Outcomes-like "framework—guiding principles, goals, and outcomes— of robustly imagined WPE [writing program education] programs" is indeed in order (Estrem and Reid 2012, 236).

However, what was additionally surprising to me was the low incidence of association between participation in faculty-development activities and the presence of a workforce of contingent or lecturer faculty, which are groups that tend to be subject to high turnover and/or uneven preparation in teaching writing. Wouldn't the existence of these high-turnover faculty necessitate a faculty-development or training program? To understand this discovery, I hypothesized that many institutions would offer faculty development if they had a WPA to lead such efforts; however, only 56.7 percent of the institutions with WPAs required any kind of training or development (compared to 44.9 percent across the

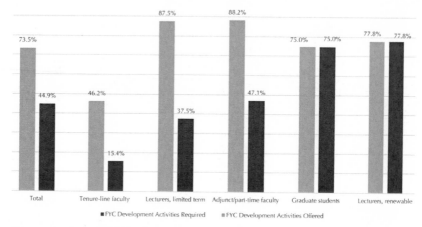

Figure 3.11. Professional-development requirements by primary FYC faculty type

population), though all of them had some kind of non-tenure-track faculty teaching FYC. Similarly, when the question shifted from required to invited, I found that 78.1 percent of WPA-led programs included such optional opportunities, compared to 59.1 percent of institutions that did not have a WPA at the helm. Beyond the scope of this study are insights as to whether WPAs and programs that do not offer or require faculty development do not do so on principle or because of resistance, workload rules, or some other reason.

I also thought the presence of graduate students teaching FYC would be associated with a required graduate course, practicum, or at least a preteaching seminar. I also hoped that significant usage of non-tenure-track faculty would be associated with the presence of faculty-development activities, which is the case. In figure 3.11 you see the nonstatistically significant trend lines for both required and offered development activities. More generally, and with the exception of institutions that employ graduate students and renewable lecturers, the data show a clear preference for *offering* over *requiring* faculty development.

The argument for optional over required professional-development activities is easy to make: it's a more collegial approach, it's likely the preferred approach for teaching faculty, and it's especially appealing when departments aren't able to offer additional compensation for such activities. However, this data raises questions about how institutions provide consistently effective writing courses without requiring faculty development, if only to bring people to consensus on assessment issues or course components. Even more questions are raised when we think about what happens at the 20.4 percent of the institutions that do not

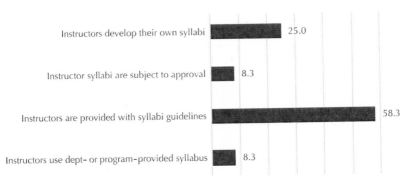

Figure 3.12. Syllabus standardization

require or offer any faculty development at all. How is consistency in teaching and assessment achieved?

COURSE STANDARDIZATION THROUGH SYLLABI

The issue of syllabi standardization evokes strong reactions from both faculty and administrators, with the former typically in opposition and the latter more positively inclined. Witte, Meyer, and Miller observe this diversity of perspectives with a decidedly neutral stance: "The effects of such a requirement can be many, and they can be either positive or negative, depending on the particular course, program, and institution involved" (Witte, Meyer, and Miller 1982, 23). They then report that 40 percent to 49 percent (24) of faculty teaching FYC at four-year public universities were required to follow a common, departmental syllabus, an increase in autonomy from what was assumed by Kitzhaber. In his study, Kitzhaber appears to take for granted that syllabi are departmental and collective (Kitzhaber 1963, 8–10), revealing how differently faculty in the early 1960s must have felt about syllabi standardization compared to contemporary views, where standardization is seen by many as an incursion on academic freedom or perhaps simply a removal of one of the chief pleasures of teaching one's own class. As revealed in figure 3.12, respondents to this study reported a middle-ground approach between total faculty independence and total control by the department or program, with 58.3 percent of respondents reporting that their faculty were provided with guidelines for developing syllabi, and another 16.7 percent reporting that faculty developed their own syllabi, subject to approval. Just 8.3 percent of institutions provided and required a specific syllabus, suggesting this practice is well outside the mainstream. The final 25.0 percent reported that faculty had total autonomy over syllabi. As

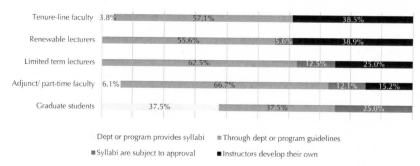

Figure 3.13. Syllabus standardization as a function of majority rank of FYC instructors

was hypothesized and is detailed in figure 3.13, autonomy over syllabi is associated primarily with the status of the majority of the faculty who taught FYC.

While this question provides only a limited view of the ways state comprehensive colleges and universities provide responsible oversight—or controlling reins, depending on one's outlook—of FYC implementation, as with the discussion of faculty development, we once again see a full range of approaches, with graduate students receiving the most guidance or oversight and tenure-line faculty receiving the least.

CLASS SIZE: BROAD RANGE, WITH SIGNIFICANT CORRELATIONS BY REGION, PRESENCE OF SPECIAL POPULATIONS, AND PRESENCE OF GRADUATE PROGRAMS

There are few numbers that mean more to writing faculty than class size. We judge a job, an institution, and perhaps even the discipline by this number, and few facts strike envy into others' hearts like the statement "our class size is fifteen," or twelve, as is the case at a few elite institutions. For those of us in state universities, such a number may well be nonexistent. Rich Haswell compiled a list in 2004–05 based on self-reporting and casual investigation that included a nonrandom sample of 177 institutions that had a mean class size of 21.49 (cited in Horning 2007, 20). This is an improvement over what Shuck reported from his two studies: a mean of 24.0 from his midwestern-schools sample (Shuck 1955) and a mean of 25.1 from his US multipurpose institution sample (Shuck 1955, 205). For this portion of my study I was able to begin with survey responses and then fill in and verify these numbers by directly reviewing course information in catalogs or online scheduling tools, which make verification easy, if laborious. The mean FYC class

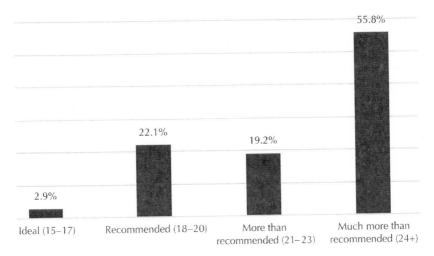

Figure 3.14. FYC class size: not meeting recommendations

size for this study was 23.3 (*SD* = 3.19), with the range running from three schools having an FYC class size of fifteen to five schools having a class size of thirty. Further, 55.8 percent had class sizes of twenty-four or higher, a finding that is disheartening.

How do these findings compare with the other studies? Given the variations in sampling methodologies used by Shuck, Haswell, and myself, little can be made of the differences over time. However, when we drill down and look at school characteristics, interesting if unwelcome associations are discovered.

My initial hypothesis about the kinds of variables that would associate with smaller class size focused on what I would refer to as *best practices*. Thus, I thought the kind of institution that had a WPA (and ideally a tenure-line WPA), had a CCCC presentation presence, and taught process writing or had a course sequence coded for process-writing instruction (see chapter 4) would be a good candidate for smaller class sizes. I hypothesized that either the presence of WPAs and faculty active at CCCC would lead to smaller class sizes or that, perhaps more likely, the same institutional forces that enabled these "best-practice" variables would also enable "good" practices around class size. I was wrong. In all these variables, I observed no associations, significant or trending. Sometimes I even observed the reverse, as is the case with the variable about tenure-track faculty: whereas I hypothesized that institutions that had most FYC classes taught by tenure-track faculty would likely have lower class sizes, in fact, the opposite result was shown. To simplify:

- When most FYC classes were taught by tenure-track faculty, the mean class size was 20.0 (SD = 3.04), n = 26.
- When most FYC classes were taught by full-time renewable faculty, the mean class size was 23.92 (SD = 2.30), n = 18.
- When most FYC classes were taught by full-time faculty, limited term, the mean size was 24.0 (SD = 2.45), n = 8.
- When most FYC classes were taught by adjunct faculty, the mean class size was 22.56 (SD = 4.0), n = 34.
- When most FYC classes were taught by graduate students, the mean class size was 22.68 (SD = 2.89), n = 8.

The higher the status of the faculty, the smaller the class size. Another way of putting it is this: 28.3 percent of the schools that had twenty-four or more students in an FYC class were institutions where FYC was primarily taught by tenure-line faculty, similar only to schools where FYC was primarily taught by adjunct or part-time faculty.

Some significant class-size associations with institutional variables were unexpected, but interesting. Significant class-size associations were found with the variables region (as defined by accrediting agency) and special-population institutions (HBSCUs and Hispanic serving), but not with graduate classification or size. In other words, contrary to what one might expect, class size did not go up as institutional enrollment went up or when graduate classification shifted "up." Once again, as with the presence of tenure-track faculty teaching FYC, we see a significantly lower class size correlated with BA-focused four-year state universities over MA-focused institutions and, to a greater extent, doctorate-focused institutions. Equally interesting discoveries, for me, are the correlations between class size and region, with the finding that the New England region had a significantly smaller mean class size than did the other regions, with the spread and differences detailed in table 3.2.

Statistically significant differences were found among these regions in respect to class size ($F(5, 98)$ = 3.26, $p < 0.05$). What is beyond the scope of this study is an understanding of why this might be the case: Do these regional trends in class size show up across disciplines? If flagship universities, community colleges, and private institutions were also profiled, would these trends still appear?

Finally, an unwelcome relationship was found when institutions are divided by identification as HBCU, Hispanic serving, or non-HBCU/Hispanic serving, as detailed in figure 3.15 ($F(2, 101)$ = 6.70, $p < 0.05$), with both HBCUs and Hispanic-serving institutions having larger FYC class sizes than do schools without these designations. Schools with no special designation had a mean class size of 22.77 (SD = 2.97); HBCUs

Table 3.2. FYC class size and regional location

Region	Mean	Standard Deviation	n
New England	18.00	2.16	4
Middle states	22.58	4.15	19
North central	23.43	2.44	34
Northwest	24.36	3.09	7
Western	24.29	2.98	7
Southern	23.91	2.86	33

had an FYC mean class size of 25.54 (SD = 3.58); and Hispanic-serving institutions had an FYC mean class size of 25.30 (SD = 2.84). The total mean was 23.34 (SD = 3.19).

Two questions are both obvious and beyond the scope of this study. First, why did HBCUs and Hispanic-serving four-year state comprehensive universities tilt more greatly toward large class sizes for FYC? Second, what is the effect of larger class sizes on students at HBCUs and Hispanic-serving institutions? As has been documented by Alice Horning (2007, 19–20), our national organizations (NCTE/CCCC and MLA/ADE) periodically and consistently call out for small class sizes of fifteen to twenty students, though unfortunately calls for reducing class size are much more frequent than are empirical studies that demonstrate the improved outcomes of smaller classes, particularly in higher education. That said, some data support the position that larger class sizes have a negative effect: a careful and large study of student evaluations of teacher effectiveness in economics courses at UC Santa Barbara found a consistent and large negative effect correlating with increased class size (Bedard and Kuhn 2008), as did another large study of class size and final grades across disciplinary areas conducted at a (anonymous) research university (Johnson 2010). In the field of writing studies, Horning relies heavily on Astin's work (Astin 1993) on the positive effect of smaller student-faculty ratios on student engagement and graduation records (cited in Horning 2007, 12). Horning also calls attention to Gregory Glau's research, tracking the basic writing Stretch program at Arizona State, from which the finding that dropping class size from twenty-six to nineteen was correlated with higher pass rates; lower drop, withdrawal, and failure rates; sequence continuation rates; and student evaluations, across instructional type (Glau 2007, 45). For most of us, the value of smaller classes is experiential—our lives as students and teachers have made that clear. This conclusion is widely shared outside

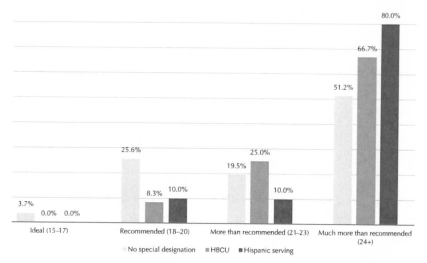

Figure 3.15. FYC class size at HBCUs and Hispanic-serving institutions

certain political arenas; as James Monks and Robert Schmidt note, lower class size is so widely valued that it "represents two of the fifteen inputs into the *US News and World Report* college-ranking formula (Monks, Schmidt, and the Cornell Higher Education Research Institute 2010, 1). Thus, though the sample sizes for Hispanic-serving and HBCUs in this study are fairly small (twelve and ten, respectively), it's nonetheless a concerning trend that deserves further research and attention.

BASIC WRITING: PERSISTING AT SCUS

Providing and maintaining basic writing courses or programs for under-prepared students is a site of great stress for writing faculty and basic writing supporters, and the political landscape is both tumultuous and frequently changing. Mike Rose describes the terrain as contradictory, with pressures that aid and undermine support for underprepared writers being exerted simultaneously: "At the same time that there is a push to get more low-income people into postsecondary education, cash-strapped states are cutting education budgets, leading colleges to limit enrollments and cut classes and student services" (Rose 2012, 15). On some level, basic writing is always under threat, and pronouncements that basic writing will be eradicated come fairly frequently. Yet where the pressure to remove basic writing instruction from four-year institutions is clearly powerful, as evidenced by actions taken in both California and in the CUNY system, to offer two familiar examples, opposing political pressures, namely retention rates and enrollment increases, also push these programs back into existence, often under new names (see Otte and Mlynarczyk 2010 for an engaging history of basic writing). This may explain how it is that 80.2 percent of the four-year state institutions in this study were found to have basic writing programs, a finding drawn from catalog and course-offerings review and confirmed by the survey. I suspect basic writing is more often renamed or repositioned than actually entirely eliminated.

It's useful to begin with a comparison to other studies, though I'll risk repetition and note that methodologies and populations vary across these studies. But a review of this data at least suggests that changes in practices around offering basic writing instruction include variation and flux, depending on the sample. The National Center for Education Statistics has not reported out on higher educational institutions' offering of basic writing since a 2003 report on data from 2000 (Parsad and Lewis 2003). At that point, 68 percent of all institutions in the study (of two- and four-year public and private colleges and universities) offered remedial writing (7), compared to 67 percent of the public four-year universities, a finding that is down slightly from the 1995 reporting of 71 percent (8). In comparison, Basmat Parsad and Laurie Lewis reported that 46 percent of private four-year universities offered remedial writing in 2000, down from 52 percent in 1995. Thus, we see that, consistently, public universities are more likely to offer basic writing than are private universities. The higher percentages found in my study are likely the result of the focus on the state comprehensive or regional university, which excludes many flagship public universities that likely share characteristics with private universities. Certainly, however, this finding of an 80.2 percent presence of basic writing instruction in the sample suggests that pronouncements of the death of basic writing at four-year public universities are premature, particularly when we take an historical view (see table 3.3).

I suspect that much of the data fluctuation in table 3.3 reflects a mix of changes in enrollment, historical trends, and varying samples. For example, the top university study is the most significant point of comparison with a similar method but a very different population, and yet we see many fewer schools offering basic writing at top universities. The top university study tilts much more toward selectivity: all institutions in that sample were classified as selective, at least (82.2 percent are *more selective* and 17.8 percent are *selective*) compared to this study, for which only 54.7 percent are either *more selective* or *selective* and 37.7 percent are *inclusive* or *unclassified*.

Table 3.3. Presence of basic writing courses across studies

Study, data collection year	Sample characteristics	Basic writing presence in sample	Author note
Shuck, 1953 survey (Shuck 1955)	Midwestern universities, $n = 26$	62%	"Most of the institutions in this 1953 survey indicated satisfaction with their remedial programs" (Shuck 1955, 207).
Shuck, 1954 survey (Shuck 1955)	Multipurpose universities, nationwide, $n = 70$	66%	
Kitzhaber, 1960–61 school year	"A fairly accurate cross-section," private and public, $n = 95$	Less than half have course on the books; a "few" offer clinics or lab options (Kitzhaber 1963, 18).	"The students who used to populate remedial English courses in the college and universities . . . now appear to be going to junior colleges" (Kitzhaber 1962, 478).
Smith, 1973 survey (Smith 1974)	Random sample survey; 70% return rate, $n = 490$	44%	
Trimmer, 1986 (Trimmer 1987)	All 2- and 4-year schools, MLA List; 35.4% returned	84%	
Gere, 2009	Survey of CCCC membership; 525 return rate; $n = 643$	71.16%	
Top university study, Isaacs and Knight, 2009	Top-university public-document study, $n = 101$	51.5% overall; 64.3% of public	
State comprehensive U study, Isaacs, 2011	Randomized from ASCU list	80.2%	

Joseph Trimmer has argued that basic writing instruction and support has been in decline ever since the heyday of basic writing in the 1970s and 80s, citing Andrea Lunsford's survey finding that 90 percent of surveyed universities had or intended to create a basic writing program (Trimmer 1987, 4). More recently, scholars have written about states' efforts to remove basic writing from four-year colleges (Goen-Salter 2008; Greene and McAlexander 2008; Otte and Mlynarczyk 2010). Certainly the threat to basic writing is well documented in the public press, yet the data suggesting the persistence of these programs is equally clear. At the conclusion of their history of basic writing, George Otte and Rebecca Mlynarcyzk (2010) address the future by countering the significant threats to basic writing instruction in four-year colleges with reports of innovation, adaptation, and, as always, the case for growing need: "It is possible but by no means certain that current threats to basic writing may be trumped by future needs as economic forces reconfigure the political landscape" (187).

BASIC WRITING: CLASS SIZE

Basic writing class-size data are as follows: the mean is 20.5 students (SD = 5.0), and the median is 20. These numbers compare with an FYC class-size mean of 23.3 (SD = 3.19) and a median of 24. Thus, while basic writing class sizes are generally higher than recommended by our national organizations (which typically cite a maximum of fifteen), they do follow the recommendation for having a comparatively smaller class capacity for basic writing instruction. In respect to range, basic writing class-size data reveal a disturbing range of twenty-seven students, compared to fifteen for FYC. Behind this range are a basic writing class size of eight at The College of New Jersey and a class size of thirty-five at Colorado Mesa University. Of interest, both these schools are medium-sized institutions, but The College of New Jersey has a staff writing-program administrator, and Colorado Mesa University does not have a WPA at all.

BASIC WRITING: PLACEMENT PRACTICES

Placement into basic writing or first-year composition has been subject to rich discussion in the scholarship, so much so that I think readers will be surprised at the primary findings, which are that 82.3 percent of schools that offer basic writing use a standardized test—ACT, SAT, Accuplacer, or a State Objective (multiple choice) test for basic writing placement. This data was gathered from the survey and catalog review; in some instances the survey respondent did not report an objective-test usage, but the catalog clearly did. For this section the catalog, which is the official record, prevailed. I should say that the data is a little more complex, as some schools that use these heavily standardized object measures appear to do so as a first cut, with additional refinement at the program level. For example, 17.7 percent (n = 14) of the schools reported they had a directed self-placement (DSP) element, with 78.6 percent of these institutions using a standardized test as well, so some of these DSP schools had a mixed-methods approach. Many schools had provisions for appeal, apparently mandated by state law, and this resulted in 45.6 percent of schools having an element of placement

Table 3.4. Placement methods

Instrument used for placement	Percentage of institutions
Placement by any standardized test (SAT, ACT, COMPASS and/or ACCUPLACER)	81.0%
SAT scores	45.6%
ACT scores	54.4%
COMPASS	30.4%
ACCUPLACER	26.6%
In-house assessment	45.6%

by what I refer to as *in-house assessment*. In looking at the figure below (which reports only on the seventy-nine institutions that offered basic writing), it's important to recognize that institutions often use more than one placement instrument.

Readers can readily interpret this data: nationally developed, typically indirect objective tests, whether from the College Board or ACT or the relative newcomers COMPASS or ACCUPLACER, have collectively worked to become the outsourced solution to writing placement at comprehensive four-year colleges and universities in the United States. Although researchers have consistently demonstrated the poor predictive value of such measures (Elliot et al. 2012; Haswell and Wyche-Smith 1994; Huot, O'Neill, and Moore 2010; Isaacs and Keohane 2012; Isaacs and Molloy 2010; O'Neill, Moore, and Huot 2009; Peckham 2009; White 2008; White, Elliot, and Peckham 2015), it appears that neither the researchers nor the reports and quotes from MIT's anti-SATs crusader Les Perelman in the mainstream press (Weiss, *Boston Globe*, March 14, 2014) have done much to persuade state universities to abandon their reliance on these sources. Norbert Elliot and his coauthors argue that the source of test reliance lies in a "national culture of remediation" (2012, 306) that relies fundamentally on the assumption that high school does not teach writing adequately, which has allowed for the rise of outsourcing assessment: "Capitalizing on these debates, both for-profit and non-profit organizations have developed tests for writing placement" (Elliot et al. 2012, 307).

Amidst the dominant story of reliance on national, objective assessments for placement is the persistence of some level of local testing: 45.6 percent of the institutions that offer basic writing include in-house assessment, which takes place in various forms: after initial cut via an objective test, as a challenge option, or as the primary and sole measure. However,

Table 3.5. Placement in-house testing

	As a percentage of institutions that include in-house placement (n = 36)	As a percentage of institutions that offer basic writing (n = 79)
Primarily objective	61.1%	27.8%
Primarily essay based	5.6%	2.5%
Directed self-placement	38.9%	17.7%
Not determined	4.0%	2.5%

the data allowed me to identify three primary types of in-house testing: primarily objective (an indirect measure, typically consisting of multiple-choice-type questions), primarily essay based (a direct measure), and DSP, with distribution across these approaches detailed in table 3.5.

It is noteworthy that 17.7 percent (*n* = 14) of the schools that offer basic writing use directed self-placement (DSP), a classification of methods introduced at Colgate (Harrington 2005; Howard 2000) and made popular by Daniel Royer and Roger Gilles (Royer and Gilles 1998), and which varies in implementation, as has been detailed in subsequent scholarship (Blakesley 2002; Gere et al. 2010; Royer and Gilles 2003).

Concern over reliance on national, standardized placement assessment is heightened when we consider research on the disparate impact of these assessments. Asoue Inoue (2015), Mya Poe (Inoue and Poe 2014), and Norbert Elliot, as well as other researchers, have been leaders in defining and bringing attention to disparate impact in writing assessment and suggesting methods for writing program administrators to develop placement methods that avoid disparate impact, which most frequently really means practices that more negatively impact students of color. For example, Inoue reports that students of color at Fresno State in California were identified as needing remediation by the English Placement Test at "dramatically higher rates than white students" (Inoue 2015, 35). For Inoue, part of the remedy for racially disparate impact was to adopt directed self-placement, a measure that was not possible when Edward White and Leon Thomas reported similar findings in 1981 (White and Thomas 1981; Moore, O'Neill, and Crow 2016, 18). Lest we assume that local assessments are always better, Mya Poe and colleague's examination of a locally designed placement assessment consisting of a two-hour writing sample evaluated by trained faculty readers found that "nearly half of African American students (47%) and over one-quarter of Hispanic students (28%)" were placed into basic writing, a result that writing faculty at Brick University found "disquieting" (Poe et al. 2014,

598). For the writing faculty at Brick City University, the solution was to place all students into the standard FYC course and to conduct an assessment two weeks into the semester, only for the purpose of providing additional writing support to identified students.

Comparing the findings of this study with two studies conducted in 1950 and 2009 suggests that objective testing has always been prevalent, though likely not as standardized or commercial and nationally managed, and that the DSP movement is indeed a new phenomenon in local placement. (The only other data on DSP prevalence I could find were on CompFAQ's "List of Schools Using DSP," which in May of 2014 listed thirty-four schools and thirty-five in March 2015 [CompFAQs 2017].) Emerson Shuck's 1950s study identifies The Cooperative English Test as the most commonly used assessment (206), which is defined as an assessment that "purports to measure ability in spelling, vocabulary, sentence structure, grammar and diction . . . [and] requires approximately 105 minutes for administration" (Shuck 1955, 82). More recently, the CCCC survey of members asked respondents to report on what was the most important criterion for placement at their institutions, finding that some kind of standardized test was the leader at 52.78 percent and that in-house assessments accounted for 29.08 percent of the responses, with 8.25 percent reporting "Guided Self-Placement" (Gere 2009). The CCCC report also gave two other interesting options, reporting that 2.89 percent of respondents identified application data as most important in placement and 0.62 percent reporting portfolio evaluation. These are important methods on which I did not seek findings.

In my own former work as a WPA, it took me years to take on placement. I remember thinking vaguely that placement probably wasn't done well, but I had enough to do and was happy enough to simply trust the in-house assessment admissions ran and to focus instead on teaching credit-bearing basic writing to students who seemed to benefit from it. When my university moved to placement by the SAT, I couldn't ignore the problem, and from there I embarked on a local assessment project that led to solutions that programmatic evaluation suggested were much better (Isaacs and Keohane 2012; Isaacs and Molloy 2010) and whose merits I could at least evaluate, though I will say they haven't stuck, as numerous higher-level changes, mandates, and conditions have made our in-house solutions impossible. But still, I am happy to support my successor WPA as she perseveres in finding placement solutions that, at very least, do no harm. Placement remains an important site for writing faculty to take control through meaningful assessments that not only place students adequately but also support strong practices in teaching and learning. While I certainly sympathize with WPAs who have not taken on placement, I want to encourage WPAs to garner the strength to attempt some local research that may open the doors to methods that are better than relying on the SAT or other national objective tests. Simply put, we are not following the evidence from our own research when it comes to placement assessment.

BASIC WRITING: CREDIT AND EXIT ASSESSMENT

Two major issues around basic writing instruction are whether or not institutions grant credit for basic writing and whether or not there is an exit assessment exam. In respect to exit examinations, 25 percent of the institutions that offered basic writing required an exit assessment for the course. (Interestingly, and to offer comparison, 5.0 percent of schools required an exit exam for FYC.) What is beyond the scope of this research is information on the specifics of these exit assessments. (For this question, I relied primarily on the survey and secondarily on websites and catalogs, which did not always provide details.) In respect to the important issue of credit for basic writing instruction, just 7.7 percent of the schools did not give students any credit for basic writing instruction, and the remaining 92.3 percent were split between giving institutional credit only (which allows for financial aid) and full credit toward graduation.

EXEMPTIONS

Exemptions for FYC are available across state comprehensive universities through multiple means and most frequently through national assessments, whether for-profit or nonprofit. With the exception of Medgar Evers College in New York,[6] every school in the sample provided ways for students to exempt out of FYC courses, as detailed below. Most schools offered many options. In my review I considered a designated cut score in the following: advanced placement (AP), international baccalaureate (IB), ACT, SAT, or CLEP. Other methods I included were: portfolio or in-house assessment.[7]

In the comparative review provided in table 3.6, a sense of historical change and institutional variation around exemption practices can be observed. First, we see that state comprehensive colleges and universities offer exemptions as a matter of course, whereas a few elite institutions (e.g., Wellesley, UPenn, and Stanford) in the top university study hold to the principle that *all* students should take their FYC courses. This is a notable departure from what Smith observed about the exemption

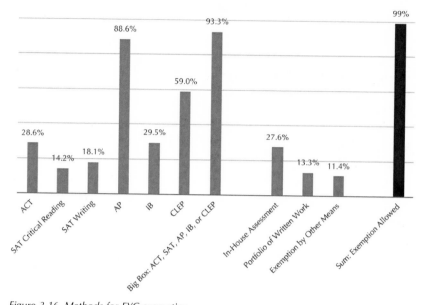

Figure 3.16. Methods for FYC exemption

practices at the institutions in his sample: in addition to observing no differences between private and public schools, Smith notes that "the higher the percentage of students exempted at schools, the likelier it is that the entrance requirements at those schools are high" (Smith 1974, 144). In fact, in many ways the picture is quite different from what was found in earlier studies. Smith and Witte et al. found greater use of in-house assessments in their 1973 and 1981 studies and less use of national, standardized assessments.

Through my catalog review, it became apparent that many schools were following state laws or regulations when it came to exemptions. We can speculate that as college costs have increased, students and their advocates are pressing for more and more ways to gain college credit outside of taking classes. The study does not help us understand what percentages of students are exempted from FYC instruction and, of course, more important, what the effects of these exemptions might be on students' development and success as students and writers.

INSTITUTIONAL SUPPORTS FOR FIRST-YEAR COMPOSITION

The data presented in this chapter suggest to me that, while first-year writing composition is essentially universal, how state comprehensive

Table 3.6. Possibilities for FYC exemption

	State Comprehensive University Study, Isaacs, 2011 data, n = 106	Top University Study, Isaacs and Knight, 2010 data, n = 101	National Survey, Witte et al., 1981 data,* n = 127	Comp Requirement Today, Smith, 1973 data, n = 491
ACT	28.6%	15.4%	29%	
SAT critical reading	14.3%	9.9%	23%	
SAT writing	18.1%	24.2%	n/a	
AP	88.6%	70.3%	34%	
IB	29.5%	46.2%	Not addressed	
CLEP	59.0%	28.6%	39%	45%
Big-box exempt: ACT, SAT, AP IR, or CLEP	92.4%	78.0%	Incalculable	
In-house assessment	27.6%	20.9%	64%	45%
Portfolio of written work	13.3%	7.7%	Not addressed	
Exemption by other means	11.4%	17.6%	24%	
Exemption by some means	99%	80.2%	80%	66%

* *Witte et al. actually present their data somewhat differently than I have referred to it here, where I have focused on comparative points. Here is Witte et al.'s excerpted report: "Of the 127 responding institutions, 102 (80.3%) indicated that they have a procedure for exempting students from required writing courses, usually those at the freshman level. We find it encouraging that 64 (63%) of the 102 directors answering this particular question said that their institutions use a writing sample, either alone or in conjunction with some other measure, to determine exemptions. Either to supplement or to replace writing samples, many institutions use "standardized" tests for exemption purposes. These percentages are as follows: 34%, Advanced Placement; 29%, ACT Verbal; 24%, other (often an in-house objective test of grammar and usage); 23%, CLEP with a writing sample; 23%, SAT Verbal; 16%, CLEP without a writing sample; 7%, ECT with a writing sample; 6%, TSWE; 3%, TOEFL; 2%, SAT Quantitative; and 2%, SAT Total Score" (Witte et al. 1981, 55–56).*

universities support and enable best instruction varies broadly. What is to account for why Salem State University (Massachusetts), Thomas Edison State University (NJ), and The College of New Jersey were able to have FYC class sizes of fifteen, whereas Nevada State (NV), Medgar Evers (NY), Cheyney University of Pennsylvania (PA), South Carolina State, and Texas A&M International University have class sizes of thirty? For that matter, why do some institutions choose to support their

---

Quick Facts: Institutional Support for FYC

In this sample's institutions . . .

- *Location*: 85.7 percent of FYC programs are housed in English or similar departments; 7.6 percent are housed in independent writing departments.
- *WPAs*: 71.4 percent have WPAs.
  - 81.1percent of WPAs are tenure-track faculty.
    - 14.6 percent of faculty WPAs are untenured.
- *Tenure-line Teaching*: 88.8 percent report tenure-line faculty teaching FYC.
  - 27.4 percent report that most of their FYC courses are taught by tenure-line faculty.
- *Adjuncts Teaching*: 94.9 percent report that adjuncts teach FYC.
  - 35.8 percent report that most of their FYC courses are taught by adjuncts.
- *Graduate Students Teaching*: 38.8 percent report that graduate students teach FYC.
  - 8.4 percent report that most of their FYC classes are taught by graduate students.
- *Faculty Development*: 44.9 percent require some kind of faculty development or training for FYC instructors.
- *FYC Class Size*: mean: 23.3; median: 24; range: 15 to 30.
  - FYC mean class size at HBCUs: 25.5.
  - FYC mean class size at Hispanic-serving institutions: 25.3.
- *Basic Writing Instruction*: 80.2 percent offer basic writing instruction.
- *Basic Writing Class Size*: mean: 20.5; median: 20; range: 8 to 35.
- *Basic Writing Exit Assessment*: 25 percent require an exit assessment for basic writing students.
- *Placement*: 82.3 percent use a standardized test to determine placement.
- *Exemption*: 99 percent provide pathways to exemption.

---

writing programs with tenured professors and others seek out staff or ask department chairs to take on this task? How is the presence of basic writing determined, and why do schools in the same state manage to vary not only on the presence of basic writing but also in whether or not they offer institutional credit or favor national objective placement instruments over in-house methods? It's hard to know because the data is broad and often unpredictable and inconsistent; a university can do well in one respect and fall clearly short in another one.

What is clear to me is that beneath the headline that all universities teach general education writing lie significant differences that not only suggest very different working conditions for those who work at these schools but also differences in instruction quality and consistency. Among K–12 parents, it's popular to say that it doesn't matter what school you get into, just whether or not you have a good teacher. Likely there's some truth to this adage, but how does one know what the likelihood is of finding that good teacher? What do we provide potential students in terms of presenting our programs, methods, and the support structures that allow for strong writing instruction? Our catalogs and websites feature our rules, our approaches, and perhaps our philosophies. Course descriptions can be found, frequently along with links to faculty and resources for negotiating the university or finding help with writing. However, little is said about our resources and how we're set up to provide strong instruction. If you search, you can find faculty-student ratios, but they very clearly speak not to class size but to a simple ratio of all students enrolled versus all faculty employed. No one advertises that adjunct faculty teach 75 percent of FYC courses or that basic writing classes have twenty-six students; for that matter, seldom did I see promotion of more positive indicators. For writing faculty, the factors that matter most are well known. We know from our scholarship and from our day-to-day experiences that it matters who runs our programs and whether or not we can have a consistent, adequately recompensed labor pool. The list goes on and on. But for many of us, gaining support for strong writing instruction is beyond our control or advocacy, and thus we work at very different writing programs, providing very different kinds of experiences in writing for students.

Notes

1. Basic Carnegie Classifications represented in this sample include three categories for doctoral institutions (very high research activity, high research activity, and doctoral/research), three categories for master's institutions (large, medium, and small), and three categories for BA institutions (BA arts and sciences, BA diverse fields, and BA/associates colleges).

2. As noted by Susan McLeod (2007) in *A History of Writing Program Administration*, citing Barbara L'Eplattenier and David Schwalm, writing program administration tasks or work existed before positions were created.

3. In respect to reporting on the WPA-type variable, late in the stage I found I had a discrepancy for one school, so I eliminated the school from the analysis. Thus, although seventy-five schools had WPAs, for the analysis of WPA type, I used an *n* of seventy-four.

4.   I should say that small institutions did report inviting students to some of the activities listed below, but only infrequently, and I think the exclusion of small schools is useful for the reasons stated.

5.   Over the years, many monographs and collections have been devoted to this topic, though the focus is almost exclusively on training graduate assistants and seldom on other faculty who teach FYC, as exemplified in Joseph Gibaldi and James Mirollo's (1981) *The Teaching Apprentice Program in Language and Literature*, Betty Pytlik and Sara Liggett's (2002) *Preparing College Teachers of Writing*, and Sally Ebest's (2005) *Changing the Way We Teach: Writing and Resistance in the Training of Teaching Assistants* (Ebest 2005; Gibaldi and Mirollo 1981; Pytlik and Liggett 2002).

6.   The case of Medgar Evers College was a surprise given that every other school had exemption possibilities. However, both the survey response and catalog review indicated no possibility of exemption. Perhaps beneath the public record there are some methods for exemption as defined in a side agreement or through the assessment office, though it is notable that survey and catalog represented exemption as unavailable.

7.   A weakness of my design is that I did not gather information about dual-credit enrollment, which is not an option catalogs and bulletins cover with any consistency, and in my experience, faculty aren't even always aware that their school has made such agreements.

4
WHAT ARE WE DOING WITH FIRST-YEAR COMPOSITION?

It has been a few years since I worked as a WPA at a state comprehensive university, but I remember well the pleasure I took each August and January when I made my plans for the semester, an exercise I urge WPAs to do at least once a year. You need to pull out time to innovate and also to evaluate and redesign your courses. It is very easy for WPAs and other busy administrators to be entirely reactive, spending their days hiring, training, assessing, responding to students, responding to faculty, responding to administrators, and the list goes on and on. But once or twice a year WPAs and their faculty need to turn off their e-mails and make time to plan for improvements to the heart of the program—the courses! What do our programmatic assessments suggest should be done better? Should the curricula change? The methodologies? Should the research component be reconfigured? Might it be time to adopt multimodal instruction? Do course outcomes appropriately reflect university values and student needs? The wonderful part about curriculum development is that it tends to be work entirely in the control of the faculty. Administrators don't attend much to course content, respecting that faculty are the keepers of the curriculum, and curricula innovation is typically cost neutral. I begin this chapter reporting on first-year composition course content with this call to make time for curricular reflection and revision because I hope readers can use what is presented herein to consider what they want to do in their own programs. I aim to further this reflection and planning by presenting the sample's course content in the context of scholarship and previous studies so as to provide historical perspectives. These contextualizing efforts are designed to reveal the ways we have changed our curricula over time and to demonstrate the relationship between scholarship and practice—and typically such relationships are found to be present, though significant absences are also revealed.

When we look broadly at FYC instruction at the state comprehensive university, as represented by these 106 institutions, we see the overall impact the discipline of writing studies has had. In the sample, 63.5

DOI: 10.7330/9781607326397.c004

percent of institutions were led by tenure-track WPAs, and 58.5 percent had someone presenting a paper at CCCC in either 2010 or 2011, two small snapshots that give a brief sense of the institutions' access to expertise in teaching writing.[1] Thus, a majority of these institutions have WPAs or other tenure-line faculty clearly enough engaged in writing studies to prioritize this conference for research presentation. Further, the broad outlines of the FYC courses in the sample reflect the writing constructs, or the principles and valued approaches advocated for, debated, or presented as guiding principles by the major organizations in the field.

Other primary findings are that FYC as a requirement is almost universal, as is some version of the research paper. Further, the language of writing as a process has been widely adopted across the sample, though there is a strong minority strain of institutions that articulate process-writing approaches and yet emphasize skills and "grammar" at the same time. Another big story is the popularity of argument and argumentation—there is very little evidence of "expressivist" approaches. Courses are most typically organized around the activity of writing, not literature, a specific discipline, or any other topic announced at the level of the course description. I suspect many of these courses are organized around topics or themes, given the popularity of thematic readers, but these foci occur below the level of course descriptions.

Before digging into the details of the status of FYC at the state comprehensive university, I want to reiterate that the data for this chapter were drawn from a variety of sources, including catalog information about FYC requirements, course descriptions, outcomes data mined from catalogs, assessment offices, department and program websites and other university documents, survey-response data on research practices, WPA information gained from website review and faculty surveys, and finally, CCCC participation (from NCTE offices). As I describe specific data points, I offer occasional points of clarification about source information to help readers weigh and evaluate the findings.

FIRST-YEAR COMPOSITION IS REQUIRED

As evidenced by data from this sample, the first-year composition requirement is alive and well, with all but one of the study's 106 institutions requiring one or two courses. Of the 105 schools that required FYC, 31.4 percent required one course in FYC and 68.6 percent required two. In reviewing these numbers it is useful to recall that FYC is the most pervasive method institutions use to provide general education writing instruction, but it is not the sole method: some schools required

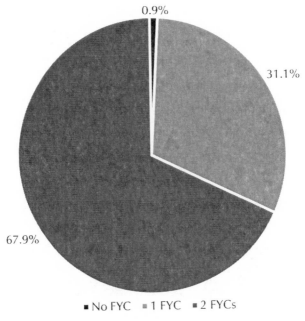

Figure 4.1. The state of the FYC requirement

writing-intensive (WI) courses within their general education curricula, so it would be incorrect to infer that schools that required one rather than two courses in FYC were necessarily less committed to writing instruction. For example, California State University–Long Beach required one semester of FYC (English composition) and a total of four other WI courses, including three WI capstone general education courses (see chapter 5 for further discussion of writing requirements beyond or in lieu of FYC). The one college in the sample that did not require FYC is the very small (under nine hundred students enrolled) New College of Florida (2011, n.p.), Florida's "honors college for the liberal arts," a state university distinctive for its absence of universal general education requirements and also letter grades; in their place, New College offers intensive advising and individual learning contracts. With this one exception noted, in 2011 the study data evidenced that FYC has become a mainstay of four-year public education, which is precisely the opposite of what Ron Smith predicted after reviewing 490 survey responses on "the composition requirement" in 1974: "All signs point to more schools dropping the composition requirement, more diminishing the one that exists, and more taking advantage of what will probably soon be better equivalency exams" (Smith 1974, 148).

This may be surprising to those following the scholarship on this subject, in particular if they have read the most famous critic of the requirement, Sharon Crowley (1998). Significantly, although Crowley's call for "abolition" of the FYC requirement was published when Crowley was at Utah State University—a call that was not heeded at either Utah State or Arizona State University, where Crowley taught subsequently—the schools that do *not* require FYC are typically elite liberal arts colleges such as Brown University. Brown eliminated all its general education requirements in 1969 (Bergeron 2009) in a move that turned out to be competitively advantageous—by the 1980s, it had climbed into the coveted *US News and World Report*'s top-ten-US-universities list. This movement reached its peak during the 1960s when "almost one fourth of four year colleges and universities dropped the composition requirement" (Russell 1988, 140). Yet, whereas discussion of alternatives to FYC have continued to have traction in our *scholarly conversation* (Crowley 1998; Goggin and Miller 2000; North 2011; Schilb 1994), these discussions have had little impact at state comprehensive universities; my findings echo Moghtader, Cotch, and Hague's (2001, 457) findings. Previous researchers also note FYC's strong presence as a required element of postsecondary education. In 1973, Ron Smith reported that 84 percent of public four-year universities required general education writing instruction, and in 1967, Thomas Wilcox surveyed English departments at public and private four-year universities, finding that 83 percent required at least one semester of freshman English (Wilcox 1968, 446). A contemporary comparison to another population, from the Isaacs and Knight 2009 study of top universities, found that slightly fewer of these "top" schools, 90.0 percent, required FYC (Isaacs and Knight 2012, 294). Beyond the changing approaches at private schools, Crowley's argument for abolition of required FYC, taken up again more recently by SUNY Albany's Stephen North (North 2011), has clearly proven unpersuasive at public four-year institutions.

At 68.6 percent of the sample, the FYC requirement tipped toward a two-course approach. When comparing one- and two-course sequences, an additional factor I considered was the oral-communication requirement. At many institutions, an oral-communication course was required, and three institutions combined oral and written communication in one requirement. Arguably, an institution that requires one FYC course and one oral-communication course is not very different from an institution that requires two FYC courses mandated to provide instruction in oral *and* written communication. At Southern Oregon University, writing and oral-communication instruction were described as occurring in a three-course requirement defined collectively as teaching students to "communicate effectively using writing, speech, and image" (Southern Oregon University 2011–2012). (In this case I coded this school as having a two-course writing requirement.) Two other institutions in the sample, Fort Valley State and California State University, Monterey Bay, included oral-communication instruction as part of courses in their FYC requirement sequences. As an example of how oral communication can be articulated within FYC, here is the description from Georgia's Fort Valley State University:

ENGL1101–Composition I
Students develop communication skills in reading, writing and speaking, with a particular focus on using expository and argumentative essays in standard written English. Basic research skills are honed. (Fort Valley State University 2011)

Notwithstanding the obvious logical advantages to teaching speech and writing concurrently, Fort Valley, which required two communications courses, and California State University, Stanislaus, which required one, are arguably less able to focus on writing instruction than those institutions that teach oral communications in an entirely separate course in *addition to* FYC. I offer these examples to suggest the ways in which, despite my simple reporting on one- versus two-course writing requirements, differences may be less clear-cut than they appear.

An effort to identify which variables have a relationship with a two-semester approach reveals a few findings and many null hypotheses. First, I hypothesized that larger universities would be more likely to have just one course in FYC compared to small universities, based on the assumption that large universities would simply not be able to manage staffing two FYC courses. The hypothesis did not bear out, but there's a lesson in statistics here, for the difference of mean enrollment for schools that required one class versus two seems large: 11,219 ($n = 32$, $SD = 8,865$) for one class, 8,644 ($n = 72$, $SD = 7,762$) for two. Yet the difference between these two means is *not* statistically significant ($t(103) = 1.5$, $p > 0.05$, two-tailed). As discussed in appendix A, it's important to recognize when differences appear significant but are not statistically so. For those who are surprised that the difference between 8,644 and 11,219 is not statistically significant, this is mostly because the sample includes such a wide range of enrollments: from 692 at New College to 42,465 at the University of Central Florida (UCF), the latter of which did in fact require two FYC courses. Notably, there are outliers to these mean differences: a total of four of the seven very large (twenty-five thousand or more) institutions managed to require two courses.

A review of earlier studies reveals that over the last fifty-plus years, US colleges and universities have maintained or increased their commitment to FYC as a vehicle for general education writing instruction, despite Ron Smith's prediction that exactly the opposite would occur. In Albert Kitzhaber's methodologically informal Dartmouth study of ninety-five private and public colleges and universities (Kitzhaber 1962, 3), "Freshman English" is reported to be nearly universally required, with just a few highly selective institutions declaring students advanced enough not to require it and another few similar institutions requiring a course in literature instead (1–2). Kitzhaber does not differentiate between institutions that require one or two courses but rather suggests that all the institutions require a full year of two or three courses, depending on the system, to make up the "freshman English sequence" (23). Yet based on his survey of private and public institutions, Wilcox found that 77.8 percent of schools required two courses (Wilcox 1972, 686), and seven years later, in 1974, Ron Smith found that 24 percent of respondents reported "no composition requirement," with 31 percent requiring one term and 45 percent requiring two or more terms (Smith 1974, 139). Smith did, however, find FYC more present at public universities, with 89 percent of these institutions requiring FYC (141). We see variation in the 1980s: Witte, Meyer, Miller, and Faigley reported that in their public and private institution sample, 9.4 percent did not require "Freshman composition" (their term), 28.1 percent required one course, and 62.6 percent required two courses. They conclude, "Data indicates that freshman composition courses are a major component of college writing programs, but more so at public universities" (Witte et al. 1981, 21). A different report comes from Clinton Burhans who, from his study of private and public university course catalogs, found that 20 percent did not require a general writing course at all (1983, 647). The most recent study is from data collected in 2008 by Anne Ruggles Gere. Commissioned by CCCC as a study of practices among its membership, a population reasonably most likely to be invested in FYC, Gere found very high numbers of some kind of writing instruction: 97.3 percent of respondents reported that their institutions required one or more "terms of writing instruction" (a more capacious category than first-year composition), with 21.0 percent requiring one term and 55.89 percent requiring two (Gere 2009). In summary, with consideration of various samples and methodologies, FYC as a requirement has increased in prevalence, and the prevalence of FYC is greatest at four-year public universities and colleges, especially at those that fall under the comprehensive or regional category.

To detail, over the fifty years from Kitzhaber to the present study, we see variations, yet in Witte, Meyer, Miller, and Faigley's study, which includes a focused review of a population most similar to this study's, we see evidence that the FYC requirement has grown in popularity (from 91 percent to 99 percent). The percentage of institutions favoring a two-semester over a one-semester approach remains fairly constant, with about two-thirds of each sample choosing a two-semester approach. What we do not see is the bearing out of Ron Smith's prediction that there would be more "schools dropping the composition requirement, more diminishing the one that exists, and more taking advantage of what [would] probably soon be better equivalency examinations" (Smith 1974, 148).

In addition to the hypothesis that two-semester course requirements would dwindle as institutions grew large in size, two other hypotheses related to the length of the requirement were also *not* confirmed: positive associations with Carnegie institutional selectivity (χ^2 (2, $n = 97$) = 4.36, $p > 0.05$) and graduate classifications (χ^2 (2, $n = 105$) = 0.53, $p > 0.05$). On the former, and based on the top university study, I hypothesized that more selective schools would more frequently decide that only one course in FYC was necessary for their students. Not the case for this sample, though a mitigating factor may be the fact that Carnegie is very rough in its sorting of schools for selectivity.[2] Figure 4.2 dramatizes the findings related to institutional selectivity and number of required courses.

My next hypothesis, about an association with Carnegie graduate classification, follows Crowley's (1998) argument that the availability of cheap graduate-student labor enables the FYC requirement to exist. This hypothesis was not borne out. In fact, doctoral institutions are significantly *more likely* to offer two semesters as opposed to one (χ^2 (1, $n = 29$) = 4.17, $p < 0.05$). However, as captured in figure 4.3, we see that MA and BA institutions are also more likely to offer two semesters than one. Further, we observe trending toward BA institutions' demonstrating greater likelihood of requiring two semesters of FYC than MA and doctorate-granting institutions—but these trends do not reach the level of statistical significance.

Where we finally see a significant association for FYC requirement length is with geographical location, a construct I defined by regional association membership (discussed further in appendix A). The number of courses required to complete the FYC writing requirement associates with statistical significance [χ^2 (5, $n = 105$) = 20.55, $p < 0.05$] to institutions' regions. As table 4.1 below indicates, the western region trended strongly toward one required course, while other regions

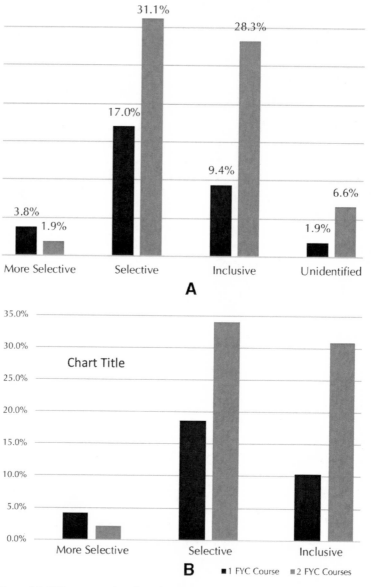

Figure 4.2. FYC sequence length and Carnegie selectivity classification

trended toward two required courses, and several were about evenly divided. Most pronouncedly, 91.2 percent of schools in the Southern Association of Colleges and Schools (SACS) required two courses, which can be contrasted with 14.3 percent for the Western Association of Schools and Colleges (WASC).

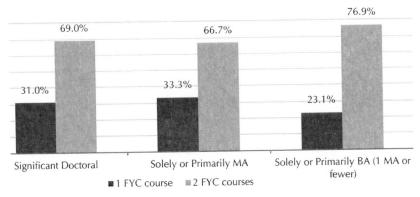

Figure 4.3. FYC sequence length and Carnegie graduate classification

Table 4.1. FYC courses required by region

	Total in region	Percentage in region that require one course	Percentage in region that require two courses
Middle states (MSACS)	19	47.4% (9)	52.6% (10)
New England (NEASC)	4	50.0% (2)	50.0% (2)
North Central (NCA)	34	32.4% (11)	67.6% (23)
Northwest (NWCCU)	7	28.6% (2)	71.4% (5)
Southern (SACS)	34	8.8% (3)	91.2% (31)
Western (WASC)	7	85.7% (6)	14.3% (1)

In considering these trends, it is tempting to explore questions that are beyond the scope of this research but that can be posed nonetheless: Although regional accrediting agencies do not appear to require specific courses, do regional accrediting agencies have informally circulated preferences? Or is it simply that regions have developed expected approaches, and institutions follow one another? Frequently, institutions within a state (e.g., New Jersey and Georgia) are in lockstep as part of state-wide articulation agreements, but since the sample includes schools from many states in each region, this compliance would not account for the near uniformity we see in the southern states. If the move toward national standards and guidelines takes hold in higher education, as it has in K–12, we can imagine these regional differences disappearing.

In respect to this issue of number of FYC courses required, another statistically significant correlation was found with historically black colleges and universities (HBCUs); in this sample, 100 percent of the

HBCUs ($n = 12$) required two courses in first-year composition. In comparison, 40.0 percent of institutions identified by Carnegie as "Hispanic serving" ($n = 10$) required two semesters of FYC, while 68.0 percent of institutions without either of these special designations required two semesters of FYC. These are small sample numbers, but questions about how our institutions differ in their approach to writing instruction should reasonably consider institutional mission and student populations as meaningful variables. At HBCUs, two semesters is universal, whereas at Hispanic-serving institutions, FYC is more likely to be a one-semester experience.

FIRST-YEAR COMPOSITION OUTCOMES

With the rise of interest in assessment both within and outside the discipline, questions about colleges' and universities' approaches to defining FYC course outcomes, goals, or objectives are important. I approach these questions through several angles. In terms of data collection, I rely on both survey answers and institutional data. For example, on the survey (see appendix D) I asked respondents whether or not they had an outcomes or equivalent statement for their FYC courses and then asked them to check if their outcomes were: (1) the WPA Outcomes (adopted or revised); (2) a program- or department-developed statement; (3) a university-developed statement; (4) a state-developed statement; or (5) left to individual instructors to develop. Respondents' answers were cross-checked against these institutional documents: the catalog, institutions' assessment reports, and institutions' general education outcomes. From these data I was able to draw out a fuller picture of use of outcomes in FYC. To date, little published reporting of use of outcomes is available, with the exception of an early study of the WPA Outcomes (Ericsson 2003) and the previously mentioned top university study (Isaacs and Knight 2012). That said, the WPA Outcomes, first adopted by the Council of Writing Program Administrators in 2000, and amended in 2008 and 2014, has been widely distributed and assessed, primarily through case-study analysis and most directly through two books: *The Outcomes Book: Debate and Consensus after the WPA Outcomes Statements* (Harrington et al. 2005) and *The WPA Outcomes Statement: A Decade Later* (Behm et al. 2012). The Outcomes Statement, and after it, *The Framework for Success in Postsecondary Writing* (Council of Writing Program Administrators, National Council of Teachers of English, and National Writing Project 2011), reflects our disciplinary leaders' efforts to broadcast constructs for postsecondary writing and writing instruction that are reflective of disciplinary values, are easily communicated to a variety of audiences, and that, ultimately, will enable assessment across institutions. However, as Diane Kelly-Riley and Norbert Elliot explain, WPA Outcomes was designed as a "formative latent variable model . . . established through consensus of experts, supported by literature review and tradition" rather than for appropriateness for most kinds of assessment (Kelly-Riley and Elliot 2014, 91). What remains a question is how well these constructs can be represented in viewable, analyzable, measurable outcomes and, therefore, if these constructs are well designed to represent and ultimately assess postsecondary writing for specific individual students, for specific institutions, or, more broadly, for institutional types.

Of the 105 institutions in this study that offered first-year composition, verified data on the use or nonuse of WPA Outcomes was gathered on all but one institution. Of these 105 institutions, 22.6 percent had adopted or adapted the WPA Outcomes, leaving 77.4 percent that had not. When we look at a cross-tabulation of WPA Outcomes adoption or adoption against participation at CCCC in either 2011 or 2010, we can see that adoption or adaption of the WPA Outcomes doesn't follow participation in the discipline as defined by CCCC presentation. Certainly, my choice to use CCCC presentation (discussed further in appendix A) is limited, and presenting at CCCC is just one means to gauge an institution's faculty's engagement with the discipline. Yet I think it demonstrates both that the WPA Outcomes penetrate to faculty beyond those who present at CCCC and that many who present at CCCC are at institutions where the faculty choose *not* to follow the WPA Outcomes in their approach to FYC. The WPA Outcomes, it seems, are not for everyone.

Universities and colleges that have not adapted or adopted the WPA Outcomes should not necessarily be seen as out of step with the discipline or unconcerned with outcomes. In fact, 91.5 percent of the institutions in the sample reported or were found to have an outcomes or equivalent statement at the state, institutional, or departmental/programmatic level. To further explain, from the combined data from survey respondents, and from catalog, assessment, and general education document review, it was found that 9.4 percent of institutions had statewide outcomes, 62.3 percent of institutions had college- or university-wide outcomes, and 76.4 percent had outcomes on the program or department level. For these variables I relied on data from three primary sources: the survey completed by college or university representatives, catalog review, and website review. A graduate assistant and I combed the catalogs and websites for the presence of language relating to

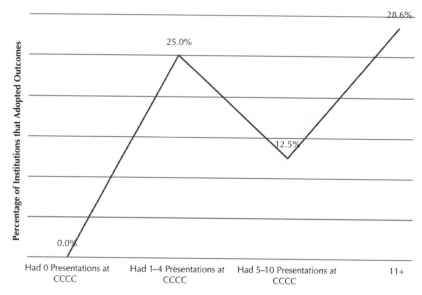

Figure 4.4. WPA Outcomes adoption/adaption and institutions' faculty presentations at CCCCs

outcomes. We did not require the presence of the actual term *outcomes*, accepting language I thought was equivalent because it indicated that the university, college, program, or department had defined outcomes for student learning. Language in place of outcomes included such terms as *competencies, goals, objectives,* and *frameworks.*

Notably, many institutions were governed by several outcomes statements that existed at the program/departmental level, the university level, and also the state level. The existence of multiple levels raises questions about how these different statements work together, or possibly do not. At the University of Central Florida (UCF), an exceptionally large institution (forty-two thousand at the time of this study) that had a two-semester FYC sequence, program-specific "Student Learning Goals" for each of two courses were found on the Department of Rhetoric and Writing's website (University of Central Florida 2012b). These goals are extensive; for example, the first unit's learning goals begin with the following: "To understand how writers construct texts persuasively (or not)" and end with "To understand the concept or rhetorical situation and be able to apply it to writing and reading situations" (University of Central Florida 2012b). At the next level, in the *University of Central Florida 2011–2012 Undergraduate Catalog,* the general education program is described and learning objectives are included. Under

"Communications Foundation" are five outcomes that proved easy to read as the source from which the more expanded course outcomes grew. The first of these outcomes reads, "Demonstrate the ability to analyze the situational characteristics of a communication act: audience, purpose, and source/author" (University of Central Florida 2011, 67). This consistency, with the program offering greater expansion on goals or outcomes than are specified at the university level, was not always apparent at other institutions.

As noted earlier, just 9.4 percent of the institutions in the sample were found to have FYC outcomes articulated at the state level. The 106 schools in the study came from thirty-eight states. Three of these states—Alabama, New York (SUNY, but not CUNY), and South Dakota—were governed by state-wide outcomes in general education writing. If the tenacity of the delocalized assessment movement continues to rise, we can imagine this number increasing as well. Among other challenges that face schools is the complexity of coordinating these different levels of outcomes. How does a program of faculty who wish to revise and improve their FYC course do so if they are beholden not only to institutional general educational mandates (read: outcomes) but also to state ones? Canaries in the coal mine might be the state institutions in the state of Georgia, where in 2009, outcomes had been adopted at state levels through the University System of Georgia Core Curriculum. Interestingly, some survey respondents from the Georgia institutions did *not* report the presence of a state-level-defined outcome in writing. However, state requirements, as indicated in the catalogs and elsewhere, clearly existed in the form of a state-wide general education program that included instruction and outcomes for the "essential skill" of writing. This state-level outcome, referred to as the Core Area A1 Learning Outcome, was defined briefly as a six-credit requirement that provided that "students [would] be able to write effectively for a variety of audiences to demonstrate collegiate-level writing development in various contexts" (Georgia Southwestern State University 2011). In this sample we find five Georgia state institutions (Georgia Southern, Armstrong Atlantic State, North Georgia College and State, Georgia Southwestern State, and Fort Valley State), all of which required two courses: ENGL1101 Composition I and ENGL1102 Composition II. Only after a close look, beyond titles and into course descriptions, can small differences among the institutions be discerned. While all the institutions' course descriptions included the phrasing "focusing on skills required for effective writing in a variety of contexts," across the five descriptions were some differences in research emphasis, reference to Standard

Written English, and attention to speaking as well as writing. In other words, though they shared general state-wide defined outcomes and course titles, faculty at individual institutions in the state appeared to have been able to develop local control in meeting the state outcomes, and it is perhaps because of this local control that survey respondents didn't perceive their course as fulfilling a state-level outcome. Clearly, further study is needed to understand if and how individual institutions are able to negotiate state requirements where they exist and how these requirements relate to assessment policies and practices.

An additional area for further study is to consider institutions' engagement with *The Framework for Success in Postsecondary Education*, an NCTE/WPA-developed and endorsed platform (Council of Writing Program Administrators, National Council of Teachers of English, and National Writing Project 2011) that seeks to define and construct writing in ways that speak not only to writing activities students need practice and experience in but also to essential "habits of mind" for college writing success. These are defined as curiosity, openness, engagement, creativity, persistence, responsibility, flexibility, and metacognition. Adopted in 2011 by various associations' executive committees, the *Framework* has had little time to be considered or reflected on, much less incorporated. For some, in fact, the *Framework* may represent yet another effort by writing studies leaders to define the field. Regardless, going forward, coming to an understanding of both the *Framework*'s influence and also the extent to which it reflects and is reflected in institution's constructs of writing will be important.

WHAT HAPPENS IN FYC?

Beyond the presence or absence of outcomes at various levels is the more fundamental question of what it is that FYC courses actually do. Clearly a *detailed* understanding of what happens in each of these courses can only come from a qualitative or observational study that includes interviews, requests for teacher documents and the like, or perhaps case studies written by participants. What this study provides instead is a review that is even-handed yet based on much more limited data on course content that reveals how writing is constructed. The data relied upon are course descriptions, program, department, and institutional outcomes or goals statements (discussed above), and responses to surveys. As described in appendix A, following grounded-theory methodologies, moving from categorizing to data and back again several times, I coded course-content data on questions relating to topic specification, research instruction, emphasis on argumentation, emphasis on skills, alignment with rhetorical approach, and emphasis on process-writing methodologies.

Limitations noted, here is the bird's-eye view: the research paper remains entrenched; in terms of course content, a focus on learning to improve or improving one's writing capacities or abilities trumps discussion of theme or genre; and, the majority of institutions' FYC courses favor process writing and rhetorical instruction and include argumentation but avoid a focus on skills-based instruction and the use of *grammar* in course descriptions.

RESEARCH INSTRUCTION AND WRITING IN FIRST-YEAR COMPOSITION

Of the 105 institutions that required FYC courses, on the basis of examination of course descriptions and outcomes, 91.4 percent of the courses included research instruction. This finding demonstrates a clear and strong link between writing instruction and research instruction. Survey responses, in comparison to the public view, indicated even greater engagement with some kind of research: 97.1 percent reported that FYC courses include some research instruction, revealing that a few of the courses not described as including research are believed to include a requirement for research instruction by their representatives. More interestingly, and to the likely dismay of composition scholars from Richard Larson, who declared war on the research paper in the eighties (Larson 1982, 816), to Carrah Hood (2010), who has recently declared the death of said papers based on her WPA-listserv study, the research paper is alive and well at 80.2 percent of these schools.[3] Imagining that some faculty and administrators familiar with the research-paper debate might value and teach a kind of documented essay instead of the research paper, the survey and document review also included a research essay category, which was defined primarily as an essay—"an essay which includes student-selected secondary sources." Respondents (85.9 percent) identified the research essay as a required part of the FYC course or sequence of courses, suggesting a trend toward research in support of writing an essay rather than research for the sake of reporting. Within the discipline, this is an important distinction. From course descriptions these distinctions are not always evident, but in looking at the schools whose respondents selected research essay over research paper, we can see some substantive differences in course descriptions.

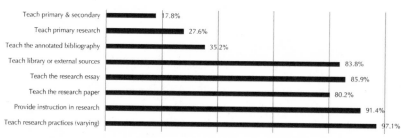

Figure 4.5. Research practices in FYC

The survey respondent from Framingham State in Massachusetts reported affirmatively to the question about the research paper but negatively to one concerning the research essay; the University of Michigan–Flint's respondent did just the opposite. An examination of the descriptions of the courses that fulfill these schools' requirement is illustrative of the difference between foregrounding the research paper (Framingham) and teaching research strategies in service of learning and writing (Michigan–Flint).

At Framingham, the catalog course description suggests that the course itself focuses on writing thesis-driven research essays, whereas at Michigan–Flint, "undergraduate research" is one of several defined "competencies" and "research strategies" among several strategies taught.

While the research paper may be entrenched, it was interesting and surprising to find two other noteworthy trends in research practices: 35.2 percent of institutions reported requiring an annotated bibliography, and 27.6 percent reported requirements for primary research, which I defined for survey respondents as "survey, interview, participation-observation." These additional data points provide a fuller portrait of the way these institutions are carrying out research activities in FYC. If the research paper is well established and research instruction virtually required, definitions and approaches to research are more varied than these headlines seem to suggest. Reference to primary-research methodologies such as those suggested in the survey cannot be found in the course-catalog descriptions, but they were found in course or general education outcomes documents. For example, California State University, Northridge provided specifications for six "student learning outcomes" for its general education writing requirement, the fifth of which states that students will be able to "select and incorporate ideas derived from a variety of sources, such as library electronic and print resources, books, journals, the internet, and interviews, and document

Table 4.2. FYC 1 course descriptions at Framingham State and University of Michigan–Flint

Framingham State (Massachusetts)	University of Michigan–Flint
ENGL 110: Composition and Research: Designed to improve the writing of expository prose needed in college and beyond. The emphasis rests on collecting, evaluating, and organizing evidence from primary and secondary sources in order to support an explicit, arguable, and substantive thesis. The course includes the writing of a well-researched and documented paper that draws on traditional and electronic sources (Framingham State University 2011, 200).	ENG 111: College Rhetoric: Introductory course in composition emphasizing written expression appropriate to successful college level work. Analytical readings; creative and critical thinking; development of a student's sense of integrity as a writer. ENG 112 Critical Reading and Writing: Intensive course in critical and analytical reading, writing and research strategies necessary for successful academic work. Techniques for essay exams; argumentative, analytical, and critical papers; undergraduate research (University of Michigan–Flint 2011).

them responsibly and correctly" (General Education Committee at California State University Northridge 2005, 6). Close to one-fifth of the schools (17.8 percent) specified students gaining facility with both "primary and secondary" research methodologies. This expectation is exemplified by Ball State University, where students are expected to develop "an argument with evidence from both primary and secondary research" through methods appropriate to research questions (Ball State University 2011a). Finally, to round off reporting on frequencies for research practices evidenced in the sample, 83.8 percent reported requiring "instruction in how to conduct library and/or external sources research," indicating the continuing strong interest in explicit instruction in finding sources.

Research practices in FYC do not associate with most institutional characteristics, though hypotheses were tested on all the institutional characteristics collected for this study. In addition, I pursued several hypotheses about the influence of the discipline on the institution's FYC courses or program, as evidenced by such attributes as the presence of a WPA, the status of the WPA, and high participation at CCCC, all of which I hypothesized would *negatively* associate with instruction in the research paper, given all the scholarship against the genre, and which would *positively* associate with instruction in primary-research methodologies, which are spoken of positively in the discipline and are thus in keeping with disciplinary values. I also hypothesized that institutions with WPAs, and especially those with tenure-track or tenured WPAs, would be more likely than other institutions to teach the research essay over the research paper. However, almost all these hypotheses were null, with statistical analyses of associations found to be insignificant.

One exception: we do see a correlation between FYC research practices that include instruction in primary-research methodologies and
presentation at CCCC [t (34.75) = 2.37, p < 0.05]. In other words,
schools that have some kind of primary-research requirement (n = 29)
have significantly more people presenting at CCCC (M = 6.24, SD = 7.99)
compared to schools that do not have some kind of primary-research
requirement (n = 70, M = 2.53, SD = 4.25).

With research papers entrenched as a practice within the entire sample (97.1 percent), and with very broad overlap among representatives
reporting on requirement of the research paper and the research essay,
few differences in practices among types of institutions or among those
that evidenced other more frequently valued approaches to writing
instruction were evident. That said, absence of associations is sometimes
important to highlight, too. In this case, that WPA presence and status
had no association with the *absence* of a research-paper requirement suggests that either there are more supporters for the research paper than
the scholarship indicates or that even with writing experts on the faculty,
many institutions are not persuaded by these resident experts to abandon this long-valued, favorite genre.

COURSE TOPIC: UNSPECIFIED BEATS OUT
LITERATURE AND RESEARCH

An enduring question that dates back to the early days of research
on the first-year composition course is: what should the topic of FYC
courses *be?* Embedded within the question of topic is the question of
whether or not FYC courses should announce a topic or theme other
than instruction in writing. From the scholarship, we find arguments not
only for a focus solely on the activity of writing but also for foci on rhetoric or literature, student-or discipline-defined foci, and, more recently,
a focus on "writing about writing" (Downs and Wardle 2007). To pursue
this question with the sample, FYC courses were categorized by topical
focus or emphasis along six categories by two raters who made classifications based on a review of both course descriptions and outcomes
statements. The six categories were literature based, discipline based,
specified theme, student generated, based on research, or nonspecified. Nonspecified is important as it indicates a school's decision that
the course focus is *writing instruction or development* and not literature,
another genre, or another subject. Of all 174 FYC courses included in
the study (this includes two courses from the schools that required two
FYC courses), 75 percent (n = 174) were found to have no topic specified

other than writing instruction. As is explained further below, this sample suggests that, in public four-year universities, focusing on a topic other than writing itself, whether it is literature or writing about writing, is not a widely practiced approach. In Doug Downs and Elizabeth Wardle's article "Teaching about Writing, Righting Misconceptions," which has been widely cited and which led to potential widespread implementation through an FYC textbook (Wardle and Downs 2010), they argue for "moving First-Year Composition from teaching 'how to write in college' to teaching *about writing*—from acting as if writing is a basic, universal skill to acting as if writing studies is a discipline with content knowledge to which students should be introduced" (Downs and Wardle 2007, 553). Compelling as readers may have found this article, as evidenced by this data, most writing courses at state universities focus on precisely what they, and many others (Downs and Wardle 2007; Ruecker 2011; Russell 1995; Trimbur 1999; Wardle 2009), argue against.

Notably, this near consensus that FYC is an activity or skills course, without a publicly defined topic, is a finding in contrast to what Taylor reported in 1929 and Kitzhaber found and wrote about in *Themes, Theory and Therapy* in 1963. Taylor reported, "At present there are signs of rebellion against the dominance of the rhetoric" (Taylor 1929, 6), and there was much curricular variety, including a significant presence of teaching writing through study of literature. He wrote that 42 percent of the total sample of state and private universities, and 35 percent of state universities, were "taught with a combination of rhetoric and literature (Taylor 1929, 13). Kitzhaber also concluded that colleges offered "a bewildering variety of content" (Kitzhaber 1963, 10), which he was able to boil down to ten main topics and several others that were "maverick courses" that couldn't even be categorized. Kitzhaber found courses based on grammar (traditional or structural linguistics), literature, rhetoric, logic, semantics, communication, public speaking, propaganda analysis, or "a kind of watered-down social science survey based on collections of essays drawn for the most part from current magazines" (13). In 1972, Wilcox concurred: "The ideal program which teachers and administrators (and textbook publishers) have sought for fifty years has not yet emerged, and the debate over freshman English continues much as before" (Wilcox 1972, 686).

Despite his strong statements, Kitzhaber did nonetheless find that for the first course (of one or of two), "better than four of five of the colleges" emphasized "expository reading and writing" (22), a finding that contrasted to Shuck's finding from a 1954 study of "multi-purpose institutions" that just 59 percent of courses were focused on "composition and literature" (Shuck 1955, 206). For Shuck, 40 percent of his respondents reported that primary readings were literature (206); for Kitzhaber, one-fifth of the first courses focused primarily on literature, and in the second course, "a little over two-thirds" focused on literature. Twenty years later, Richard Larson reported that "roughly 30 percent of the institutions rest some part of the curriculum in composition on assignments in literature"; his analysis was less clear as to what the remaining 70 percent focused on. Notably, the lit-comp debate has remained alive and well in the scholarly literature, not only in the 1993 debate between Erika Lindemann and Gary Tate, but again in 2006 and 2007 (Anderson and Farris 2007; Bergmann and Baker 2006) and through to the present (see, for example, Isaacs 2009; Kalbfleisch 2016; Odom 2013; Raymond 2010). However, in this sample I have found that the study of literature was not present in the vast majority of course descriptions, with just 8.6 percent of the FYC courses in this study evidencing literature as their topic.

First-year composition, as constructed in the brief, contractual form of the catalog description, was thus presented as an activity or skills course primarily, with a minority presenting a focus of either literature or research. Courses defined primarily as courses in research writing frequently included the word *research* in their titles. Across the sample, courses defined as research-writing courses were found at universities that required one or two FYC courses. The FYC course at Framingham State University (see table 4.2) is a good example of a research-writing course description at a one-course FYC requirement university. A good example of reserving research writing for the second-semester course is USEM 1–2 University Seminar at Southern Oregon University: "Students choose appropriate topics and issues to research; use various research strategies to find, evaluate and integrate authoritative information and data, including academic databases; write and revise extended researched and argumentative essays; hone citation and documentation skills (MLA, APA, or Chicago); design and deliver a formal presentation of research . . ." (Southern Oregon University 2011). At Lewis–Clark State College in Idaho, the standard second-semester research course was described in greater detail in the course description, revealing an investment in broadcasting and perhaps regulating an approach toward teaching research writing.

ENGL-102 RESEARCH WRITING (3 CR.)

A continuation of ENGL 101 with an emphasis on general research techniques with applications to various academic disciplines. Successful students will be able to: 1. Continue to demonstrate competency in the

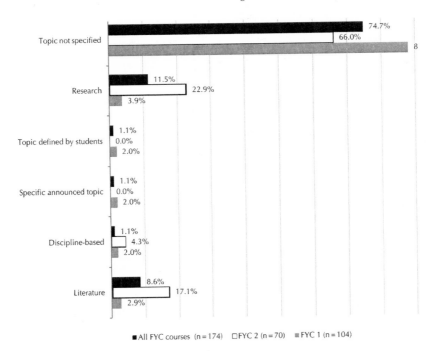

■ All FYC courses (n = 174)   □ FYC 2 (n = 70)   ■ FYC 1 (n = 104)

Figure 4.6. FYC topical focus across sample

course outcomes for ENGL 101; 2. Locate, identify, and participate in academic discourse; 3. Read critically, synthesize, and evaluate information; 4. Use a variety of research tools (databases, indexes, the Internet, etc.) to locate appropriate information sources; 5. Develop a focused research topic or project; 6. Conduct a review of the literature for a specific topic; 7. Understand what constitutes evidence in a particular discipline; 8. Use valid evidence to support claims; 9. Understand and use APA and MLA formats for organizing and documenting multiple source papers; 10. Understand and demonstrate the ethical responsibility of the research writer to explore multiple perspectives on a topic and to cite sources and report findings accurately. Writing integrated; computer intensive. Prerequisite: A grade of "C" or better in ENGL 101 or satisfactory placement score. (Lewis-Clark State College 2011, 292)

In this sample, research (itself an activity) as a course topic led the list of named topics at 11.5 percent, most frequently showing up in the second course and therefore most frequently at schools that required two FYC courses. As detailed in the figure above, courses with other topics or foci discussed in the literature—discipline-based topics, section-specific topics, or student-defined topics—were seldom evident in course descriptions.

To flesh out these findings further, discipline-based FYC writing requirements were found most frequently in the second-semester course, as at the University of Alaska Anchorage, where students were directed to select an FYC course in their discipline, or through courses that specifically directed teachers and students to cover *several* disciplines, as articulated in this course description from North Carolina Central University (2011, 258–59): "Emphasis on the reading of texts from literature, the sciences, and the social sciences; expository writing, documentation, and research in response to texts from a variety of disciplines." Courses were seldom defined by a specific topic, with the almost sole exception being at the University of Central Florida, where the previously mentioned Elizabeth Wardle directed the writing program at the time of this study. The first course in a two-course sequence was defined, in part, as follows: "In ENC 1101 students read research findings from Writing Studies intended to help them gain both procedural and declarative knowledge about writing that they can generalize ('transfer') to later writing situations" (University of Central Florida 2012a). Rounding out the range of topics represented, we found just two courses that could be said to be of the expressivist school that puts student self-definition at the center, as at the University of Arkansas at Little Rock, which began as follows: "Practice in writing, with an emphasis on personal, expressive writing . . ." (University of Arkansas at Little Rock 2011, 12).

In summary, discussions of topic, though frequent in scholarship (and teacher conversation), remained largely invisible to the formal structuring of FYC courses in this study, which, in their course descriptions and outcomes (state, university, and/or program or department), were defined by the activities, processes, or skills they focused on. Finally, we see little mention of emphasis on expressive writing, recognition, perhaps, of the end of the expressivist era.

HONORS OPTIONS FOR FYC

A seemingly minor topic in the field of writing studies is honors composition. The presence of honors programs is widespread in this sample at 81.1 percent, yet twenty-five of the colleges and programs in the sample do not extend honors to include a specialized honors course in composition. These students thus either take a regular section of FYC or else, as is the case at Montclair State University, they are simply exempted from the FYC requirement.

Perhaps not surprisingly, there is a statistically significant association between the presence of an honors program and institutional selectivity

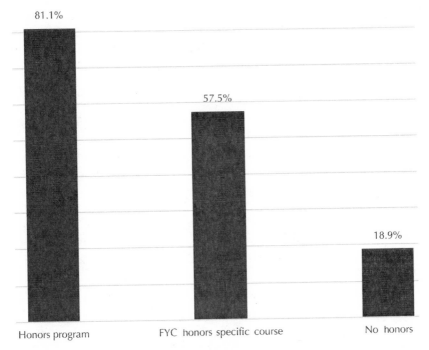

81.1%

57.5%

18.9%

Honors program   FYC honors specific course   No honors

Figure 4.7. Honors programs and FYC honors-specific courses

($\chi^2(2, n = 97) = 1.96, p > 0.05$), size ($\chi^2(3, n = 104) = 4.30, p > 0.05$), and Carnegie Classification ($\chi^2(8, n = 104) = 10.21, p > 0.05$). It is easy to hypothesize that the presence of an honors program would be more frequent at more competitive institutions that strive to provide a tailored experience for their strongest students, and that larger schools would both be more able to do so because they'd have the numbers to develop a sustainable cohort and be especially interested given the attractiveness of providing a college within the university for select students.

APPROACH TO TEACHING WRITING

To develop the bird's-eye view of state comprehensive universities' approaches to teaching writing, I used a two-rater system to examine and code course descriptions and outcome statements. As discussed further in appendix A, I moved back and forth between my knowledge of the scholarship (from which I knew, for example, that issues like process writing and skill-based instruction were important) to the primary data (from which I knew, for example, the kinds of language institutional writers were using to describe FYC courses and their outcomes) to develop a long "wish list" of categories or "dimensions" (Geisler 2004) to code the data on. From testing on course descriptions and outcomes statements from universities outside the sample, I realized I needed to reject several interesting categories because the data wasn't capacious enough to really let me see them (e.g., I wasn't able to code for modes). Further testing led to refinement of the coding directions or, when interrater agreement was too low, dropping a dimension altogether. While I originally wished to characterize courses broadly for approach, such as skills based versus rhetorically based, there were too many gray areas, particularly when courses signaled both attention to rhetorical instruction *and* an emphasis on skills instruction. In the end, following the overall principle of leaning toward using a method that was transparent and replicable, or Haswell's (2005, 201) RAD—I chose to be more specific and reportorial.

To preview the more detailed discussion that follows, the big finding here is that 68.6 percent ($n = 72$) of the institutions evidenced use of process-writing methodologies in their first-year composition courses, and 63.5 percent ($n = 66$) indicated rhetorical instruction. Argumentation, a subject of increased attention in the scholarship and in textbooks, at least since Andrea Lunsford and John Ruszkiewicz first published *Everything's an Argument* in 1998 (now in its sixth edition; Lunsford and John Ruszkiewicz 1998), was referenced in the FYC course descriptions or outcomes texts at 62.5 percent ($n = 65$) of the institutions in the sample. On the other side of the spectrum, skills instruction was evident at 25.0 percent ($n = 26$), and references to grammar was at 22.1 percent ($n = 23$). As will be discussed at the end of this section, these findings represent a very different portrait of approaches to FYC than are represented in the studies conducted by Burhans, Kitzhaber, Larson, and Witte et al. If the emergence of the discipline of writing studies has not produced legions of teachers whose primary education is in the field, as Bartholomae calculates persuasively in his millennial review for *PMLA* (Bartholomae 2000, 1953–54) and Joseph Harris (2006) confirms with his analysis of the survey by the Coalition for the Academic Workforce (American Historical Association 2007), our collective presence in administrative and faculty positions has, I would assert, changed the outlines of public four-year universities' approaches to teaching writing.

PROCESS WRITING

To begin this discussion, what follows is the definition my rater and I used to code a course as evidencing process-writing instruction:

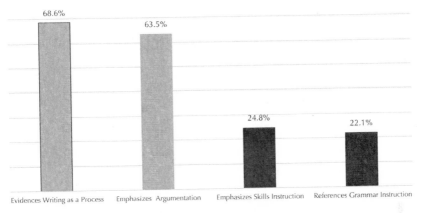

Figure 4.8. Articulated outcomes for FYC

"presence of process writing terms and approaches; that is, mention of several of the following: deliberate attention to generating writing, drafting writing, revising writing, editing writing (not only editing)." What this definition aimed to do was to identify concrete shorthand for teaching writing as a process—that very familiar, but not yet clichéd, idea that first gripped so many of us in the discipline when we read Donald Murray's (1968) articulation of it and that has remained a core and widely held value, as evidenced not only by my deeply felt sense from twenty-five years in the field but also through its embodiment in the WPA Outcomes (Council of Writing Program Administrators 2008), *The Framework for Postsecondary Education,* and as one of eleven core "NCTE Beliefs about the Teaching of Writing" (first published in 2004; revised 2016 and retitled "Professional Knowledge for the Teaching of Writing"). In the several paragraphs in the section "Writing is a process," NCTE's definition is much deeper and richer than mine, including not only a set of skills—"routines, skills, strategies, and practices, for generating, revising, and editing different kinds of texts," which are like the ones I suggested—but also habits of mind such as the "development of reflective abilities and meta-awareness about writing" (National Council of Teachers of English 2016). Had I included some expectation for these kinds of reflective abilities and meta-awareness, I would have coded many fewer schools as evidencing process writing, but I think my more limited definition makes sense for this study, as course descriptions and even outcomes statements are most frequently couched within the language of knowledge and skill attainment.

What does writing as a process look like in a course description and outcomes? What does its absence look like? Let's begin with absence, which essentially means the description focused exclusively on product over process. What follows are examples from schools that were different in regional location and size but that were similar in projecting "product" approaches in their course descriptions and outcome materials, albeit with different emphases. The first type of product focus, which reflects a utilitarian notion of writing instruction, was exemplified in the material from Thomas Edison State University in New Jersey. As is evident, there is one reference to revising, found in the ninth "course objective" for the second course—not enough to rise to the level of "several" required by the developed coding sheet.

THOMAS EDISON STATE COURSE DESCRIPTIONS
Thomas Edison State University: Course Description and Outcomes Excerpt

Course Description: ENC-101 English Composition I

Emphasizes basic expository writing skills that enhance the skills needed for academic and business writing. (Thomas Edison State University 2011a, 26)

Course Description: ENC-102 English Composition II

Presentation of expository writing skills that expand upon skills learned in English Composition I. Emphasizes research-paper writing. (Thomas Edison State University 2011a, 26)

Course Objectives for ENC 101:

Describe and utilize common techniques used in expressive, narrative, and descriptive writing;

Demonstrate the ability to use analysis of a subject to inform a reader.

Effectively write an explanatory paper.

Evaluate audience type and writing format.

Effectively compose both analytical and evaluative papers.

Write a clear thesis statement and support it with related, logical supporting arguments.

Write meaningful and effective introductions and conclusions.

Effectively write a problem/solution paper. (Thomas Edison State University 2011b)

Course Objectives for ENC 102:

Demonstrate the ability to use appropriate library and Internet resources when researching a topic.

Effectively compose a short research proposal.

Compile an annotated working bibliography and a complete bibliography in correct MLA or APA format.

Demonstrate the ability to write a formal topic or sentence outline.

Formulate a thesis for an essay or research paper.

Compose effective introductory, body, and concluding paragraphs.

Use quotations and paraphrases to strengthen your own thesis in essays and research papers.

Correctly document sources in either MLA or APA style.

Analyze and revise essays for greater effectiveness.

Spot common grammar, punctuation, and mechanics errors and explain how to correct them. (Thomas Edison State University 2011c)

As is clear, the key terms here are "effective" and "skill," words that come up repeatedly in courses my rater and I coded as those that do *not* exhibit process-writing methodologies. In a second example, below are two levels of outcomes for first-year composition at Georgia Southwestern State University (the course descriptions are fairly generic, left out for brevity's sake), which cover many aspects of writing instruction but do not speak to teaching the processes of writing.

First, the program level:

Course Objectives and Learning Outcomes [for ENGL 1101: Composition I]:

The purpose of Composition I is to help students improve their ability to write clearly and to read with understanding. The student will be able to:

1. effectively communicate ideas related to assigned material in both a written and oral format;

2. write well-defined and adequately developed expository essays;

3. demonstrate a comprehension of assigned readings;

4. demonstrate the use of proper grammar, diction, and mechanics.

(Georgia Southwestern State University 2004a)

Objectives and Learning Outcomes
[for ENGL1102: Composition II]:

The student will be able to:

1. write longer and more sophisticated essays than in Composition I with the continued emphasis on writing and reading;

2. discuss literary works and analyze in-depth and will read to develop critical and analytical thinking and writing skills;

3. use literary works of various genres to promote ideas for writing;

4. have the opportunity to master the techniques of researching, reporting, and documenting a thesis.

(Georgia Southwestern State University 2004b)

Looking at the university-level outcomes for writing, which are found in the catalog, we again see a product-focused perspective: "Students will be able to write effectively for a variety of audiences to demonstrate collegiate-level writing development in various contexts" (Georgia Southwestern State University 2011, 26). At Georgia Southwestern, as at its northern counterpart in New Jersey, we see writing *effectively* as a powerful and controlling idea but also note the significant attention to three other favorite priorities included in what Burhans refers to as the "grab bag of concerns" (Burhans 1983, 642) FYC courses are often expected to address: *reading comprehension, literary understanding,* and *research abilities,* all packed in with "effectiveness."

Once again, it is important to recall the limitations of a bird's-eye study; in this case it may well be that some or even many of the teachers at these institutions teach writing as a process. However, in these courses process writing is not presented as a course objective; further, these statements convey a dominant focus on final product.

Before turning to discuss the schools that did articulate process-writing instruction methodologies from this study, it will be useful to look back to two earlier studies. Based on data collected in 1986, Richard Larson, through examination of syllabi and other documents, concluded that 30 percent of the programs (public and private) in his study taught "writing as a process" and "55% pa[id] attention to revision" (Larson 1994, 24). Notably, however, although Larson originally surveyed 575 randomly selected institutions, by the time he drilled down to document review, he had 240 participating schools (5), raising the likelihood that the individuals who chose to send more materials to Larson were self-selected and, I would guess, were among those who saw themselves as more rather than less invested in teaching expository writing. The other significant study to discuss here is Clinton Burhans's study of 263 college and university catalog descriptions (from 1982–83 and 1983–84), the results of which led him to find "writing processes mentioned or implied" in only 3 percent of the FYC courses (Burhans 1983, 646). Compared to these findings—different as their findings are, despite their close time frame—I interpret the finding that 69.8 percent of schools in my sample evidenced process-writing instruction as a sign of considerable change and improvement for those of us who see process-writing instruction as valuable to FYC instruction.

WRITING AS MASTERY OF SKILLS

Articulation of teaching the writing process was most frequently demonstrated through relatively brief mention in course descriptions, as in this concise and clear description from Austin Peay State in Tennessee: "Development of the student's writing skills through a process of thinking, researching, planning, writing, revising and editing expository essays" (Austin Peay State College 2011). However, as is frequently the case, this course description was expanded in the outcomes, which at Austin Peay are referred to as the General Education Outcomes for Communication. This institutional statement on communication outcomes includes five points, the fourth of which reads, "Understand that the writing and/or speaking processes includes [sic] procedures such as planning, organizing, composing, revising and editing" (Austin Peay State College n.d.), suggesting some of the reflective aims NCTE articulates in "Professional Knowledge for the Teaching of Writing."

Across the country I found process-writing language articulated in catalogs and outcomes statements. Here, as another example, is Virginia's George Mason University's course description that foregrounds process writing in the first sentence of its first FYC course description: "Intensive practice in drafting, revising, and editing expository essays of some length and complexity" (George Mason University 2011). In addition to reference to attention to prewriting, drafting, and revising processes, course descriptions provide ample evidence that many institutions also value work in editing and improving students' writing to conventions, nimbly or even discordantly pairing the language of writing process with the language of skills. Elizabeth City State University in North Carolina begins as follows: "This course emphasizes the development of basic and intermediate writing skills, including mechanics, sentence clarity, coherence, organization and vocabulary. Special emphasis is on the role of revision in the writing process" (Elizabeth City State University 2008,

335). Writing as a process appears to have become institutionalized, though likely the ways in which it is emphasized and practiced vary by institution and individual instructor.

The coupling of process-writing language and skills language raises the question of association between variables within the sample, the headlines of which are as follows: process-writing features were more likely to occur in course descriptions and/or outcomes materials from research universities than from BA-granting institutions, with a highly significant correlation ($r = 0.422$, $p = 0.000$). For size, we see that larger institutions were statistically more likely to include process-writing language ($r = 0.279$, $p = 0.019$) than were smaller institutions. Further, more selective institutions were similarly more likely to include this language than were less selective institutions ($r = 0.279$, $p = 0.025$). Finally, as shown in the table below, and as the Elizabeth City State University course description illustrates, process-writing language was *not* negatively correlated with skills-instruction language or with the explicit referencing to grammar, contrary to what I had hypothesized. I reiterate the point because it is so striking: *process-writing language and skills-instruction language were not mutually exclusive.*

As can be extrapolated from the data presented in table 4.3, sixteen of the 72 (22.2 percent) of the schools that included the language of process-writing also specified skills instruction. This coupling, however, wasn't constant. Looking just at the sixty-four institutions that had two FYC courses, there is a statistically significant negative association between skills-oriented instruction and process-writing instruction; that is, when we look only at the second courses, as we see evidence of skills-oriented instruction rising, we see evidence of process-writing instruction declining ($r = -0.356$, $p = 0.003$). Thus, we see some mixed results: overall, there is no negative association between skills instruction and process-writing instruction, but when we hone down to only those schools that require two courses in FYC, we do see a negative association, as would be expected.

SKILLS AND GRAMMAR

I am confident that readers of this book have spent countless hours trying to explain their views on teaching grammar and skills as *part* of the writing process, only to explain it again and again, most often with the end result of being completely misunderstood by altogether too many other educators and members of the general public. The twin myths around students' inabilities to write clearly and teachers' neglect of "basic skills"

Table 4.3. Coexistence of process writing methodologies and skills instruction

		FYC sequence: process-writing methods evident		
		No	Yes	Total
FYC sequence: skills instruction specified	No	21.9% (23)	53.3% (56)	75.2% (79)
	Yes	9.5% (10)	15.2% (16)	24.8% (26)
Total		31.5% (33)	68.5% (72)	100% (105)

like writing grammatically are powerful, politically motivated ones, as Adler-Kassner discusses in her book *The Activist WPA* (2008). One measure of the persuasiveness of our field, then, is the extent to which writing instruction is still articulated as skills instruction and as about "grammar." Depending on your level of cynicism, you will either take comfort in or feel discouraged by the finding that skills instruction in FYC was evident at 24.8 percent ($n = 26$) of the schools in this study. To come to this finding, my co-rater and I used the following definition:

> Course description and/or outcomes materials indicate that the course has an *emphasis* on teaching/mastering specific lower-order general skills; address of writing as fixed/defined; skills instruction thus appears dominant in the course description and defines the course as one that addresses deficiency in concrete, lower-order, fixed skills.

Grammar, which was coded by examination of course descriptions alone, and which was defined simply as the specification of *grammar*, *grammatical*, or use of a word with a similar root, was present at 20.0 percent ($n = 21$) of the schools. Not surprisingly, there is a strong association (χ^2 (1, $n = 105$) = 24.74, $p < 0.05$) between schools coding for lower-order skills and presence of the word *grammar*. Further, grammar instruction in the FYC sequence is associated with two institutional characteristics: Basic Carnegie Classification and Carnegie Classification size. The association between grammar instruction and Basic Carnegie Classification is also strong (χ^2 (8, $n = 105$) = 23.052, $p < 0.05$); as institutions rose up the research-intensity ladder, they were less likely to include grammar in their construction of writing, as evidenced by FYC course descriptions and outcomes.

We see the same phenomenon in respect to grammar and Carnegie size; again, as institutions grew larger, they were less likely to reference grammar instruction in their FYC course descriptions: (χ^2 ($n = 105$, $df = 3$) = 9.5423.052, $p < 0.05$). From this we can see that specification of grammar instruction was more prevalent in smaller schools and BA-granting institutions. Looking at grammar instruction in the first FYC course alone, as opposed to the whole sequence, we see more associations. There is a strong association between schools *not* referencing grammar in FYC course one and Carnegie Graduate Classification, with schools with doctoral programs showing the least likelihood of referencing grammar ($r = .239\ p = .015$); further, this is the case even though there is no correlation between skills-based instruction (in the first FYC course or in the sequence) and institutional selectivity (i.e., admissions standards), as one might hypothesize. In other words, institutional size rather than institutional selectivity is associated with avoidance of an emphasis on grammar.

Previous research makes clear the long history of tension between research on teaching writing and its practice in classrooms. An effort to compare my findings on practice with respect to skills and grammar with other researchers' work brings us back first to Kitzhaber's 1962 study, then to Witte, Cherry, and Meyer at the University of Texas at Austin's 1980s study of four-year and two-year college writing programs (private and public), and finally to Laron's 1994 study. Kitzhaber's second major finding, as reported in *College English*, was to declare that the "so-called 'review of fundamentals,' a traditional feature of the freshman English course, [wa]s being dropped at many schools" (Kitzhaber 1962, 476); for Kitzhaber, in this respect, progress had been made. Reflecting a different perspective, Witte, Cherry, and Meyer, in their report entitled "The Goals of Freshman Writing Programs as Perceived by a National Sample of College and University Writing Program Directors and Teachers," revealed the extent to which directors and writing teachers felt compelled and pressured to prioritize the teaching of "writing mechanically correct prose" and even "writing coherent prose" (Witte, Cherry, and Meyer 1982, 29) rather than writing for "different audiences," "different purposes," or to gain the ability to "evaluate one's own writing and the writing of others," among other more rhetorically oriented goals. Witte, Cherry, and Meyer found great differences between what participants identified as their ideal goals (what they believed should be their goals) compared to their real goals as teachers and directors of particular courses and programs. Comments directors made about "writing mechanically correct prose" occurred only 13.5 percent of the time when they were discussing their "ideal" goals but 69.2 percent of the time when they were discussing their "real" goals (Witte, Cherry, and Meyer 1982). What is more, the researchers found directors were more concerned about mechanical correctness than were teachers, speculating that "the difference might also be attributed to the greater frequency with which directors encounter complaints from colleagues in their own and other disciplines regarding students' inability to write with mechanical correctness" (7–8). Today, faculty leaders continue to encounter such complaints, and I speculate that the pressure from external colleagues and the society outside academia puts some pressure on writers of course descriptions and outcomes. Ultimately, these documents reflect a negotiation between disciplinary faculty and the several faculty and administrative committees that review, revise, and vote on them before they are published in catalogs and university websites. The authors of these documents are experienced writers, well aware of the multiple audiences that can be expected to read these documents: students, other faculty, parents, administrators, external reviewers, and even those outside the institution and higher education who have been known to examine academic documents for the purpose of making fun of them (Straussbaugh, *New York Times*, Dec. 27, 2004).

Whereas Witte, Cherry, and Meyer avoid making judgments about their findings on the priority teachers and administrators place on mechanical correctness, Richard Larson's approach is different, though he too finds much emphasis on correctness. In his study, Larson finds 30 percent of syllabi "focusing directly on grammatical categories" (Larson 1994, 23), concluding that "attention to form dominates the advice about revising" (26). Of his primary conclusions, Larson lists as second the concern that there is a "predominant emphasis on teaching forms of writing, patterns of arrangement, compliance with formal requirements (in paragraphs and sentences)" (18). In fact, Larson is so disturbed by his findings that he ends up agreeing with the Ford Foundation—which commissioned his work—that there is no "center of gravity" (18) to the teaching of writing in higher education, and worse yet, no system for assessing writing-program effectiveness (46–47). Ultimately, he recommends that the Ford Foundation not waste its money on "the improvement of college writing programs" based on his inability to discern any real agreement "on what a college writing program should be or should teach" (40). Based on my data from state comprehensive universities, I believe we are in a different place today: we have come to much greater (if not perfect) agreement that writing instruction should not focus primarily on teaching correctness.

AREAS OF EMPHASIS IN FYC: ARGUMENTATION

Through examination of course descriptions and outcomes, 62 percent ($n = 65$) of schools were coded as emphasizing argumentation. Argumentation emphasis was defined by "evidence of instruction in argumentation through the use of the words (or words with the same root): argument, persuade; through language such as: take and support a position, provide evidence for one side of a debate." Argumentation was not found to have associations with any other institutional or instructional characteristic. Argumentation was found in the title of just one course, ENGL145 Reasoning, Argumentation, and Writing (California Polytechnic State University 2011, 349) but was emphasized in course descriptions and detailed in course outcomes in various ways. For example, at the University of Illinois Springfield, argumentation was linked with civic engagement in the second FYC course, articulated in the description as follows:

> ENG 102: College Writing and Civic Engagement Explores analytical and argumentative writing written for the public sphere. Students will develop their abilities to articulate rhetorical strategies found in texts and to produce carefully constructed arguments in multiple genres and for multiple audiences.

Although the focus on civic engagement was unique to this course, what is typical is this positioning of argument as one of a few prioritized genres (here, with analytical writing). Repeatedly, the argumentative essay was listed as either the only genre or one among just a few (most often coupled with analytic, expository, persuasive, or research genres), often suggesting that the argumentative essay was the academic preferred form. Here are snippets from a variety of schools' FYC courses:

> ENGL 1101: English Composition I: A composition course focusing on skills required for effective writing in a variety of contexts, with emphasis on exposition, analysis, and argumentation. (North Georgia College and State University 2011)
>
> ENG 103 Rhetoric and Writing. (3) Introduces and develops understanding of principles of rhetoric; basic research methods; elements, strategies, and conventions of persuasion used in constructing written and multi-modal texts. (Ball State University 2011b, 354)
>
> EN 102 is a study of analytical and interpretive skills necessary for constructing a well-supported argument. (Mississippi University for Women 2011)

This focus on argumentation as the most commonly taught genre likely reflects values not only in the discipline, which are not always embraced by practitioners across the nation, but also values within higher education more broadly. It appears that argument has won the day both in and outside the discipline.

Although few studies look at this question directly, a strong case can be made that attention to argumentation reflects a change from earlier periods, as reported in 1929 by Taylor and certainly since the 70s and 80s. Taylor noted that 41.3 percent of the institutions in his study reported including argumentation instruction in their freshman English courses, declaring, "Argumentation, without question, is taught less frequently than it was even a decade ago. It has lost ground with the wane in popularity of college debating" (Taylor 1929, 13–14). I don't believe we have good data to support Taylor's position that argument was more common prior to 1929, though that may well have been the case. However, we know a little more about practices after 1929. Jumping forward to the 1980s, Burhans reported widespread emphasis on exposition (not exactly argument), with 59 percent of the courses in his study having this emphasis (Burhans 1983, 646). In 2008, Andrea Lunsford and Karen Lunsford reproduced research from Connors and Lunsford (1993) based on their examination of student writing collected from across the country, leading Lunsford and Lunsford to conclude that "emphasis on personal narrative ha[d] been replaced by an emphasis on argument and research," with 32.7 percent of the 877 papers they collected favoring "researched arguments or reports" (Lunsford and Lunsford 2008, 793). An indirect indicator of argument's rise can be found in Richard Fulkerson's fairly scathing review of the field in which he argues that the field is split into three theoretical camps but that all three tend strongly toward teaching argument; further, he states that argument-based textbook sales have become "phenomenal" (Fulkerson 2005, 670). Fulkerson's analysis of textbooks slides quickly into an argument for, among other things, argumentation. I think Fulkerson was on to something: in reading through the many course descriptions and outcome statements in my sample, it's hard not to think that argument has, for now, won the day, despite the powerful voices of Peter Elbow, Wendy Bishop, Doug Hesse (Bishop 1997, 1999, 2003; Elbow 1973, 1990, 1995; Hesse 1993, 2003, 2009), and many others for the place for creative and expressive genres. Bishop quotes Robert Connors, who says, "Exposition and argument quickly were accepted by teachers as the most important modes." (Bishop 2003, 265), in her plea for writing faculty to embrace creative nonfiction and other creative forms. Elbow is perhaps the most well-known advocate for exploratory, creative, and expressive genres, not as replacements for argument but as complementary genres; and, though his books and essays that argue for expressivism are still popular, as are creative writing and other nonargumentative genres in courses and programs outside FYC, the infrequency of references to expressive writing coupled with the dominance of argumentation suggests that the expressive period is, indeed, on the wane.

TEACHING WRITING AS A RHETORICAL ACT

For many, argumentation is closely related to rhetoric—the explicit or inexplicit teaching of it or at least a pedagogical approach that reflects a deep belief that writing is always rhetorical. It is therefore not surprising that the sample reflected high percentages, 62.9 percent ($n = 66$), for rhetorical instruction, the presence of which was marked when course(s) and/or outcomes

> indicate[d] that writing is rhetorical, that it requires an awareness that individuals make choices, that there isn't one set of procedures for writing well in all situations; that writing is always situationally dependent. Key words include (presence of which is not sufficient): rhetoric, rhetorical, audience, purpose, invention, strategies, context. (Coding Sheet; see appendix D for full copy)

Presence of the word *rhetoric* in the title was not judged sufficient to qualify a course as including rhetorical instruction. In this sample of the schools whose FYC sequence was identified as emphasizing argumentation, 40.9 percent (43) were also identified as emphasizing rhetorical instruction. The signifying of a rhetorical orientation took many forms, from evocation of ethos, pathos, and logos, (University of Northern Colorado 2011) to "kairos" (Missouri Western State University 2012), to more contemporary language and application, such as the following:

- "1. Discern a writer's argument or purpose . . . 5. Write in a manner appropriate to the audience and context." (University of Nebraska at Kearney 2011, 42)
- "[E]mphasizes critical thinking as well as traditional rhetorical skills because only insight can generate substance for the writer's craft to shape." (East Carolina University 2005)
- "Organize central ideas and supporting material in unified, coherent patterns, using various methods of rhetorical development (e.g., argument, comparison and contrast, process and analysis); . . . Write to a variety of audiences." (Department of English, Lock Haven University of Pennsylvania 2011)
- "Students will be able to write in different ways for different audiences." ("Core Curriculum" University of Texas at Dallas 2011)

For some rhetoricians, these articulations of rhetorical practices will seem thin, though recalling that course descriptions and outcomes are written with a broad range of audiences in mind may help explain the language many authors of course descriptions and outcomes chose to use. I think Albert Kitzhaber, whose own study led him to conclude that "few English teachers show any awareness of the tradition [of rhetoric], much less recognize that the freshman course in composition is or properly should be a part of that tradition" (Kitzhaber 1962, 481), would be pleased that so many courses have taken on teaching rhetorical awareness and strategies, explicitly or implicitly, in FYC. On the flip side, that 35 percent of courses that focus on argumentation do not also identify inclusion of rhetorical instruction suggests that these courses may emphasize argumentation without also emphasizing rhetoric.

In terms of finding statistically meaningful associations with courses having a rhetorical emphasis, we see some marginal significance between evidence of rhetorical writing instruction and Carnegie Classification of Selectivity. As schools were classified as more selective, it was marginally *more likely* that their FYC courses would have a rhetorical bent (χ^2 ($n = 97$, $df = 2$) = 4.91, $p = 0.086$). In addition, we also see a *negative* association between rhetorical instruction in the FYC sequence and grammar ($r = -0.207$ $p = 0.034$), an expected finding. There is also a marginally significant trend when we look at the association between rhetorical instruction and process-writing instruction (χ^2 ($n = 105$, $df = 1$) = 2.65, $p = 0.103$), also an expected finding.

WPA INFLUENCE ON INSTRUCTIONAL APPROACH

I suspect the direction of FYC courses, and therefore the language of course descriptions and outcomes, is shaped first and foremost by the primary authors of these documents—the writing faculty and the WPA, when there is one, or the chair of the FYC or equivalent committee when there is not. Although far beyond the scope of this study, I suspect we might also see these writers' own personal institutional histories: tracks of the graduate programs WPAs studied with, for example. As a proxy for this more detailed kind of work of uncovering the influence of writing program administrators, I have selected the variable WPA faculty status and cross-tabulated this information against the variables relating to approach to teaching first-year composition, as detailed in figure 4.9.

What we see throughout the variables is that institutions with WPAs on the tenure track were *more likely* to have course descriptions and outcome statements that indicated process-writing instruction and rhetorical instruction and included argumentation but that did not emphasize skill or reference grammar (in their course descriptions). However, more likely/less likely is quite different from always/never: that 18 percent of the institutions with tenure-track faculty in the WPA position oversaw courses that explicitly referenced grammar and had a skill-based component is significant, as is the fact that so many did not include reference to either rhetorical or process-writing instruction.

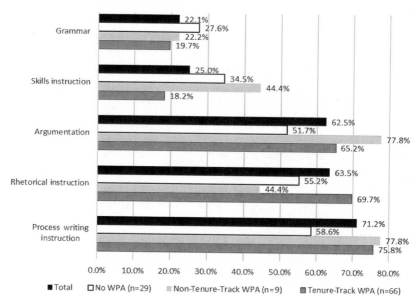

Figure 4.9. FYC course description references and WPA presence

To conclude this chapter, I call attention to several of the most significant findings:

- the uniform presence of research versus the absence of expressivism
- the majority adoption of the language of argumentation and rhetorical instruction and process writing
- the persistence of skills language
- writing most frequently defined as a generalized activity to skill, without explicit connection to topic, genre, or discipline

In these findings we see the outlines of first-year composition in the US state comprehensive university. Of all the discoveries discussed here, the one I found most surprising is the near absence of engagement with the language of expressive or personal writing, which was so core to my experience learning about teaching writing at the University of Massachusetts/Amherst in the 1990s. UMass Amherst was and is known for highly valuing expressive writing, but expressivism was also given significant attention in my experiences at Colby College, where I was taught writing by literature and creative-writing professors, and in high school in the suburbs of Boston. The value on writing personally to express oneself, and on providing instructional time for and attention to that work, was clearly present in my high-school, college, and graduate-school experiences, and I can't help but be sorry that the acknowledged, articulated role of expressive writing has so diminished. I think many of us who went to high school and college in the last quarter of the twentieth century would attest to similar experiences. Perhaps today, across the country, writing teachers still place priority on and hold time for expressive writing, but it is a shame that this work that clearly people who write have always valued has been relegated to the unofficial, unarticulated landscape.

Quick Facts: What Is Happening in FYC

In this sample's institutions . . .

- *FYC Requirement:* 67.9 percent require two courses in FYC, and 31.1 percent require one course.
- *FYC Outcomes:* 91.5 percent articulate outcomes for FYC in such publicly available documents as catalogs and general education, assessment, or program websites.
- *WPA Outcomes:* 22.6 percent of those that require FYC have adopted or adapted the WPA Outcomes Statement.
- *Program-Level FYC Outcomes:* 76.4 percent have outcomes articulated on the program or department level.
- *Institution-level FYC Outcomes:* 62.3 percent have outcomes articulated on the institutional level.
- *State-level FYC Outcomes:* 9.4 percent have outcomes articulated on the state level.
- *Research Instruction:* 91.4 percent specify that research instruction is provided in FYC.
- *Focus of Course:* Only 25 percent of institutions identified a topic, genre, or discipline (e.g., learning, argumentation, or literary study) as the focus of the course; 75 percent identified writing as the primary activity of the course.
- *Focus on Literary Study:* Just 8.6 percent of the FYC courses focused on literary study.
- *Focus on Expressivism:* 2 percent of the courses focused on expressivist writing.
- *Process Writing:* 68.6 percent evidenced emphasis on process-writing methodologies.
- *Rhetorical Instruction:* 63.5 percent evidenced emphasis on rhetorical instruction.
- *Argumentation Instruction:* 62.0 percent evidenced emphasis on argumentation.

- *Skills Instruction:* 25.0 percent evidenced emphasis on skills instruction.
- *Grammar:* 22.1 percent specifically identified grammar as an area of instruction.

Notes

1. Beyond institutions that had someone present at CCCC in those two years are likely many institutions who had an individual attend CCCC, suggesting broader engagement with contemporary scholarship.

2. In the 106-institution sample, 7 (6.6 percent) were "more selective," 51 (48.1 percent) were "selective," and 40 (37.7 percent) were "inclusive"—the remaining 8 (7.5 percent) were unidentified by Carnegie Classification—with one and two-course sequences breaking down across selectivity as a percentage of the total.

3. In this section reporting out on research practices within FYC, I relied first on the survey reports completed by representatives from 92 of the 105 institutions that require FYC and second on course descriptions and outcomes or equivalent statements. These documents provided corroboration, and, where a survey was not completed, sometimes additional answers. For example, at two institutions for which I did not have survey responses, a research paper was defined in the course description, but I could not find and therefore report out on several other questions, such as an annotated bibliography assignment or inclusion of primary research as part of the research instruction.

5

BEYOND FIRST-YEAR COMPOSITION

In this chapter I offer a view of what the four-year public colleges and universities in the sample are doing with writing beyond first-year composition: for all students through upper-level requirements, for students who are looking for individualized instruction in writing through a writing center, and for those students who seek greater immersion in the discipline through a writing minor, major, or other program. As a discipline, we have focused primarily on FYC and secondarily on writing centers, writing across the curriculum (WAC), and graduate education. Most recently we have turned to vertical writing programming; that is, on developing upper-level writing/rhetoric programming for undergraduates, a move many have seen as overdue: "It is past time that we fill the glaringly empty spot between First-Year Composition and graduate education with a composition major" (Yancey 2004, 308). This last arena is the focus of much excitement, at least since Kathleen Blake Yancey's 2003 CCCCs chair's address, quoted here, which I recall receiving enthusiastic applause.

This section's highlights include finding documentation for writing-across-the-curriculum programming at 33.0 percent of the schools in this sample; if you look at writing requirements from matriculation to the end, students are required to take an average of 3.03 courses in writing ($SD = 1.5$) to graduate. Further, survey respondents reported more WAC initiatives than are found in catalogs, suggesting unofficial programs or the presence of programs not articulated at the university-catalog level. In respect to support for student writers outside class, I found presence of writing centers or individualized tutoring in writing at *all* the sample schools, though they vary in their administrative locations, with many at general tutoring centers within a division of Student Affairs. In the area of vertical writing programing, just 10.4 percent of the institutions in this sample have majors in writing, but 69.8 percent of the schools offer some kind of vertical program in writing—a minor or concentration most typically. In these programs writing is variously defined and imagined, with programs in creative writing, journalism,

DOI: 10.7330/9781607326397.c005

technical communication, and rhetoric. Interesting statistical relationships include the general finding that variables associated with a strong FYC program do not necessarily lead to a strong WAC presence; that is, for example, neither process writing nor argumentation in FYC, use of DSP, or adoption of the WPA Outcomes, all qualities that suggest university strength in trained and influential writing faculty, are associated with WAC presence. Strong writing faculty have more of an effect when it comes to writing majors, it seems, as writing majors exist when other indicators of writing-faculty leaders are present. For example, writing majors were more likely to be present at schools that had adopted the WPA Outcomes and had individuals presenting at the Conference on College Composition and Communication (CCCC).

In this chapter I begin with a discussion of WAC, followed by what I call *writing robustness*, then writing centers, and finally vertical writing programming. What is clear from this review of the research is what I think experienced writing faculty know: whatever difficulties we encounter with FYC are small compared to the much greater challenge of engaging faculty and students with writing after FYC.

WRITING ACROSS THE CURRICULUM: STATE COMPREHENSIVE UNIVERSITY STUDY IN CONTEXT

Writing across the curriculum, writing in the disciplines, writing to learn, and other efforts to extend writing instruction beyond FYC have a long history, beginning with the dawning of the modern university in the early part of the twentieth century. David R. Russell, writing first in 1991 in *Writing in the Academic Disciplines, 1870–1990: A Curricular History*, takes a rather dim view of the success of WAC movements, chronicling several different efforts that have not been sustained.

> There have been literally hundreds of cross-curricular writing programs since the turn of the century at institutions of every type. Indeed, each generation has produced its own versions of cross-curricular writing programs, yet none, except perhaps the last, has made a permanent impact on the modern university curriculum or on literacy in America. Sooner or later these programs were marginalized for many of the same reasons general composition courses were. Because administrators and faculty did not perceive the central role of writing in modern academic disciplines and professional work, they tended to make writing instruction an adjunct to a course or program rather than an integral part of it. (Russell 2002, 8)

Russell is pessimistic, despite his expressed hope that the WAC movement that began in the 1970s would be more durable, asserting that

WAC requires universities to radically reorganize their disciplinary-silo approach and to abandon what Mike Rose has coined "the myth of transience" (Russell 1990): the belief that students can simply be cured of their writing ills once and for all.

In contrast to Russell, and writing ten years later, Susan McLeod (2000, 2002) and Chris Thaiss and Tara Porter tend toward greater optimism for both the possibilities of widespread adoption of WAC (Thaiss and Porter 2010) and the spread of WAC in postsecondary education. In large part, McLeod's belief in WAC's growth is corroborated by two studies that document this growth. She cites a 1985 MLA survey that found "46% of all Ph.D.-granting institutions, 48% of all BA/MA-granting institutions, and 28% of all two-year colleges had a WAC program of some sort" (McLeod 2000, 1) and her own survey data from 1988, compiled by Susan Shirley, which found that "of 1,113 respondents (2,735 institutions queried), 427 (38%) reported having some form of WAC program" (quoted in Thaiss and Porter 2010, 535). Chris Thaiss and Tara Porter, in a study published from data collected in 2008, also document growth in WAC programming. From surveys sent to twenty-six hundred institutions (including one hundred sent to Canadian institutions) that yielded a response rate of 51 percent (537), they found that 47 percent of these institutions had WAC programs (540), another 27 percent were planning to develop WAC programs, and only 27 percent were "neither having nor planning a WAC program" (541). Like McLeod, Thais and Porter are measured in their declarations of victory, concluding, "WAC is still a 50-50 option in American higher education—and a distinct minority presence in the community college—and, as a program depends on the co-operation of more-stable entities (i.e., departments and deans' and provosts' offices), can rather easily be diminished, if not eliminated" (563).

WRITING BEYOND FYC IN THE STUDY

For this state comprehensive university study, and as detailed in figures 5.1 through 5.3, I sought to understand the presence of WAC through two different means: a survey of identified leaders of writing programming or courses and my review of catalogs and other public documents. In the survey I attempted to distinguish between writing courses and requirements that were part of majors and between additional general education writing courses and requirements. Interestingly, the survey results (figs. 5.1 and 5.2) suggest greater engagement with required writing experiences across the sample than I was able to find through

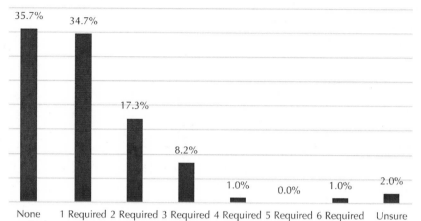

Figure 5.1. General education writing requirements beyond FYC: survey responses

documentation in catalogs or bulletins. Figure 5.1 represents answers in response to this question: Beyond the FYC requirement, how many additional writing courses (e.g., a writing-intensive course or a junior-level writing course) or writing experiences does your institution require as part of students' general education?

From the survey, two-thirds of respondents indicated additional general education writing requirements beyond FYC, a finding not confirmed by catalog review (fig. 5.3), suggesting that the survey question yielded a flexible interpretation of the question. Greater similarities between the two sources can be found in respect to the question of presence of additional requirements within the major, which respondents reported to be present at about one-third of the schools in the sample. For this question, I asked: Is there an institution-wide requirement for writing courses or experiences within students' major courses of study? If so, how many?

Through course catalogs and other documents, I found that only 32.1 percent of the colleges and universities had any writing requirements beyond FYC. Important to note, I didn't distinguish between courses in the major and courses in general education (see fig. 5.3), so it's truly the case that two-thirds of the schools in the sample did not choose to require writing after the first year. I looked long and hard for additional requirements, including at those schools affected by the California State University Board of Trustee's decision to require students to pass an upper-division writing requirement (taken after fifty-six semester units are completed) not met by a lower-division course (Ball State University has a similar requirement). Document review revealed that writing

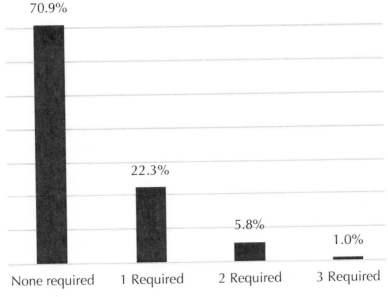

Figure 5.2. Writing requirements within the major: survey responses

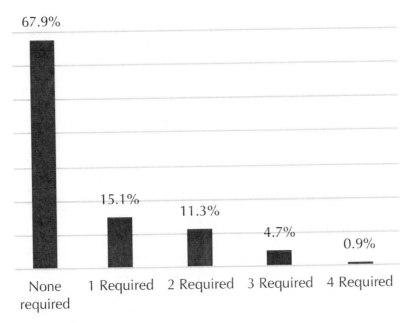

Figure 5.3. Number of requirements beyond FYC: catalog review

requirements beyond FYC were most frequently articulated through writing-intensive courses defined by Grand Valley State University as "meaning that writing quality is a major component of both the classroom requirement as well as the grade," (Grand Valley State University 2011, 9). Additional writing courses are located within majors, occasionally as capstone courses, and in one instance as part of a university thesis requirement for majors (New College of Florida 2012).

The catalog review provided more detailed information about official policies, noting, for example, that the schools that have a college-level proficiency requirement typically provide an alternative to passage of a test through successful completion of a writing course. In addition, catalog review revealed that seven schools have both a general education writing requirement and a requirement for writing in the major. For example, as explained on the web page devoted to WAC at East Carolina University,

> Students enrolling at East Carolina University must fulfill the writing across the curriculum requirement prior to graduation. To do so, each student must complete a minimum of 12 s.h. of writing intensive courses, including ENGL 1100, 1200; at least one 3 s.h. writing intensive course in the major; and any other 3 s.h. writing intensive course of the student's choice. All second degree students will be required to complete at least 3 s.h. of writing intensive course work in the major." (East Carolina University 2011)

Catalogs from schools that require additional courses vary in their specificity, though a handful articulate writing-intensive or other writing courses in some detail, as is exemplified by Eastern Illinois University. At Eastern Illinois, the catalog informs students that all its general education courses are "writing-active courses," whereas at least one required course is writing intensive.

> In such courses several writing assignments and writing activities are required. These assignments and activities, which are to be spread over the course of the semester, serve the dual purpose of strengthening writing skills and deepening understanding of course content. At least one writing assignment is to be revised by the student after it has been read and commented on by the instructor. In writing intensive courses, at least 35% of the course grade should be based on writing activities. (Eastern Illinois University 2011, 37).

While frequently requirements were explained briefly in catalogs, such details as noted here at Eastern Illinois were also present at several other schools.

Another good example of a comprehensive approach to WAC beyond a two-semester FYC comes from SUNY Buffalo State, which is classified as a Carnegie Master's Large university, where the requirement is focused on writing outside the major. After completing the two-semester FYC sequence, students have a WAC requirement that includes two courses designed to "enhance and reinforce basic writing skills learned" in the FYC sequence (Buffalo State College 2011, 37). In the catalog the WAC program is further described, emphasizing a wide range of goals for upper-level writing courses, from writing to learn to demonstrating writing competency.

> Like many other courses offered at this campus, W courses include both formal and informal writing. W courses, however, emphasize writing as a major course component for both instruction and evaluation. Instructors employ writing-to-learn techniques as a major way of teaching. In such courses, students learn how to use writing as a tool that can be used in all their learning processes. A significant portion of the coursework, and subsequently grades in these W courses, will be allocated on the basis of the student's writing performance. (Buffalo State College 2011, 37)

This statement is followed by an articulation of minimum writing standards for written work, a list that ranges from higher-order to lower-order concerns and that I imagine being the end product of an interdisciplinary faculty committee discussion and negotiation of instructional priorities for these writing courses. At Buffalo State, nearly every department offers W courses, with some offering eight or more different courses. As might be expected, course descriptions range in their emphasis on writing and the extent to which the content—its focus and also its breadth of competencies or skills covered—appears like a good choice for a writing-intensive course.

There are a number of potential explanations for understanding why this review of catalogs and websites uncovered a lower prevalence of WAC programming than was discovered by McLeod or Thaiss and Porter. These explanations include differences in choice of target populations (theirs targeted all or most postsecondary institutions and included community colleges), sampling strategies, and data sources. My hunch, supported by the differential in findings I gained from the survey as compared to the document review, is that surveys that call for self-reporting are going to generate more responses from schools that participate in WAC. When I report that one-third of the schools in the sample had requirements for writing beyond FYC, I am thus following the definitional categories established by Thaiss and Porter, who break down their data in various ways and report a 47 percent finding as a sum of either WAC or WID programs in their study.

Another methodological point is that Thaiss and Porter (2010) and McLeod (2010) were deeper and more thorough in their data collection, asking many questions including those related to staffing configuration, age of program, funding source, and components of the program, whereas my investigation was primarily limited to institutions' programmatic descriptions and course descriptions and findings about numbers of courses or "experiences" (which I included to capture data on portfolio or other requirements), as will be discussed further below. Briefly, to mention one of Thaiss and Porter's important findings not addressed in my study, they found that 47 percent of respondents were associate or full professors, a representation fairly close to the percentage I found for FYC directors, 57.1 percent (forty-eight of eighty-four confirmed WPAs), discussed in chapter 3. They also observed that WAC leaders most typically report to deans or central administrators (559), receiving funding from a variety of sources, with central administration and college or division as most commonly reported sources (555), a notable difference from the way most FYC programs are structured (see chapter 3).

WRITING BENEATH UNIVERSITY REQUIREMENTS

The document review from this state comprehensive university study indicates that the majority of colleges and schools do not mandate advanced writing courses as a matter of college or university policy. In reviewing the catalogs of the schools that do not have articulated WAC or WID programs, I observed only a handful of upper-level requirements of any kind: requirements in diversity, global studies, service learning, and interdisciplinary study were most frequent. Instead, curricula at the sample schools are comprised of two primary components: breadth general education courses and major programs, a system that effectively relies on the majors to define and provide writing instruction and support as desired or needed. And, of course, the institutions in the schools that do not have articulated writing requirements beyond FYC may well have departments that take it upon themselves to teach disciplinary writing, despite Russell's (2002) contention that universities are organized with such a focus on disciplinary knowledge so as to preclude this likelihood.

As an example, it's useful to look at Alabama Agricultural and Mechanical University, a Carnegie Large Master's university that does not have a WAC program to follow its two-semester FYC sequence. However, in reviewing the catalog, I found that about a dozen majors from a list of forty-three (in addition to certification programs) required upper-level writing courses, including all six majors in the business school. Course descriptions suggested a variety in the intensity of writing instruction and support but included several courses similar to what would be required for a WAC course at a WID/WAC school; for example, at Alabama A&M Business School, majors are required to take two courses, Business Communications and Business and Professional Writing, both of which emphasize writing instruction in their course descriptions. For example, BSM 315 Professional Writing is clearly focused on writing: "This course is specifically designed to meet the needs of students who will perform research and write business and technical reports and proposals pertinent to any area of business, industry, or government" (Alabama Agricultural and Mechanical University 2008, 273). It seems likely that the business school is responding to national or regional accrediting requirements from their disciplinary organizations. In contrast, many other course descriptions for required writing courses for specific majors at Alabama A&M were comparatively sparse in the attention allotted for writing; writing is presented as a skill addressed along with many others. In this description for Social Research Methods, a course required for students in the social work program, we see the following full plate of course goals: "It is designed to present the basic principles of social science research (scientific method). It covers all aspects of the research process from problem formulation to writing of the research proposal. It introduces students to qualitative, quantitative, and single subject methods of conducting research are also covered. Ethical issues . . . [and] The use of research . . ." (173). In summary, the Alabama A&M University catalog reflects no systematic attention to upper-level writing instruction and support and only spotty and varied approaches in specific programs (including what appears to be at least some robust approaches). My review of these catalogs and my experience suggest that many universities, without a comprehensive approach, would have a similarly wide range of approaches to upper-level writing.

The nature of this study precludes me from making any statements about the strength or even the nature of these WAC programs. An excellent source for this kind of understanding can be found in Dan Melzer's examination of WAC, a study that had a sampling method similar to mine for identifying institutions and that also relied on publicly available information, although Melzer collected writing assignments directly rather than relying on course catalogs. As Melzer discusses fully, 83 percent of the assignments were transactional in nature, with the majority of these focusing on writing to inform (Melzer 2009, 245). Nonetheless, Melzer concludes that where WAC is "a formal part of the institutional culture . . . the transformation of writing pedagogy is impressive" (Melzer 2014, 72), underscoring the value of a requirement that still so few schools have embraced.

VARIABLES PRESENT AND ABSENT AT WAC SCHOOLS

I was able to pursue several hypotheses about what variables might positively associate with the presence of WAC programs, finding many surprising-as-expected results. For this part of the analysis, I began by identifying variables I thought suggested strong writing faculty or programmatic presence of writing to develop my hypotheses. My hypotheses originated in my belief—no longer held after this study!—that there would be a productive bleed from FYC to WAC: with a strong faculty WPA, evidence of best practices in FYC course curricula, and undergraduate curricula in vertical writing, there would be greater likelihood of developed upper-level writing. The variables listed below are among those I hypothesized would be positively associated with WAC but that were *not* found to have any statistical association:

- undergraduate programming (writing major, minor, concentration)
- FYC WPA presence
- faculty WPA for FYC
- evidence of process-writing methods in FYC sequence
- presentation at CCCC

These null hypotheses are significant and interesting because they suggest, in total, that there is no apparent spillover effect from one area of writing strength to WAC strength. For example, I thought the presence of a WAC program would be related to having a vertical writing program, but in fact my statistical analysis found this was not the case. In addition, I anticipated that the university that hired a faculty WPA, developed undergraduate programming, evidenced process-writing instruction in FYC, or presented at CCCC would be more likely than those that didn't have these qualities to also have an articulated WAC program. To my view, the presence of these variables indicates a faculty and university supportive of writing instruction and that this support would also lead to WAC programming. However, these hypotheses were not borne out in my sample.

I did find statistical associations for the presence of WAC with three important variables, one of which is related to an institution's support for writing and two of which are not. These variables are institutional size, number of first-year composition courses and, perhaps most interestingly, placement by directed-self placement (DSP). I predicted there might be an association between WAC and institutional size because I believed leaders at small institutions have fewer policies to enforce teaching behaviors, relying instead on persuasive faculty and other leaders to inspire more focus on writing (or any other emphasis). Or perhaps it is simply the case that formal articulation and regulation of

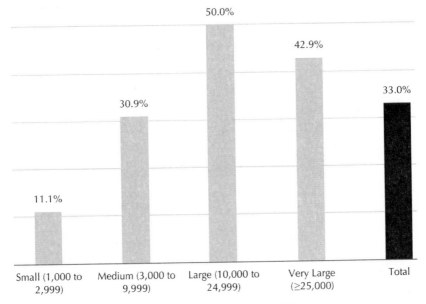

Figure 5.4. Percentage of WAC requirements by institutional size

principles increases with size. As is shown in figure 5.4, with the exception of very large institutions, we see that WAC is increasingly likely to be present as institutional size increases, a finding that is statistically significant ($\chi^2(3, n = 105) = 7.71, p < 0.10$). This discovery is a reminder that some of what is possible for writing programming has nothing to do with writing interest, pedagogy, or developments in the field, but is, rather, reflective of institutional characteristics.

With respect to my examination of WAC by looking at variables related to other data I collected on writing, I hypothesized that schools that had powerful writing faculty who were able to advocate successfully for FYC resources or to take on DSP (an assessment methodology that runs counter to institutional norms and is unique to writing studies) would also be more likely to have a WAC program. My hypothesis might be said to be based on a power theory. In fact, the findings split. On the one hand, I observed a statistically significant association of WAC presence and use of DSP to place students in FYC, with WAC significantly more likely to be present at schools that use DSP for placement ($\chi^2(1, n = 79) = 5.11, p < 0.05$.). On the other hand, as detailed in figure 5.5, schools that require two courses of FYC have a marginally significant trend toward being *less likely* to have WAC programs than do those that require one course, as shown in figure 5.5 ($\chi^2(1, n = 105) = 3.18, p < 0.10$).

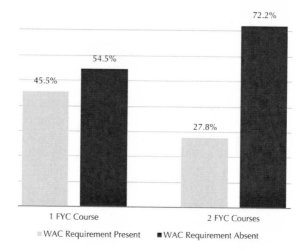

Figure 5.5. WAC requirement presence and number of FYC courses required

This finding is precisely opposite what I had hypothesized, which was that WAC would be more likely to be present at institutions that had two rather than one FYC course. My hypothesis about powerful writing interests being able to lead to more resources for WAC/WID was not supported by the data; however, it's not difficult to develop a countering theory to interpret the data findings: it may well be that institutions can only support so many writing requirements and that the economies of the 120-credit system and the pressures for large-credit majors mean that a second course in FYC makes a WAC requirement more difficult, and vice versa.

When it comes to the issue of the FYC program using directed self-placement (DSP), I found a positive and significant association between WAC/WID presence and use of DSP($\chi^2(1, n = 79) = 5.11, p < 0.05$).

Interestingly, the use of DSP isn't a resource issue, but it is a measure of political power. DSP is typically inexpensive, but it requires persuading administrators to go against the cultural authority of standardized tests, which is no easy feat. This is therefore an interesting finding, though I note that the total number of institutions in the study that use DSP is fairly low (14). Further, while I see a link between DSP usage and WAC/WID programming on the basis of the two variables presented, indicating that the institution has faculty or staff with writing expertise and institutional power, there are many other factors that come to play in the creation of these two complex programs. Still, these two variables

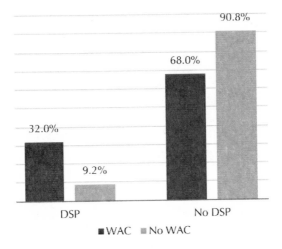

Figure 5.6. WAC at schools that use DSP for FYC

both reflect well on these schools' advocates for writing having been per-suasive on these fronts.

REQUIREMENTS BEYOND FYC

In addition to WAC-course presence, I sought to find out how robust institutions' requirements in writing were in terms of all courses or writing experiences required from matriculation to graduation. This broader approach, developed when Melinda Knight and I coined *writing robustness*, is a way to recognize that schools make different choices about where to place writing requirements. For this state comprehensive university study, the range included institutions that only had one requirement to the University of Northern Colorado that had eight requirements! The mean was 2.60, the median was two courses, and the mode (most frequent) was two (46.2 percent); 46.2 percent of institutions required three courses, whereas 10.3 percent required one course, and 43.3 percent required three to eight courses. Thus, the majority of the sample's universities (70.7 percent) required two to three writing courses or other experiences.

Schools that require more than FYC and one other writing course typically do so through a writing-intensive requirement. For example, CUNY's Lehman College requires four writing-intensive courses, Clarion University of Pennsylvania requires two "writing flag" courses, and Truman State articulates their requirement as "writing-enhanced"

Figure 5.7. FYC and beyond: required writing

courses, directing students to complete one enhanced junior interdisciplinary seminar (JINS) course along with two other writing-enhanced
courses from across the curriculum.

These findings are similar to what Witte and colleagues found in their
1981 research. In their study, Witte and his colleagues asked respondents about whether or not they required at least one course at the
sophomore, junior, and senior levels. Excluding private schools and two-
year schools, they reported as follows about public four-year colleges and
universities that participated in their study:

27 percent required at least one sophomore class
19 percent required at least one junior class
2 percent required at least one senior class (Witte et al. 1981, 14)

Their study and mine are different—not only in how we attempt to
count upper-level instruction but also in sampling methods—so it's difficult to assess whether we can declare an increase or decrease from
Witte's study.

Again, I think there's more to knowing about the culture of writing and
writing instruction at a school than studying requirements, as I've done.
A good example of this observation can be found at the New College of
Florida, which does not require any writing courses per se, though a thesis is required for graduation. My view is that this is a case of a school's
eschewing requirements and specific courses more than an indication of
a school lacking interest or commitment to student writing. New College
of Florida, "The Honors College" of the state system, requires students to

work with advisers to develop a series of seven contracts in lieu of credit hours, offers narrative evaluation instead of grades, and ends with a two-semester senior thesis (New College of Florida 2012). I suspect students at New College of Florida do a lot of writing, more so than the mere one-course credit I was able to credit the school for the required thesis. It is an unusual school, without doubt. More typical are the many schools that require two FYC courses and nothing more. Alternatively, schools such as William Paterson in New Jersey, for example, require one of two FYC courses and either a WAC course or a range of writing-intensive (WI) courses. At William Paterson, WI courses—of which four are required as part of the core—include the following components: writing-to-learn strategies, "drafting, revising, editing and other writing processes to develop final products appropriate to the discipline," and research and documentation skills that are similarly discipline appropriate (William Paterson University 2010). Thus, in this case, WI courses build off a two-semester FYC sequence, with a total of six writing courses required.

This state comprehensive university study clearly provides only a snapshot of WAC in US four-year state colleges and universities. With an understanding of the limited data collected, I offer the summary view that state universities vary widely in their approach and implementation of upper-level writing instruction and programming and that, as a class, they are about as likely to have upper-level writing classes required as are those surveyed by previous researchers.

WRITING CENTERS

Writing centers, or some kind of tutoring in writing, are present at *all* the state comprehensive universities in the sample. This level of presence is consonant with the 96.0 percent presence reported for the top university study (Isaacs and Knight 2014, 44). I also collected data on administrative and fiscal location, revealing a range of locations of writing and tutoring providing individualized writing instruction. Writing center location is important, reflective of the long debate about what is appropriate and possible for writing centers, which have a history of emerging as much from the world of student services as from the discipline of composition and rhetoric (Balester and McDonald 2001; Diamond 1999; Ervin 2002; Griffin et al. 2006; Healy 1995; Lerner 2009; Mauriello, Macauley, and Koch 2011; Riley 1994). As is revealed in figure 5.8, the majority (54.7 percent) of writing tutorial services in this study were provided via student-support centers from within the larger area of student development and campus life.

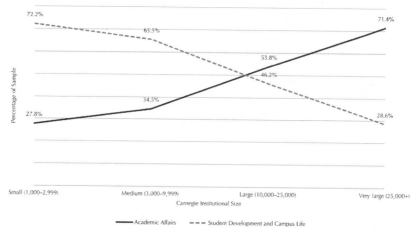

Figure 5.8. Distribution of writing centers by institutional size

In comparison, the top university study sample had fewer writing centers located in student development and campus life, at 37.6 percent (2014, 46),[1] suggesting some differences in how the colleges and universities in these samples approach the important work of providing students with tutorial services in writing.

For this study I did not collect data on writing center directors—their position types, titles, or membership in academic departments—so I do not have evidence of any relationships that might exist between administrative placement and formal affiliation with faculty, and therefore, presumably, a closer tie to the research community. However, based on the comparison of the two studies, I hypothesized that there would be relationships between both institutional size and writing center location and also between graduate classification and writing center location. These hypotheses are demonstrated in the following two figures.

As figure 5.8 demonstrates, smaller schools are more likely to house individualized tutoring in writing in student development and campus life than in academic affairs. As schools get larger, academic affairs takes a larger role, with 71.4 percent of schools with twenty-five thousand or more students running their writing centers out of the academic side. As figure 5.9 demonstrates, at BA-granting institutions, writing centers are much more likely to be located in student development, whereas at doctorate-granting institutions, we see a split, with roughly half the writing centers in student development and the other half in academic affairs. A fuller explanation for the trends represented by these two charts lies beyond the grasp of my data collection and analysis, but these findings

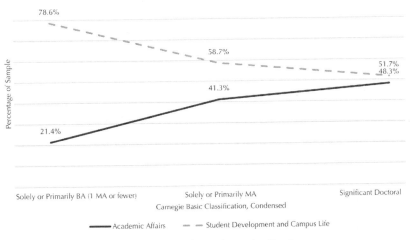

Figure 5.9. Distribution of writing centers by graduate classification

suggest that institutional size and graduate classification of a college or school have an impact on how close writing centers are to the departments that house writing. Writing center scholarship has debated the comparative value of placement of writing centers gingerly and inconclusively (Diamond 1999; Healy 1995; Isaacs 2008; Lerner 2000, 2009; Olson and Ashton-Jones 1988), with most focusing on the importance of local context. I'll hazard my own essentially undocumented view: placement of writing centers closer to the academic side serves to increase the chances of a closer connection to research in the discipline of writing studies, whereas placement closer to the student-services side increases the chance of stable and adequate funding and support.

In reviewing catalog descriptions of writing centers or tutorial centers that include tutoring in writing, this hypothesis has some support. Although I did not code and evaluate writing center description data as I did FYC data, I did collect and review all catalog description language, sorting centers by types of fiscal and administrative locations. From the catalog and survey data, I sorted tutorial centers by their fiscal/administrative locations: in an English, writing, or another academic department; in an independent academic center grouped in the academic-affairs category; in an academic support center or another nonacademic department grouped in the student-development-and-campus-life category.

English departments were most frequently the home for writing centers in this sample, with the catalog description for the writing center at the University of Arkansas at Monticello typical of the students-tutoring-students model:

Table 5.1. Administrative and fiscal location of writing centers

Fiscal and administrative location	
English department (n = 31)	29.2%
Other academic department (n = 7)	6.6%
Independent writing program or writing department (n = 4)	3.8%
Provost's office (n = 3)	1.9%
Stand alone (n = 3)	2.8%
Student support centers (n = 58)	54.7%

Table 5.2. Writing centers: top university study sample versus state comprehensive university study sample

	State Comprehensive University Study	Top University Study
Academic affairs	40.5% (n = 43)	62.4% (n = 53)
Student development and campus life	59.5% (n = 63)	37.6% (n = 32)

The Writing Center services are free to university students. English majors assist students during all stages of the writing process. Writing is recognized as a recursive, overlapping activity that involves pre-writing, drafting, revising, proofreading, and publishing. Whatever the academic discipline or class assignment, peer tutors provide feedback and suggestions that help students understand the essential elements of academic writing. (University of Arkansas at Monticello 2011, 13)

From this text we see a writing center that projects that it is built on traditional writing center theory and practice, with a clear nod to the hallmarks of drafting and recursiveness, but that also includes notice that tutors will help students improve their "proofreading skills" and, somewhat oddly, their skills in word processing. Presumably, this writing center's location in the English department makes the staffing of the center with English majors easy.

In contrast, the majority of the colleges and universities in the sample address writing tutoring through a tutoring or learning center within student life. In these centers tutoring is typically provided for all areas of general education and always for math and writing. At Lake Superior State University in Wisconsin, the learning center is part of the Division of Academic Services, along with Career Services, the library, Testing Services, and also the liberal arts program for undeclared students. The learning center is located in the library, and the catalog description indicates that it provides peer tutoring, "organized study groups," seminars in student success, and access to computers equipped with "tutorial and instructional software." As is typically the case, the learning center highlights its services for math and writing, for the latter noting its ability to provide assistance "with all types of writing at all levels for all disciplines" (Lake Superior State University 2011, 61).

Finally, a brief look at one of the few writing centers located within a writing department is interesting, as it is clear how the influence of a writing department is shown in the text that presents the center in the catalog. At Georgia Southern University, the University Writing Center is part of the Department of Writing and Linguistics. The writing center entry in the catalog is longer than most, and it has a number of distinguishing features. First, in the catalog the director of the University Writing Center, Michael Pemberton, is identified, which is atypical. Second, in this case the staff are graduate students. Third, I observed another common trend, which is to warn students about staff members' limited availability for editing: "The Writing Center staff will not proofread papers or do any of the actual writing" (Georgia Southern University 2011, 20). The description of the services provided includes the following language that reflects the field's values: "[Tutors] will teach students effective ways to use evidence and detail, to anticipate and meet audience needs, and to streamline the structure of their arguments" (20).

My reporting on writing centers from this sample is clearly limited, but I am hopeful that this data might be useful in helping writing center scholars more closely investigate the relationship among institutional characteristics and writing center placement and for faculty and writing center staff to think strategically about what is possible and best at their own colleges and universities.

PROGRAMS IN WRITING: CONCENTRATIONS, MINORS, AND MAJORS

Whether writing studies' disciplinary undergraduate programs, or what is sometimes called *vertical programming*, will continue to be the source of as much conference-corridor excitement in the future remains to be seen, but for many years now such possibilities have been subject to great interest at conferences, as I well recall when I attempted to enter the 2008 CCCC session devoted to the writing studies major and had trouble getting through the door. Proponents of writing majors frequently argue for the writing major on intellectual and historical bases, emphasizing rhetorical theory and history and the former prominence of rhetoric as a field of study in higher education. Arguments for a writing major are also made on practical, applied grounds for a career-ready major. For the profession, Janice Lauer argues that undergraduate majors in writing provide other benefits: a more prepared graduate-student population, better undergraduate tutoring, a broadening of the discipline, and a greater variety of teaching opportunities for writing studies graduate students and faculty (Lauer 2010). Although some readers may believe that the movement for writing majors began with the frequently cited Peggy O'Neill, Angela Crow, and Larry Burton's *A Field of Dreams* (O'Neill, Crow, and Burton 2002), Linda Shamoon et al.'s *Coming of Age* (Shamoon et al. 2000), or Downs and Wardle's (2007) *CCC*'s article proposing FYC as an introduction to the discipline of writing studies, the public scholarly conversation has actually been ongoing for several decades.

EARLY PROPONENTS OF VERTICAL WRITING

An implicit argument for the writing major was made in a 1975 *CCC*'s article by George Tade, Gary Tate, and Jim Corder of Texas Christian University, who offered up a new rhetoric major "for sale, lease or rent" (20), having failed to see the program they developed accepted at TCU. In presenting their new rhetoric major for others to adopt, they argued forcefully, if humorously, for the value of a highly inter-disciplinary major that would address many facets of rhetorical study. Several years later, Arthur Shumaker argued for a composition major based on the experience at DePauw University. He described DePauw's composition major, which had been in existence "over seventy years" (Schumaker 1982, 139) and remains, in 2015, under the title *the writing major*. Schumaker, writing in what was then a new journal, *JAC: The Journal of Advanced Composition*, asserted that a few other colleges and universities offered composition majors, though he didn't provide specifics. Schumaker laid out the case for and against the composition major, with fourteen points for and only five points against. The arguments for and against are largely familiar, and it may amuse (or distress) readers to read the top reason given for not having a composition major: "If too many members of the Department are afraid of the idea because they think that neither they nor anyone can really teach writing, or, if they feel that it would possibly prove to be a threat to entrenched courses in literature, obviously no major will be created" (Schumaker 1982, 145). Schumaker described a composition major that sits alongside a literature major in an English department and consists of a variety of topics or foci, including expository writing and advanced composition, linguistics, journalism, creative writing, teaching methods and grammar, theory and practice of criticism, and a senior seminar.

The authors of these two articles don't reveal frustration or hostility toward literature or their literary-focused colleagues, but they do suggest that the practical business of persuading other faculty to accept and approve of writing, rhetoric, or composition majors was challenging. Notably, these articles were published not long before Maxine Hairston's famous "Breaking our Bonds" essay, in which she calls for writing to break its dependence or subservience to literature, declaring, "If we want to cause change instead of wait for it, if we want the profession of teaching writing to become a recognized and respected discipline, we are going to have to believe in ourselves and in what we do strongly enough to be willing to take a chance and break with the power structure if necessary" (Hairston 1985, 281). Of course, Hairston was focused on teaching writing and FYC and not on a major, yet the assertion of disciplinary legitimacy and the call for equality with literary study runs throughout all these articles.

In the 1990s, Sharon Crowley's essays and speeches against the universal FYC requirement introduced the idea of a vertical curriculum to a new readership ready for the argument. In a *JAC* article from 1995, Crowley ends her argument against the universal requirement, which she sees largely responsible for "discourses of hierarchy and exclusion," with this proposal: "Let us, rather, articulate the practices that do legitimate us: the study, practice, and teaching of writing. We can devise vertical and diverse curricula in writing that aim at the achievement of critical, public literacy" (Crowley 1995, 238). John Trimbur, citing Crowley, repeats the term *vertical*, in his call for the development of vertical writing programs. For Trimbur, the goal of "concentrations, majors, minors, certificates, whatever designation is available" (11) is driven by a desire to move beyond what he sees as excessive focus on one course (FYC) and toward providing students with an interdisciplinary program that allows study of many theories and practices of writing. Trimbur, as a precursor to Yancey (2004), notes that "between graduate studies and the first-year course is an ill-defined terrain" (15). He confesses uncertainty as to what to recommend for curricular aims of such a program, ultimately resorting to a generality: the plan calls for "designing courses and programs to intersect with multiple constituencies and to serve multiple purposes (25). This challenge of what exactly vertical writing programming should be devoted to remains to this day.

DISCONTENTMENT WITH ENGLISH: THE CASE FOR
INDEPENDENCE THROUGH DISCIPLINARY LEGITIMACY

In these 1990s discussions, authors appeared unable to discuss writing majors or other vertical writing programs without also discussing comp/lit wars and English departments. These were hard times for composition/rhetoric faculty, and clearly the problems writing faculty experienced working within English departments were great enough to challenge implementing—and even imagining—vertical writing programs. David Chapman, Jeanette Harris, and Christine Hult, reporting on a survey about opportunities for English majors to "specialize in composition and rhetoric" (Chapman, Harris, and Hult 1995, 421), ultimately devoted the majority of their article to reporting on the difficulties writing faculty faced within English departments, concluding: "The challenge we face is not simply to replace the old hegemony of literature with a new hegemony of composition but to construct a new English department where reading and writing are mutually valued and mutually supported activities" (429). And, as David Fleming argued in another article from the 1990s, rhetoricians of this period felt urgently the need for a place for the study of rhetoric, whether it be through a major, minor, or sequence of courses (Fleming 1998). Today I hear graduate students and those new to the field expressing bewilderment when they read these writers' words on the comp/lit wars and English departments, but it is important to read these essays in the context of the often hostile climates in which they worked, as witnessed by this survey respondent: "Most of the faculty here view English as the study of literature only and believe that writing is a non-, if not anti-, humanistic activity. Opposition to writing has always been fierce" (Chapman, Harris, and Hult 1995, 425).

I imagine faculty who have experienced the greatest disdain from humanities faculty have been those involved with developing technical communication programs which, as Charles Bazerman notes, have developed independent of the influence of first-year writing programs (Bazerman 1995, 259). Thomas Pearsall, who founded the Council for Programs in Technical and Scientific Communication in 1974, writing with Thomas Warren, documented the history of this organization's development and the growth of technical and scientific programs. Pearsall reported that in 1973 he was able to locate 20 programs in technical communication, spanning two-year, four-year, and graduate study. In 1984 the organization had 70 programs (143), and by 1994 it reportedly had reached 190 (Pearsall and Warren 1996, 145). Pearsall and Warren were light in tone in their reflections on the status and political challenges that faculty teaching in technical and scientific programs faced: "Discussions of political relationships recorded in the proceedings centered on dealing with colleagues in the home department, many of whom, putting it mildly, were uncomfortable with the intrusion of technical communication into the department. No clear-cut advice other than learning to live with the problem seemed to emerge" (143).

More recently, Jim Nugent combed membership lists, finding duplications and also additional programs through an extensive web search, and reported the existence of "172 U.S. technical communication programs" overall (Nugent 2013, 65) and 114 programs that offered a BA degree, concentration, or certificate of a graduate degree (68). Nugent, echoing others, remarked on the difficulties of achieving recognition and autonomy: "Technical communication's frequent lack of practical and political distinction from English suggests it has yet to attain many of what Gerald J. Savage [1999, 2004] enumerated as the defining feature of a modernist profession, particularly the features of market closure, self-regulation, and a formalized body of knowledge" (76). Quite simply, the challenges for those creating vertical writing programming in the twentieth century have been many and persistent.

TWENTY-FIRST-CENTURY WRITING PROGRAMS: ARRIVED?

In the first decade and a half of the twenty-first century, discussions of vertical writing programming have increased, beginning with the frequently cited *A Field of Dreams* (O'Neill, Crow, and Burton 2002) and an article by Eileen Cushman, who argued for "the need for vertical writing programs to be taught in writing departments by fully enfranchised writing professors" (Cushman 2003, 125). In 2007, *Composition Studies* devoted an entire issue to the writing major, and Downs and Wardle argued for an FYC course focused on writing studies scholarship. The year 2010 saw publication of *What We Are Becoming: Developments in Undergraduate Writing Majors* (Giberson and Moriarty 2010) and a status report (Balzhiser and McLeod 2010) in *College Composition and Communication* on the number and type of writing majors. In 2012, Christian Weisser and Laurie Grobman published the results of their survey of professional-writing-major alumni, providing a neat bookend to this discussion (Weisser and Grobman 2012). Finally, the writing major had become enough established to provide data for an alumni survey.

The essays in *A Field of Dreams* typically focus on the issue of independence—the often rocky, always political and locally specific road to an administrative position in which writing is not in a department of English or in another academic area. Reading through these essays again, it often feels as if the primary impetus for independence is something other than creating a major in writing studies. The impetus varies but centers on the urgent desire to get out of the House of English to protect first-year composition, to improve the working conditions of adjunct and other nontenured faculty, and/or to improve the psychological well-being of tenured writing studies faculty who feel frustrated from years of listening to disciplinary put-downs and professional slights. The authors of these stories of independence write candidly of their struggles to imagine the right vertical curricula for their students, program faculty, and institutions. At Grand Valley State, the faculty settled on a major that allows concentration in either creative writing or professional writing, the former of which required some careful negotiation with the English department and the latter of which was criticized as beneath the liberal arts, a "trade" (Royer and Gilles 2002, 35). At Metro State University in Minnesota, which Anne Aronson and Craig Hansen describe as atypical in that it is "distinctly entrepreneurial" and "an institution where change is fundamental and present" (51), two majors are offered: writing with emphasis in creative or professional writing and technical communication. Aronson and Hansen define the disciplinary venture of their department clearly, though they also recognize that developing disciplinary purpose took discussion and time and that the faculty had to negotiate tensions between the desire for disciplinary study and the call for service through general education instruction (Aronson and Hansen 2002, 59). The stories that describe majors or minors in writing vary, though throughout the collection, at least one trend emerges: programs in creative, technical, and even professional writing are fairly easily imagined, but the broadly conceived "writing" major, which often combines theoretical work in rhetoric alongside applied writing instruction, requires more truly creative thinking and ultimately results in programs that vary greatly.

The 2007 *Composition Studies* issue devoted to the writing major functions, in the words of editor Heidi Estrem, "as a record of 'where we are' as a discipline *right now* in our development of writing majors" (Estrem 2007, 12). In this issue Tony Scott is cautious in his endorsement of the writing major, arguing for the development of a scholarly vision for writing majors closely tied to what he calls the "ecologies" of postsecondary writing instruction (82–83). He asks, "If professionals in rhetoric and composition who are in a position to do so 'carry forward' from First-Year Composition, will it be as managers and theorizers of a project that further expands the de-professionalization of teaching in academia? (Scott 2007, 83). Another voice of caution comes from Hill Taylor, who works at a historically black state university, the University of the District of Columbia, and expands Scott's concern that curricula take into account context by considering students, particularly but not only black students. In addition to the master canon of courses in writing, Taylor suggests the need to include a "localized and admittedly political curriculum" (2007, 108) that would prepare students not just to be, for example, proficient technical writers but also writers aware of "notions of skills sets and positionality along lines of race, gender, and socioeconomic status, which necessitates a critical inquiry into access as it relates to institutionalized systems of oppression" (Taylor 2007, 109). In "Against the Writing Major," Kelly Lowe does not actually argue against the major as a concept but rather notes that there may be significant and even insurmountable challenges in obtaining enough staff and in designing a curriculum sufficiently stable and defined from the start (Lowe 2007).

Within the *Composition Studies* special issue, Estrem also presents many writers who reflect more positively on the writing majors at their colleges and universities. For example, Dominic Delli Carpini writes from his experience with developing a writing major within the English Department at York College in Pennsylvania, noting that a rhetorical education has expanded literature students' work in literature and that the professional writing majors' education is also deepened by their literary study. Based on his study of student perspectives at York College, Carpini concludes, "Our students' achievements underscore the growing understanding among writing majors that literary inquiry need not be mutually exclusive with profession-based goals, lending credence to the expanding mission of writing majors" (Carpini 2007, 31–32). Finally, Rebecca Moore Howard, long a proponent of the writing major, remains enthusiastic, arguing that the writing major "challenges the hierarchical ideology in which writing instruction socializes the Great Unwashed"[2] (Howard 2007, 46). Again, we see plans for disciplinary writing variously complicated or enriched by competing visions, priorities, and, as always, practical and political challenges.

Giberson and Moriarty's 2010 collection *What We Are Becoming* continues the focus on local conditions and political realities, though in many ways the assembled writers are more positive and celebratory, by and large pleased with what they have accomplished at their various institutions. Throughout the collection, we see some of the range of how writing majors are constructed in the twenty-first century, with programs varying in their emphasis on rhetoric, creative arts, and professional

writing. Despite the typical references to political, fiscal, and practical difficulties, and with the exception of a cautionary tale (Lowe and Macauley
2010) and David Beard's (2010) argument that rhetorical study is too
fragmented across the disciplines, the writers in *What We Are Becoming* are
positive and even jubilant. Susan McLeod summarizes, "With the publication of this book, we can now say that the undergraduate major is not
just a good idea: it has arrived, and it is big. We have cause to celebrate"
(McLeod 2010, 287). Notably absent in this collection are any chapters
on technical and/or scientific communication, an omission that is unfortunate. Technical and scientific communication programs have a long
and robust history, as discussed previously; that the authors would inad-
vertently leave out a discipline that has been frequently marginalized,
and while discussing the marginalization of writing by literature, is ironic.
However, the emphasis in this collection on newly formed majors may
account for the absence of technically focused programs.

The only chapter in the collection that seriously addresses technical
writing is by Lee Campbell and Debra Jacobs in their attempt to define
the focus and common elements of writing majors through their review
of all the writing majors they could locate at the time. Campbell and
Jacobs provide a useful "map" of programs (2010, 280), reproduced
below, to graphically present the range of topics and courses along two
axes: general to specific and liberal to technical.

General

Liberal   Technical

Specific

By Campbell and Jacobs's definition, curricula in liberal courses are
"grounded in no particular fields or technologies beyond word processing but instead present writing as primarily a literacy act of an individual
addressing a broad audience interested in the literary aim" as compared
to curricula in technical "courses in which writing is studied in specific
fields or studied in terms of the demands of specific technology or media,
such as the computer and Internet" (Campbell and Jacobs 2010, 282).
As their map suggests, the writing majors they reviewed covered several
emphases: "creative nonfiction, rhetoric and journalism, professional writing, and technical writing" (284). Campbell and Jacobs's analysis under-
scores what critics of independent writing programs have observed, which
is that the notion of a "writing" major's content is not well established.

From reading the literature arguing for and describing the writing
major, I have come to believe that whereas minors and concentrations
tend to develop around a genre of writing—journalism, creative writing,

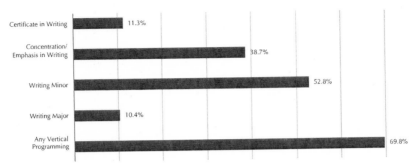

Figure 5.10. Programming availability for disciplinary writing

professional writing—that has a predictable set of aims and courses, the writing major is much less clear. A writing major might begin with a collection of minors or it might expand upon just one genre such as professional writing. However, frequently, it seems authors of writing majors begin their move toward independence as a solution to the problem of living within English departments and focusing on literature, and thus the work of developing curricula and defining the discipline begins at the ground floor.

STATE COMPREHENSIVE UNIVERSITY STUDY RESULTS: MAJORS RARE, SMALLER PROGRAMS COMMON

Returning to my study, it appears that for these schools, the writing major is still a rare phenomenon although many programs have some vertical programming. Specifically, as detailed in the figure below, just 10.4 percent of the universities in the sample had a writing major, though almost 70 percent had some kind of vertical program—a major, minor, an emphasis or concentration, or, least frequently, an undergraduate certificate program.

This finding of 69.8 percent vertical writing programming across the sample is significantly higher than what Donald Stewart found in 1989; Stewart reported that 38 percent of the English departments he surveyed offered students the opportunity to specialize in some aspect of writing in addition to literature (reported in Chapman, Harris, and Hult 1995, 421). However, in 1995, Chapman, Harris, and Hult surveyed a larger population of English departments and found that 70 percent offered "writing concentrations" (422). I will note that Chapman, Harris, and Hult only surveyed English departments, whereas my catalog-review method allowed me to identify vertical writing programming present in

Table 5.3. Titles of writing majors and minors at state comprehensive universities

Major names	Minor names
Comprehensive English writing and literature	Applied and professional writing
Creative writing	Business and technical writing
English writing	Composition
Professional writing	Expository writing
Professional and technical writing	Rhetoric and language
Rhetoric and composition	Technical and scientific writing
Rhetoric and writing	Technical writing
Writing	Writing and publication
Writing arts	
Writing and linguistics	
Writing, rhetoric, and technical communication	

any department. Further complicating matters, their survey return rate of 23.3 percent (421) suggests the possibility of a skew toward departments that offered some kind of writing-concentration options. Thus, it's hard to meaningfully compare the 1995 Chapman, Harris, and Hult study with this present one, other than to say there isn't evidence that options for vertical programming have increased since 1995.

A review of names of majors alone indicates a wide variety of programming, revealing that writing as a curricular area remains if not "ill-defined" (Trimbur 1999), not tightly defined. In table 5.3 is a listing of the majors, revealing the different genres and foci faculty have selected. When I extended the title examination to names of minors, even more genres and foci were uncovered.

These names indicate what lies beneath: courses that span the range suggested by Campbell and Jacobs. Thus, a writing major (or minor) isn't such a clear thing, and writing programming might lean more or less toward any of the following: creative writing, journalism, rhetoric, professional writing, and linguistics.

Deborah Balzhiser and Susan McLeod followed another method to measure the growth of vertical curricula; they cataloged the growth in the major by soliciting information on several listservs, noting that their count grew from forty-five in 2005 to sixty-eight in 2008 (Balzhiser and McLeod 2010, 416). Balzhiser and McLeod also observed a wide range of terms for describing these writing majors, and in their review of courses, determined that there are two main types, which they "refer[red] to . . . as 'liberal arts' and 'professional/rhetorical' writing majors" (418) but acknowledged that still "we have little consensus about what a writing major should look like in either one of the two kinds of majors" (422). This observation concurs with how I analyze the majors in this sample: there isn't a consensus yet. Of course, I hasten to add that an English major isn't particularly closely defined either, and perhaps this is true of many other majors that, from a distance, we might assume are more uniform than they actually are.

WRITING MAJORS: ASSOCIATIONS WITH OTHER VARIABLES

The presence of a writing major is not associated with any of the institutional characteristics or Carnegie Classifications I have frequently identified. That is, when discussing other findings, its presence is not correlated with regional location, or institutional size or selectivity, or Basic Carnegie Classification, as has frequently been the case in other associational reporting throughout this book. In fact, my hypotheses found statistically significant associations between the presence of writing majors and just a few noteworthy variables: the location of first-year composition at the institution ($\chi^2(2, n = 105) = 37.53$, $p < 0.05$.), the adoption of the WPA Outcomes by the FYC program ($\chi^2(1, n = 106) = 7.13$, $p < 0.05$), and the presence of individuals at the institution presenting papers at CCCC in the years 2010 and 2011 (Spearman's rank order, $t(10.64) = 3.04$, $p < 0.05$; variances adjusted for homogeneity). These relationships speak collectively to the notion that a strong FYC program is closely aligned with the national professional association that endorses the WPA Outcomes Statement and sponsors an annual conference related to the development of a writing major.

In the sample there are eleven schools with writing majors. The cross-tabulation shown in figure 5.11, below, demonstrates the importance of FYC location in indicating whether or not a school is likely to have a writing major. Risking the annoyance of repetition, I'll note that, of course, association or correlation does not equal causation.

The schools that had writing majors and housed FYC in a department other than English, humanities, or writing housed their FYC programs in either a professional and technical communications department (Montana Tech) or through central administration (The College of New Jersey and Buffalo State College). Clearly the big winners of the writing-major race are at schools that house FYC in a writing department; these schools are the University of Arkansas at Little Rock, Georgia Southern

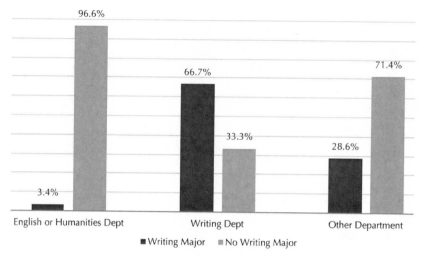

Figure 5.11. Presence of writing major by location of FYC

University, Grand Valley State University, Rowan University, and James Madison University. Writing majors that house FYC in English or humanities departments are few—from this sample, just the University of Wisconsin–Platteville and Wayne State College.

The other two FYC-related variables that associate with the presence of a writing major are the use of DSP for placement and the inclusion of instruction in primary-research methodologies when teaching research writing! These associations suggest that the same kinds of schools that have faculty or staff interested in and *able* to adopt practices discussed in the pages of *CCC* and on the conference circuit are also interested in and able to propose and pass majors in writing. Which comes first—the major or the adoption of these approaches to placing students in FYC classes and teaching research methods in the FYC sequence—is clearly beyond the scope of this study. But these are not surprising results. Directed self-placement is a fairly new idea, born from deep within the disciplinary conversation. Similarly, the idea of having first-year students take on the research methods that many of us learned in graduate programs in composition-rhetoric is far away from the dominant, traditional approach of focusing on learning MLA form. On their own, that these hypotheses were supported by the data says a little; together with the data on the organizational location of FYC, they say more. And they say even more when we consider the correlation between the writing major and presentation at CCCC (Spearman's rank order, $r = .329**$ $p = .001$). Thus, in this way, we can see more connection between the scholarly conversation about writing program administration and its practices.

More needs to be said about how I measured schools' involvement with the profession. Without the availability of CCCC attendance, I used participation (a speaking role, as listed in the convention catalog) in CCCC as proxy. As discussed in appendix A more fully, while there are many limitations to this method for measuring an institution's involvement with the profession, by using two years of data, I was able to limit some of the variation due to chance scheduling. Further, I observed significant variation in participation: over the two-year period, institutions had between zero and twenty-eight people represented by speaking roles in 2010 and 2011, with a mean of 3.61. Slightly more than half the schools in the sample, at 58.0 percent ($n = 62$), were represented in speaking roles at CCCC over these two years. Schools with writing majors ($n = 10$) had significantly more people presenting at CCCC in 2010 and 2011 [$t(10.64) = 3.04$, $p < 0.05$; variances adjusted for homogeneity]. Schools that had a major had a mean total of 11.27 ($n = 11$, $SD = 9.17$) people presenting, and in comparison, schools without a major had a mean of 2.73 ($n = 95$, $SD = 4.78$) people presenting. Significantly, 90.9 percent of the schools that offer writing majors presented at CCCC, with a mean of 14.4 for these schools (see fig. 5.12).

Clearly, engagement with the profession, as measured by the imprecise but I would argue relevant measure of CCCC participation, is highly correlated with the presence of a writing major. It is worth repeating that institutional size was not correlated with the presence of a writing major and that many of the large schools in the sample did not have writing majors.

Writing programming and instruction beyond the first-year composition experience vary widely across the schools included in this study, but that nearly 70 percent of the sample provided students with some way to develop expertise in an area of writing studies is important and demonstrates that the subject of writing studies is not simply first-year composition, as critics and the naïve have been known to assert. Likely, faculties have developed these programs in response to students' and their own interests and also to the ever-present, if always vague, demand that college graduates "write well." Given that there are always students who excel at writing and wish to do more of it, writing programming makes obvious sense.

Why, then, are there so few writing majors? It may be that proponents of other disciplines—literature, of course, but also likely other well-established disciplines—have prevented these developments on the

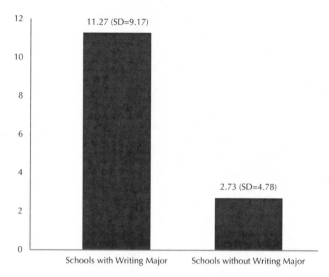

Figure 5.12. Mean number of presentations at CCCC (2010 and 2011) by presence of writing major

grounds that a major in writing will lessen enrollments in existing majors. However, it's also the case that colleges and universities are reluctant to develop new majors without closing existing ones, making those who might like to start a major in writing additionally cautious about the likely payoff for such effort. It is also true that a case can be made that majors in English, communications, and various other disciplines are so attentive to language and require so much writing that they, too, provide opportunities for these students, and one only has to read through the websites of contemporary English and humanities departments that encourage students to select their major on precisely these grounds to see this is true. The familiar language encouraging students to choose the English major at Indiana State University, which does not offer a writing major but does offer a minor in creative writing, is illustrative: "The study of English develops essential skills for professional success and personal fulfillment: an understanding of language and its functions in society; fluency in written communication, in both practical and artistic applications; . . . The most common career paths for English majors are writing, editing, and publishing; advertising and public relations; business administration and management; technical writing; and teaching at middle school, high school, or college levels" (Indiana State University 2014).

The question really is, then, what is a writing major? Not only how it is different from an English major, which promises similar outcomes and career trajectories, but what exactly is it at heart? What will students learn? What is its disciplinary core and what are its required components? As this study reveals, we are figuring that out locally, individually, and one program at a time. From the view of this study, while coursework and opportunities to study writing beyond FYC are widespread, we have not yet developed even a short list for what constitutes major study in writing studies.

In this chapter I have sought to better understand what is happening at state comprehensive colleges and universities beyond first-year composition. As it turns out, a lot is happening. In these state comprehensive universities whose missions include providing applied skills and programming for postgraduate career success, it is no surprise that writing figures prominently as an option for further development through a minor or concentration, and, less frequently, through a major; it is also no surprise that these institutions anticipate students will need further help in writing through a tutoring center, whether it's dedicated to writing or not. In this class of institutions, WAC appears to be less robust than at some other institutions, and I speculate that the challenge is the resource heft such an endeavor requires. At Montclair State University, I often thought about attempting to launch a strong WAC program, even considering following the UMass Amherst model of trading a second-semester in FYC for a junior-level writing requirement, but I didn't see how we could possibly raise the money needed to support disciplinary faculty in teaching writing well through a dedicated director, faculty-development monies, and staff support. In summary, I'll risk some generalization in this characterization: at state comprehensive universities, the tilt in writing programming and support beyond FYC is in some ways locked in a deficiency model in which the priority for writing programming is getting students up to the bar—good enough for college work, good enough for advanced college work, good enough for disciplinary work—rather than helping them soar over it.

Quick Facts: Beyond FYC

In this sample's institutions . . .

- *WAC Presence:* While survey respondents suggested two-thirds of the institutions, syllabi and document review indicated just one-third presence.

- *Writing Robustness:* The mean number of required writing numbers or experiences is 2.6; the mode is 2; 70.7 percent require two or three.

- *Centers that Support Writing Tutoring:* 100 percent of the institutions.

- *Centers Located within Student Life and Student Affairs Divisions:* 59.5 percent of the institutions.

- *Centers Located within Academic Affairs:* 40.5 percent of the institutions.

- *Writing Majors:* 10.4 percent of the institutions.

- *Vertical Writing Programs:* minors, majors, concentrations, or other vertical programs at 69.8 percent of the institutions.

Notes

1. For this figure, I recalculated the writing center location data provided by the top university study (Isaacs and Knight 2014), excluding "Unknown," to provide comparable percentages to the state comprehensive university study.

2. The *great unwashed* is a phrase coined in the nineteenth century by members of the upper class to refer to the lower class.

6
WRITING AT THE STATE COMPREHENSIVE U

This study reveals wide implementation of several guiding principles of contemporary writing practices in US four-year state colleges and universities. In FYC we see clear evidence of writing as process, articulated outcomes for writing courses, rhetorical instruction, and the importance of argumentation. Further, I found evidence of majority adaptations of several developments in respect to writing programming beyond FYC: the existence of upper-level writing instruction; the presence of experts in writing instruction at faculty or administrator levels; the overwhelming presence of writing centers for individualized writing instruction; and the presence of minors, majors, and other undergraduate writing programs of study. These are positive developments, as I think all readers would agree. What we do not see is widespread adoption of our most provocative or disruptive ideas: independent writing departments or programs, the abolishment of the FYC requirement, or nationally defined outcomes, to name a few.

Based on my data, it is clear that the influence of the field is felt across the country, at both large and small universities and in every region. This is evident through the robust offerings the study reveals to be found in curricula and programming and in alignment with many, though certainly not all, of the goals for writing articulated in such statements as the "Principles for the Postsecondary Teaching of Writing" (Conference on College Composition and Communication 2015) or the *Framework for Success in Postsecondary Writing* (Council of Writing Program Administrators, National Council of Teachers of English, and National Writing Project 2011). In just fifty years since the 1966 Dartmouth Seminar, we have accomplished a great deal, and we should be pleased! Major conceptual gains can be seen in terms of evidence that courses and requirements are developed with the understanding that writing is rhetorical, varying by genre, and requiring instruction and support at every level. The influence of argumentation is also significant. Collectively,

DOI: 10.7330/9781607326397.c006

those of us who fear the scholarly conversation exists in a bubble that does not extend to the field at large as practiced at US state comprehensive universities can breathe a sigh of relief: it has had an influence.

It is also clear that the discipline hasn't touched every institution and that a small but significant number of schools demonstrate no impact from the discipline, seemingly caught in a time warp, serving up an arhetorical understanding of writing in "freshmen English." Predictably, these schools also have public documents that suggest a fixed notion of writing that is rooted in the binary of correct versus incorrect. Judging by the public documents, students at these schools are presented with a view of writing that is not only inaccurate to but that is also contrary to educated people's understanding of writing as socially constructed and evolving; this view is also clearly and predictably inclusive of those of us who were raised in Standard English language communities and exclusive of those of us who were not. It's a set-up for reproducing existing patterns of inequality based on language dominance by those who are native speakers and writers of a narrow definition of Standard American English. This is as regrettable as it is a descriptively inaccurate view of the English language both in and outside the academy. Further, these institutions are light on training for and hiring expectations of their FYW faculty. This study demonstrates, through findings of significant variable associations, that these institutions trend toward those that did not have representation at CCCC over a two-year period and do not have a WPA or tenure-track writing faculty. Also, these institutions tend to be smaller and to be BA granting in their institutional focus.

Yet beyond this serious problem within FYC, we see something quite different. Perhaps greater testament to the acceptance of writing studies as a discipline are the findings related to vertical writing programming within the sample. In 69.8 percent of the sample, we find some kind of vertical programming in writing, and in 10.4 percent of the sample, we see a writing major. These writing majors vary in focus, falling variously within the two continua Campbell and Jacobs (Campbell and Jacobs 2010) introduce: liberal to technical and general to specific. As an illustration, here are the names of the majors at these ten schools:

- professional and technical writing
- writing and linguistics
- writing (two)
- professional and technical communication
- journalism/professional writing
- writing arts

- writing, rhetoric, and technical communication
- technical communication
- professional writing

Thus we see that the vertical writing programming in the sample reflects an interdisciplinary understanding of writing, with roots in linguistics, journalism, creative writing, technical communication, and rhetoric and composition (though note the absence of the word *composition*). In reviewing these names, it is also easy to imagine how the acceptance of writing studies at the state comprehensive university may be tied to acceptance, and even the embrace, of applied studies common among comprehensive universities. Bruce Henderson, author of *Teaching at the People's University: An Introduction to the State Comprehensive University*, the only book I could find devoted to the study of this institutional class, writes that preparing students for work is part of the mission of the comprehensive or regional university, and thus SCUs emphasize applied curricula (Henderson 2007, 7). The acceptance of the discipline of writing studies, then, is part of the culture of the regional colleges and universities that make up the sample, a culture different from that of the colleges and universities that belong to the Association of American Universities (AAU), an organization that represents the most elite research.

The study also reveals that several of the core values of the discipline have deeply influenced the curricula of first-year composition. Major conceptual inroads can be seen in terms of evidence that courses and requirements are developed with the understanding that writing is rhetorical, that it varies by genre, and that it is best taught as a process. The influence of argumentation is also significant. That so many of the FYC courses emphasize these elements—rhetoric, genre, process writing, and argumentation—demonstrates that these values have been disseminated fairly successfully, particularly when we consider how young our discipline is. Nearly twenty-five years ago, in 1994, Lad Tobin dated the writing-process movement to the late 1960s and early 70s, arguing that the writing-process movement was as much about what it critiqued as it is about what it offered; in his words, the writing-process movement was a "critique (or even an outright rejection) of traditional, product driven, rules-based, correctness-obsessed writing instruction . . . of a particular kind of product—the superficial, packaged, formulaic essays that most of us grew up writing and teaching" (Tobin 1994, 5). He speculated that this influence had been great, but he really didn't know—he was not of the empiricist school. Since then we have wondered about the influence of this great movement and have come up with various reports on our success. Much more recent than the writing-process movement is what might now be called the "WPA Outcomes movement" (it is in its fifth version), which began with its first publication in 1999 and which I found to be adopted or adapted at nearly a quarter of the schools (22.6 percent) in this study, with many other institutions with programs that reflect similar tenets. Collectively, then, we see the presence of many of the discipline's core qualities in FYC programs across the country. What I find gratifying in the relatively high degree of emphasis of these core qualities in the FYC courses I reviewed is that these were not self-selected schools but a random sample of regional four-year state institutions.

It is also clear that the discipline hasn't touched every institution and that a small but significant number of institutions demonstrate no impact by the discipline, seemingly caught in a time-warp, serving up a rhetorical understanding of writing in "Freshmen English," or with very large classes, among other unwelcome possibilities. Predictably, these schools also have public documents that suggest a fixed notion of writing rooted in the binary of correct versus incorrect; further, these institutions are light on training for and hiring expectations of their FYW faculty. My study demonstrates, through examination of relationships among variables, that these institutions trend toward those that did not have representation at CCCCs over a two-year period and do not have a WPA or tenure-track writing faculty. Of course, there are many exceptions, going both ways. Still, in majority, these institutions tend to be smaller and to be BA granting in their institutional focus. These trends are linked to institutional characteristics that, from my study, are revealed to be particularly important indicators for the kinds of approaches institutions take in writing programming. Important indicator variables include region, size, presence of a writing program administrator, and engagement with the field as marked by participation in CCCC.

Further, at state comprehensive institutions across the country, there is much evidence that universities and colleges are not looking to disciplinary expertise or national statements for guidance in writing-assessment decisions, as is evidenced by widespread use of large-scale testing for placement and exemption decisions. While practices in first-year composition on the local level suggest a much wider range of assessment practices, with many institutions engaging in practices in keeping with organizational guidelines and scholarly discussion, the bird's-eye view suggests that areas of admissions, placement, and exemption remain very much controlled by nonfaculty administrators.

Thus, as I suggested in chapter 1, how you view this analysis of writing at the state comprehensive university depends very much on what your impressions of and hypotheses about the field were prior to reading this book. In what follows, I suggest a range of next steps.

NEXT STEPS: AT OUR COLLEGES AND UNIVERSITIES

On the local level, I think writing faculty and WPAs especially can do much more to institute training programs for their FYC faculty and perhaps for other faculty as well. Providing training is not especially expensive, so it is about presenting the case to a dean or provost that a small amount of funds for professional development will reap huge benefits in terms of student writing outcomes. Showing that this is the case through comparing faculty-retention data, student-evaluation data, withdrawal/D/F grades, syllabi, or other measures of faculty who participate in professional development versus those who don't should be highly persuasive. I am particularly surprised that there are so many schools with WPAs on the job that do not require any professional-development activities. Why not? I suspect it's the culture of academia—requirements beyond office hours and class attendance are eschewed by so many academics. I suppose I sound impatient because I am: from the student, parent, or citizen perspective, that it is so difficult to require even a one-day workshop to align pedagogy and course goals, discuss trends in student writing or in the field, and collectively assess and respond to a few student drafts is incomprehensible and definitely unfortunate.

Another local-level action I suggest is to interrogate what tests are used for placement and exemption. WPAs and writing studies faculty should start by studying their catalogs to find out exactly what tests are in place at their own colleges. There may be surprises, as would certainly be the case for many of the representatives in this study who completed the survey and were apparently unaware of some of the tests used to place or exempt students. If you question the test, or think the cut score doesn't make sense, talk to the office where this decision is made and investigate the research completed to make these decisions. Likely, there's an office on campus that would be very happy to be relieved of some responsibility for testing. At the very least, if your school is using the SAT, Accuplacer, or another nationally developed test that does not work well, supplement these tests with in-house assessments that can be used to recalibrate students. Consider options for correcting initial assessment: boost programs that make is possible for successful basic writing students to skip over the next requirement, allow midsemester switches for strong students or provide midsemester or subsequent-semester additional support for weak students. I suspect writing studies faculty often just shut their eyes to the whole problem of placement and exemption, and I can understand why, having done so myself for several years. The issue can seem impossible to take on—time consuming and politically difficult, as so often these assessment matters are in the hands of admissions, student retention, or another entity. However, placement and exemption are curricular decisions, at heart, and in these decisions faculty have a clear and definite role. Many years ago I found it was relatively easy to have a big impact at my school by making and winning the case to change the cut score for AP exemptions. It was not that I didn't want any students to receive exemption but that I found many English majors in my program who were exempted from FYC appeared to suffer for it. I'll note from personal experiences that it is much easier to supplement weak assessments with stronger assessments, and to research and alter cut scores, than it is to fight for abolishment of all standardized testing. As discussed in chapter 4, an important area of concern Mya Poe, Norbert Elliot, John Cogan, and Tito Nurudeen, and Asao Inoue (Inoue and Poe 2014; Poe et al. 2014) have made us more aware of is the area of disparate impact, which strikes me as a potentially powerful tool for improving consequential assessment instruments; if students of color or of particular demographic characteristics are, as a group, being impacted differently by a particular assessment, staff and administrators in other programs will become allies in changing methodologies.

For those who are interested in vertical writing programming, and in light of the program titles of the many vertical programs found in this study, I suggest alliances with existing areas of writing that are typically but not always outside English departments: technical communication, professional or business writing, journalism, and creative writing. Administrators and faculty across campus are familiar with these disciplines, so to develop these further, toward majors and with attention to rhetoric, is not as politically and administratively challenging as to go it alone, fashioning an entirely new major in writing studies. Rather than fight for independent department status—which is asking a lot of colleges and schools that typically want to consolidate rather than expand because of the expenses associated with departments—this route focuses on curricula. There is no reason a tenured professor in the English department couldn't work with faculty in communications or business and even regularly teach courses that *belong* to these other departments.

On the local level, faculty and staff concerned about writing studies should engage in organized, department, or committee-supported self-assessment, defining both areas of greatest pride and also areas of great concern, using the latter to create a bucket list of areas to address. WPAs most often work alone, especially at SCUs and small BA-granting institutions, and it's very easy to become overwhelmed by daily tasks and to be unclear about how to best use supporters and allies who have time for a meeting once a month but aren't thinking about the program on a daily basis. These people are sounding boards, and they can help with developing priorities and refining nascent ideas.

As an administrator for many years, I've developed strategies to make sure I make room for my big goals. Typically, on a day later in the week, after I have spent Monday, Tuesday, and perhaps Wednesday and Thursday as well, battling all the incoming e-mails and "must-dos," I pull away from e-mail and all the things that must be done to keep the program running, and I think about my big goals. What have I done to achieve these? I can enjoy administrative work because I'm always moving forward. For me, as a writing program administrator, then department chair, and now associate dean, my mandate boils down to this: what can I do to help students learn more and better? By asking that question of myself, I point myself toward low-hanging fruit, toward doable processes and activities that I can engage in without permission or funding (e.g., reading student evaluations and devising workshops that address persistent comments) or that can be transformed into proposals I can share with colleagues and then present to administrators.

NEXT STEPS: NATIONAL LEVEL

As an outgrowth to this study I would like to propose a series of actions that might help foster improved practices in writing instruction, support, and administration at state comprehensive universities, and likely others as well, particularly in categories of schools that the data suggests remain untouched by the field. We appear to be in a national moment in which the desire for greater accountability for postsecondary education is enabled by more data collection and reporting; what is more, the public and Congress appear ever more interested in "some degree of standardization across higher ed institutions" (Moore, O'Neill, and Crow 2016, 22). What support and outreach can CCCC, NCTE, and the Council of WPAs provide to encourage and support these colleges and universities in improving their practices? The typical model for institutional improvement in writing studies is for faculty at a particular college to advocate for actions at their institution and then work alone, drawing on our professional organizations, and with support from a rich body of scholarship, to support their arguments. I would assert that this model isn't supporting many of our more "remote" institutions—and here I use remote in nongeographical terms—and that we ought to be more active in our offers of support and guidance. Responses to my survey at many of these more "remote" institutions were enthusiastic; faculty and other representatives wanted to know what other institutions were doing, and several articulated the hope that this research could help them advocate more forcefully for positive change on their own campuses. At a simple level, as researcher and writer, I can and will share the findings of this research with my survey respondents, but, more broadly, with this book I call for national and state organizations to develop strategies to practically support and advocate for all colleges and universities to teach and support writing programs well, in accordance with the findings of our research and the values of our community, as articulated in a host of official statements.

Many disciplines have been very effective at this kind of advocacy by using accrediting bodies to pressure institutions to changes their practices. In my recent work as an associate dean, I have seen how powerful accrediting agencies are. Exceptions to university and college policies or conventions are regularly made because of accreditation. There's no better way to lower a class size than to argue that the university's program will lose accreditation otherwise. Typically, it's the faculty that let administrators know of an accreditation problem. Notably, there's a great difference in the effect of citing a recommendation by a professional organization and citing an actual accreditation requirement. NCTE, CCCCs, MLA, and the Council of WPAs have issued no end of recommendations and position statements—on class size, workload, assessment, online writing instruction, dual credit, and working conditions, to name just a few. Can we think about seriously moving toward disciplinary accreditation? With much work already completed by the Visibility Project (Phelps and Ackerman 2010), could disciplinary accreditation be added to the list?

One avenue for improvement of writing-instruction practices across the nation that already exists is through our regional accrediting agencies, as Moore, O'Neill, and Crow (2016, 20–22) document. Beyond or perhaps before accreditation, which is admittedly very challenging, we might think about building off the Writing Program Excellence certificate CCCC sponsors. At present, the program provides guidelines but few requirements. Would it make sense to include a few carefully selected specific requirements? Further, the certificate should have an expiration date, and I offer ten years as a suggestion. Colleges and universities change, and it would be helpful if those programs that have gained certification would have to reapply; the occasion of these reapplications would be useful to local writing studies faculty and staff in their efforts to retain good programming and to address ongoing concerns.

Another set of strategies should be developed for the colleges and schools whose policies are discordant with best practices across many levels. How can we help them? First, of course, we'd need to identify these schools in a fair and reasonable manner, for which I'd suggest state-level support. It would not be very difficult for state leaders in writing studies to use a checklist of minimum requirements to identify those schools in their state in need of more support. For this checklist, I would focus on a bare minimum of needs: some presence on campus of writing studies expertise; a greater-than-ideal but livable class size for FYC and other writing courses; course curricula that include some attention to process writing, reflect an understanding of the rhetorical nature of writing, and avoid defining writing as primarily mastery of grammatical and mechanical skills; and a writing center that provides instruction and support guided by principles of teaching writing through individualized instruction. The writing studies state leadership committee would need to reach out to faculty or staff at the institution, who would likely welcome help if it was communicated in the spirit of being supportive. Next steps would be informing university leadership of areas of concern and suggesting remedies.

A great remedy that the Council of WPAs or CCCC might organize is grant funding for WPA consultant-evaluator services. Most grants require excellence and achievement to receive funding; in this vision, the exact opposite would be required. Let's think about needs-based grants for college and university writing. An alternative to WPA consultant-evaluator services would be a matching grant to colleges and schools to send a representative to the WPA workshop for writing program administrators. This is a popular workshop as it is, but due to costs and limited size, it is not available to many of the faculty and staff across the country who need it most. The WPA-GO CWPA Conference Travel Grant is obviously a valuable program, and it does a good job of getting people trained before they go on to their first jobs. What we need is an additional grant that supports people already in positions, likely with their formal schooling completed. I would guess that the vast majority of writing program administrators at state comprehensive universities have never gone to the WPA workshop and would go if the funding was provided.

Of Use

With *Writing at the State U,* I have attempted to provide a baseline for other researchers and teachers who advocate for particular writing-programming approaches and analyze trends in the field. For researchers, I hope I have made a persuasive case against the self-selected survey I perhaps impolitically have likened to a Facebook survey. We live increasingly in a climate in which we are virtually surrounded by people like us through opting in and out of social and professional memberships, so to seek information via listservs and associations may seem open and available—*forward, link, just click*—but it's not really. We have the tools now to go find things out ourselves—to reach in and select samples rather than sit back and see what comes to us. I also hope I've made a case for teaming up with statisticians and educational researchers when working on big data, particularly if you're not entirely confident of your own training in this regard. No reason to go it alone. Finally, I have tried to follow the advice of Haswell, Smagorinsky, and Bazerman and Prior (Bazerman and Prior 2009; Haswell 2005; Smagorinsky 2008) by expending much ink space on methodological explaining and revealing—throughout the text but also via the appendices. Perhaps the extensive appendix is the way to more fully account for one's methodology. And, when space is tight, the online appendix methodology compendium might be the right choice.

For WPAs and faculty, by presenting findings on this class of institutions within the context of our scholarly discussion and other empirical researchers' findings, I hope I have contributed usefully both to a discipline and to people at a class of institutions that have always exhibited an impressive practical bent and a can-do spirit. In the face of "no money," we devise work-arounds. In the face of "not interested," we do it anyway. In the midst of it all, we teach writing day in and day out, reading drafts and responding to student writing, a powerful experience that makes students remember their teachers forever and makes teachers truly know where students are and what they need. I hope this research presentation is in the same vein: useful. Most of all I hope it will be useful to writing faculty at state comprehensive colleges and universities across the country who wish to understand better the trends and possibilities at institutions like their own for practical, local considerations.

APPENDIX A
Methods

In this appendix I have expanded upon the methodological notes I provide in chapter 1. To begin, it's useful to offer my methodological training, which began formally when I was a graduate student at the University of Massachusetts Amherst. I was trained in qualitative methodologies primarily, working with Anne Herrington on a dissertation that consisted of case studies of three writing teachers for which I drew on course observations, interviews, and paper analysis. Once a psychology major, I also dabbled in statistical analyses early on, drawing on my undergraduate coursework in statistics and a penchant for counting, classifying, and measuring, likely an unsurprising outcome for a child of a librarian and a computer-systems person. Relevant to this project was the practice and training I received on reading streams of text for themes and patterns, drawing first and foremost on Anne Herrington's careful guidance and also on Marshall and Rossman (1989), Huckin (1992), Doheny-Farina and Odell (1985), and LeCompte and Goetz (1993); more recently, for this project, I also found Geisler (2004) and Saldana (2012) very useful. My dissertation work poring through interview transcripts of students and faculty was helpful in building the skills I needed to identify important variables early on in the analysis process so I could develop coding sheets for characterizing courses. That initial careful work completed during graduate study—when full days could be spent devoted to spreading my notes across the floor, sorting, color coding, and writing on index cards—was critical for me in helping me develop the kind of cross-checking, retracing, recursive process that is important when working with data that looks different as you alternate between theorizing about it and sorting through it.

In the twenty years since graduation from UMass, I have slowly added more quantitative components to my research, most frequently in respect to assessment projects, which often require rudimentary frequency reporting and cross-tabulations. In August 2011, with this project in the planning stage, I went to Christiane Donahue and Charles Bazerman's Dartmouth Summer Seminar for Composition Research,

DOI: 10.7330/9781607326397.c007

where I learned about nonparametric statistics (Chris Hass), coding (Cheryl Geisler), and basic statistics (John Pfister and Les Perelman) and received invaluable individual feedback on my research in progress from all these people and also Chris Anson and Neal Lerner. From this experience I took on more work with quantitative methodologies, learning SPSS through the help of a graduate assistant (Vera Lentini) and an education psychologist (Emily Dow). Through it all, Norbert Elliot also provided extremely useful help in the development of my methods.

SELECTING THE SAMPLE

In the fall of 2010, I began to develop an approach to selecting a sample of four-year state universities to work from, having decided I wanted a more random and broadly representative sample than what Melinda Knight and I had come up with by using *US News and World Report*'s various "best" lists.[1] At this same time, I was in the data-analysis phase of the empirical top university study, and thus I had a basic methodology to work from. The crucial decisions Melinda and I made together—to focus on publicly available information and to develop our sample independent of willingness to respond to a survey request—were principles that continued to make sense to me and that I carried over to this study.

I wrestled with what master population of four-year state universities list to choose, ultimately deciding on the AASCU (American Association of State Colleges and Universities) membership list, chosen for two reasons. First, AASCU is the organization most identified with the idea of comprehensive universities, an underexamined class of institutions, as discussed in chapter 1. AASCU describes itself as an association whose members share a "learning-and-teaching-centered culture, a historic commitment to underserved student populations, and a dedication to research and creativity that advances their regions' economic progress and cultural development" (American Association of State Colleges and Universities n.d.). Second, AASCU's membership has significant breadth and variety in terms of size, geographical location, and type, as defined by Carnegie, so I knew that the lean toward the comprehensive university wouldn't preclude examination of important subclasses, including research universities and BA-focused colleges.

Once I had my AASCU membership list, I pulled data on all these schools from the Carnegie Foundation.[2] I pulled the following classification information for each school: state, numeric enrollment, size category (extra small, small, medium, large, and extra large), size and setting, full time/part time faculty, selectivity, graduate students, Basic Carnegie

Classification, type, and special populations served (Historically black and Hispanic serving). At this point I removed a handful of schools from the population: one school that was essentially a two-year school, seven schools that were located in territories (the Virgin Islands, Puerto Rico, and Guam), and one engineering special-focus school, leaving me with a sample of 382 schools. My first thought was to make sure I had proportional representation along most of these categories. My target sample size was one hundred, but the statistician who guided my sampling, Montclair State University math professor Andrew McDougall,[3] explained that the sample size was not large enough to stratify along so many categories. I substituted region for state, using regional accrediting-agency membership to represent region. These agencies effectively divide the fifty states into six higher education regions; given the power and influence these accrediting agencies have, and their independence from one another, it was important to have proportional representation of schools using this category. The remaining category for proportional stratification was size (as defined by Carnegie), condensed to small, medium, large, and extra large for sampling purposes and selected to enable me to investigate the hypothesis that institutional size would be an important factor in determining how writing is taught, administered, and supported.

Andrew McDougall stratified the population for region and size and generated the sample, which turned out to include 106 schools that draw from thirty-eight states and includes the following basic Carnegie Classifications: research U (high-research activity), doctoral research, master's large, master's medium, master's small, BA colleges-arts and sciences, BA colleges-diverse fields, and BA/AS colleges. Thus, the spread of institutions by size and region in the sample corresponds directly with the size and region spread of the population (all member schools in AASCU, after exclusions). See tables A.1 to A.5 for characteristics of the sample: in the second column of each of the tables, I have listed what percentage of institutions of each identified type is in the sample, and in the third column I have listed the percentage of the identified type in all four-year state universities, drawing on the IPEDS complete list, pulled four years after the initial data was collected, in March 2015.[4] I collected this information after selecting the sample, and I present it here to give readers a sense of how the state comprehensive college and university population I chose compares with the full population of four-year state universities. As the tables suggest, the state comprehensive colleges and universities are fairly similar, with these differences: SCUs are larger and less selective, and more tend toward the classification of MA-granting institutions.

Table A.1. Characteristics of the sample: Carnegie size

Size	Percentage in sample	Percentage in Carnegie's All Four-Year Publics, with Specified Exclusions
Small (1,000–2,999)	17.0% (n = 18)	25.6% (n = 159)
Medium (3,000–9,999)	51.9% (n = 55)	40.2% (n = 249)
Large (10,000 or more)	31.1% (n = 33)	34.2% (n = 212)
Total	100% (n = 106)	100% (n = 620)

Table A.2. Characteristics of the sample: Carnegie institutional selectivity

Selectivity	Percentage in sample	Percentage in Carnegie's All Four-Year Publics, with Specified Exclusions
More selective	6.6% (n = 7)	15.3% (n = 95)
Selective	48.1% (n = 51)	45.2% (n = 280)
Inclusive	37.7% (n = 40)	30.1% (n = 192)
Not listed	7.5% (n = 8)	8.5% (n = 53)

Table A.3. Characteristics of the sample: Carnegie graduate classification, condensed

Classification	Percentage in sample	Percentage in Carnegie's All Four-Year Publics, with Specified Exclusions
Significant doctoral	27.4% (n = 29)	28.4% (n = 176)
Solely or primarily MA	59.4% (n = 63)	43.4% (n = 269)
Solely or primarily BA (1 MA or fewer)	13.2% (n = 14)	28.2% (n = 175)

Table A.4. Characteristics of the sample: Carnegie special populations

Population	Percentage	Percentage in NCS—All Four-Year Publics, 2009 Data*
No special designation	79.2% (n = 84)	82.4% (n = 511)
Tribal college	0.0%	0.1% (n = 5)
Historically black (HBCU)	11.3% (n = 12)	6.5% (n = 40)
Hispanic serving	9.4% (n = 10)	10.3% (n = 64)

* Carnegie's data, at the point of review, no longer provided information on institutions' status as Hispanic-serving or historically black, so I went to NCES and downloaded data available for the period closest to the original sample capture, fall 2009 and fall 2011, and counted all four-year public universities that were designated as HBCU or Hispanic-serving (National Center for Education Statistics 2010, 2011).

Table A.5. Characteristics of the sample: region as defined by accrediting agency

Accrediting Agency	Percentage	N
Middle states (MSA)	17.9% ($n = 19$)	22.3% ($n = 138$)
New England (NEASC)	3.8% ($n = 4$)	6.8% ($n = 42$)
North Central (NCA)	32.1% ($n = 34$)	31.3% ($n = 194$)
Northwest (NWCCU)	6.6% ($n = 7$)	7.6% ($n = 47$)
Southern (SACS)	33.0% ($n = 35$)	26.3% ($n = 163$)
Western (WASC)	6.6% ($n = 7$)	5.8% ($n = 36$)

Obviously, many higher education institutions that teach writing are not reflected in the sample. These include several important institutional types: two-year colleges, non-US institutions, and private institutions, all of which I suspect have different characteristics from many of the schools in the study sample. Two-year colleges are especially relevant to the population of colleges and universities I am studying, as such a large population of students who graduate from SCUs likely were taught FYC at state community colleges. Another notable omission is that I wasn't able to figure out a good way to collect a measure of the fiscal health of my institutions, though I would guess fiscal health would be an influential factor in the decisions faculty and administrators make about writing. All these sampling choices and omissions suggest areas for future research.

VARIABLES

Sample selected and baseline data downloaded from Carnegie and regional accrediting agency state lists, I was ready to begin collecting data. But first I had to establish my variables for data collection. I had several variable lists to consult and to work from: the top university study, but also previous studies; especially relevant for me were studies by Kitzhaber, Burhans, Larson, and Witte et al. Identifying variables was important to determining my sources for data, though over the course of the study I had to abandon some variables because I couldn't find reliable data. For example, early on I had identified that I wished to find out the mission or philosophy of institutions' writing programs. However, while all schools in the sample had a clearly identified institutional mission, only a few writing programs had mission statements articulated and available for public access. I decided the data were too inconsistent, and I abandoned the variable. As this example suggests, I focused on data I could pull consistently (see appendix D), following these general categories of data: institutional data (e.g., size, focus), data on aspects of FYC that are primarily faculty determined (e.g., course content), data on aspects of FYC that are primarily institutionally determined (e.g., class size), data related to writing experiences beyond FYC (e.g., WAC), data related to writing center or individualized writing instruction, and data on aspects relating to vertical writing programming. Ultimately, I came up with 153 variables, all of which are tied to one or more specific data points, though some of them are duplicative.

One other variable deserves special mention: the number of presentations given at CCCC. I wished to understand to what extent involvement in the field was associated with other variables, or to put it another way, I wished to find out whether an institution's faculty and staff involvement with the scholarly conversation had an impact on practice. Charles Bazerman, who advised me on this project at the Dartmouth Summer Seminar, put it this way: what is the level of knowledgeability of the faculty at each institution? My challenge was in figuring out how to measure or quantify the extent to which an institution was connected to the scholarly conversation without relying on self-reporting. I wished to quantify this data so I could make distinctions between institutions with high levels of involvement with the scholarly conversation and institutions with low levels. I first attempted to use membership in CCCC as a proxy for knowledgeability, but this information was unavailable. I settled on participation at CCCC, which, while hardly a fully adequate measure of an institution's engagement with the field, would be meaningful. NCTE's Eileen Maley was not able to provide me with records of all those who attended, but she was able to provide a list of all those who presented for two years: 2010 and 2011. I selected two years to correct for attendance anomalies due to conference location or other factors. By matching lists with institutions and then isolating and counting individuals who presented from sample institutions for two years, I was able to develop what struck me as a meaningful spread: from forty-four institutions that had no presentations over those two years, to the University of Arkansas at Little Rock, which had twenty-eight presentations (the mean was 3.61, with a standard deviation of 5.95).

DATA COLLECTION: EMPHASIS ON PUBLICLY AVAILABLE INFORMATION

What is unique about my sampling approach is that the sample was not determined by the presence of an individual who was willing to respond to a survey, which has typically resulted in a response rate of between 30 and 50 percent, or who was a member of an organization or on a professional listserv; rather, like Dan Melzer's study, my sample and methodology were selected to provide a national view, "not just a snapshot but a panorama" (Melzer 2009, W242), and therefore needed to rely on publicly available information. Following Haswell's call for empirically based scholarship (Haswell 2005), I sought a method that would enable me to speak broadly about national trends. In the interest of triangulation and gaining some information that publicly available information would not allow, I did develop a survey I sent to identified and confirmed local leaders (WPA or other staff or faculty). This Institutional Review Board–approved survey (see appendix B) was sent directly to confirmed representatives at each of the 106 institutions under study, resulting in ninety-eight usable surveys (92 percent) completed. Identifying and confirming a representative contact at each institution ensured a higher-than-typical survey response rate—and one that did not lean toward one kind of institution over another. Thus data from sample institutions were collected through two primary means: review of public documents such as catalogs or bulletins (my most common data source), common data-set reports, assessment documents, other institutional reports, and documents posted on department or writing-program websites; and, second, from the targeted multiple-choice and short-answer survey. The goal of this empirical method that relies on publicly available information from a stratified sample, and seeks clarification and amplification from informant surveys, has been to gain a broad, bird's-eye view of writing instruction, support, and administration, one not based on a "skewed sample" (Anson 1988, 12). The view afforded by this methodology complements the more intimate, insider view most existing research provides.

To collect primary data, I set about locating and downloading or otherwise capturing information from the 106 institutions. The rise of the use of websites in higher education enabled me to collect data directly and also to make all my data assertions verifiable and replicable by subsequent researchers who have similar access to this publicly available information. Data reliability and veracity was sought through triangulation and other methods developed by writing studies scholars and educational researchers (Abbott 2004; Cooper 1983; Doheny-Farina and Odell 1985; Geisler 2004, 2011; Herrington 1993; Huckin 2009; McKee and DeVoss 2007; McKee and Porter 2008). Data collection was pinned to the academic year 2011–2012.

The first step was to pull university and college catalogs and bulletins. Clearly, catalogs and bulletins reflect communally negotiated decisions on what colleges and universities provide for students, and thus they are reflective of a deliberative process, though also of political pressures. These documents provide a great deal of information, and they have an authority to them, as they represent a contract between student and institution. Each catalog was combed closely to collect data on the variables. Guided by the variables, sometimes with the help of a research assistant, I scoured other areas of institutions' websites. Using the list of variables I had identified, we were able to locate data through extensive searching and a fair amount of sleuthing. For example, recognizing the limitations of course-catalog descriptions for determining course foci and coverage, I included outcomes data in my analyses of courses. I examined and selected outcomes data from several sources and levels. First, as FYC courses are typically part of general education programs, I reviewed outcomes or learning statements for general education programs, pulling any specific statements that pertained to FYC courses. For example, in the Southern Arkansas University catalog, there was a section entitled "Goals for General Education," with the following language relevant to the school's FYC courses: "1. Communication—Students will communicate effectively. 2. Critical Thinking—Students will think logically and creatively to solve problems and make informed decisions" (Southern Arkansas University 2011, 31). This information, along with what was found in the course descriptions of the two courses that were required to meet these goals, was then used to analyze the FYC requirement for this school. Second, I reviewed websites for further articulation of general education outcomes. For example, Troy University has a department devoted to general studies, and in this area of the university's web page, I located the "Student Learning Outcomes" for the general studies program, which is described as "an interdisciplinary program that educates and empowers students to become effective communicators and critical thinkers" (Troy University 2011). Language specific to the writing requirement, which is met through the required FYC course, was pulled from this website for inclusion on my spreadsheet for outcomes statements and/or equivalent. The next source I reviewed for outcomes-or-equivalent statements was the department and/or program in English, writing, or the equivalent. In these pages I sometimes found more details than what was provided in course descriptions or in outcomes statements found in catalogs. For example, the California State University–Long Beach had a composition page that tells readers that students should leave the composition courses with several "Areas of Focus." Sometimes outcomes were articulated on program- or department-mandated syllabi. The language for these areas of focus was then included in my analysis. Next, I combed the colleges' and universities' websites for Offices of Assessment, using such search terms as *assessment, outcomes, learning,* and *goals.* Finally, through the survey, I had information about whether or not schools had outcomes statements or similar statements and whether individual instructors, programs, universities, or states determined them. This information provided further guidance in searching for and locating specific text to include for analysis.

Data gathering was time consuming because I followed my variable list to guide my inquiry. It was also incredibly fun, as I almost always found something! A lot of eureka moments, not entirely unlike finding a misplaced file you are sure must be somewhere on your computer. As discussed previously, some variables had to be abandoned simply because I couldn't find reliable data. Other data I *could* find, but it took searching and putting up with many dead ends until I had the pleasure of discovering what I needed. For example, ultimately I was able to find class-size data for every school, but the data weren't always in the same place. Sometimes this information was found in the bulletin or catalog, but more frequently I had to enter into an institution's scheduling software, sometimes looking directly at how many seats were taken and used. This kind of digging is great for those of us who are obsessive (the phrase *dog with a bone* is certainly applicable to my approach), and I found that persistence paid. University websites are typically very deep and very open.

When it came to identifying where writing centers and first-year composition programs (or courses) were located, I often had to do a certain amount of sleuthing for those programs that appeared to stand alone, not obviously attached to an English department. Essentially, my task was to understand the organizational and fiscal structure that enabled a writing program to end up with a stand-alone, or at least seemingly department-independent, website. I found that all this information really is available, sometimes through organizational charts or other sources that allowed me to follow an individual's reporting lines through university structures, or through reading institutional reports from managers reporting on the activities of their units. Of course, once again, I had survey data to help me in making these determinations. Similarly, the status of the WPA was determined via two methods: the survey and also through website sleuthing. Once a WPA was identified, it was not difficult to determine that individual's title and position type, and if faculty, to determine track, tenure status, and rank. Of course, at many smaller schools there was not a WPA, and the survey helped me figure out who was doing the work of running the writing program or courses—the chair, another individual, or, in rare cases, a committee of faculty. Thus, in summary, my search for primary data began with the catalog but often went much further beyond it.

DATA ANALYSIS

In preparation for analysis, I collected all my data in a large, heavy spreadsheet, with a sheet devoted to linking cell data to specific sources. I also collected hundreds of pdf files of catalogs and bulletins and also web pages I'd captured and printed for later referral and documentation. My default position was to begin with the primary data I had collected directly and to use the survey data for verification or backup. If there was a conflict, I could look further into the source material and resolve it. For example, when it came to identifying what tests were used to exempt students from FYC, the catalog trumped the survey, as it's the legal record for this sort of issue. Thus, I had to use judgment in negotiating between sources of data. For some variables, as is noted in the text, I only had data from the survey, and ultimately it was for these variables that the survey proved most useful. Essentially, I employed methods from content analysis, closely reading written text, most often mining it for answers to specific, concrete, and objective questions but also to look for patterns. I analyzed the data by prioritizing methods for high reliability of interpretation, either through descriptive reporting, in terms of presence or absence of particular variables (features), or through a two-rater coding system. To explain, some data are very easy to report on with just one rater of the data: for example, a single rater was sufficient for determining whether an institution required one or two courses of general education writing; similarly, a single rater could identify whether the term Standard English was used in course descriptions or whether an institution had a writing center available to students. However, for reporting that relied on interpretation, a second rater was added to provide greater reliability. The second rater was given coding directions—for example, if an institution's approach to course instruction included a "rhetorical," "skills," or "research" emphasis, the two raters' ratings were compared and matched to achieve a high rate of agreement (85 percent or higher). These coding sheets (appendix C), developed following Geisler (2004, 2011), may be useful to future researchers who wish to code and analyze course descriptions and outcomes documents. This mixed-method approach to data reporting, coupled with triangulation of source data (e.g., course-requirement information was gathered by both review of course bulletins and response to the participant survey), should strengthen the confidence readers can have in my reporting and analysis. The scoring system includes many interpretive questions, which were defined and coded through close textual analysis. The scoring system was created dynamically through a process that involved going back and forth between the data and developing the tools for analysis: selecting specific dimensions, identifying language and features that represent constructs, and articulating coding language appropriate to both construct and primary data. Scoring sheets were used on the sample data only after they were tested using data from outside the sample (data from other schools).[5]

STATISTICS

The next part of the process was to move my data from a spreadsheet to statistical software, in this case IBM's SPSS 21 (statistical package for social scientists). I am largely self-trained in SPSS, and for that reason I worked closely with Emily Dow, an adjunct professor at Montclair State University who has taught Introduction to Statistical Methods in Psychology for several semesters and who was a doctoral candidate in developmental psychology at CUNY during her involvement with this project. I also worked with a graduate student, Vera Lentini, who was formally trained in SPSS in a graduate course at my university. The first step of the process was to load data into SPSS. My data were most frequently categorical, but some data points were also numerical. As discussed earlier, the bulk of the statistical work was descriptive: that is, I reported frequencies and means (where there are numbers) and displayed cross-tabulations to describe and summarize the data I had collected. Beyond reporting descriptively, I also selectively sought to address hypotheses about associations or correlations among variables. My hypotheses were developed from my reading of the literature in writing program administration and also from my experiential and observational sense of what was more or less possible in the field. For example, as discussed in chapter 3, I hypothesized that the presence of a tenure-track writing program administrator would be positively associated with a range of desirable attributes, including an emphasis on rhetorical instruction in FYC courses and the development of undergraduate vertical programming in writing studies. As this manuscript makes clear, these kinds of hypotheses were often not supported by statistical analyses. To test these hypotheses, I ultimately relied on Emily Dow. While I ran lots of correlation and association tests in early drafts of the chapters, in the end, Emily Dow checked every single statistic, allowing me much greater confidence in my reports. The tests we used were various but were primarily what are called *nonparametric*: they are used to investigate associations among categorical (rather than numerical) variables. These tests allowed us to figure out if what we suspected—our hypothesis—about nonrandomness was valid.

While most of my variables were categorical—for example, region is a categorical variable—a few were continuous variables, such as class size. For categorical variables, percentages or frequencies are reported for each group within that particular category. For continuous variables, means and standard deviations are reported. It is important to pay attention to standard deviation because the larger the standard deviation, the greater the variability or distribution within the variable. In addition to descriptive statistics, I used some inferential statistics, which are what enables comparison between groups and establishes relationships between variables. Most readers have probably heard this before, but it bears repeating: *the inferential statistics presented in this book are in no way an indication of causation but simply a way to describe the relationship between two variables.*

F-test, *t*-test, chi square, and correlation analyses were the inferential statistics used to answer the research question of interest and to test the hypotheses I developed based on the literature in the field, my experience, and my own internal thinking. A *t*-test compares the means of a continuous variable between two groups. For example, it might be hypothesized that institutions with a WPA present more frequently at CCCC compared to institutions without a WPA. Institutions with a WPA had a mean number of presentations of 4.52 (SD = 6.39) compared to institutions without a WPA, which had a mean number of 1.47 (SD = 4.04). A *t*-test can compare these two means to determine whether they are statistically significantly different from each other. And, when we ran a *t*-test for this example, we did find that the means of institutions that had and did not have a WPA were statistically different: t (83.39) = 2.93, $p < 0.05$. In comparison, an F-test, or an ANOVA, can statistically compare means among more than two groups. If a statistical difference is found, post hoc Tukey tests are reported to indicate where—among what groups—those significant differences are. F-tests and *t*-tests are used when there is a hypothesized relationship between a categorical and a continuous variable. These tests were used infrequently. The most frequently used test was the chi-square (χ^2) test. When two categorical variables are hypothesized to have a relationship, a chi-square (χ^2) test is conducted. The chi-square test evaluates the ratio relationship between the groups in each category. Similarly, when two continuous variables are hypothesized to have a relationship, a correlational test is conducted. A correlation provides information about the strength of the relationship between the two variables, the direction (positive or negative), and the significance of that relationship. Throughout the book, specific standardized statistical formats are provided for those readers who are more familiar with these statistical tests. These statistics sound complicated, but on some level what they are really doing is looking mathematically at the hunch one comes to easily when looking at a simple cross-tabulation chart and observing, for example, fruit-buying patterns and noticing that bananas, apples, oranges, and cherries are bought by different people in what appear to be nonrandom distributions.

LIMITATIONS

The limitations of this study and chosen approach are clear: what was gained from the bird's-eye view is also what was lost. In order to see widely and without reliance on individual participation, I couldn't see closely, and I couldn't see nuance. Christiane Donahue of the Dartmouth Summer Seminar was helpful in giving me language to describe what I was gaining and what I was losing in this methodology: I provide an analysis based on publicly available information, thereby emphasizing that how we present ourselves publicly is important. What I am not able to provide is a view of local experts' self-presentation— individuals' perspectives on what they are doing at their schools is not represented in this study at all. The surveys provide some individual perspectives, but by design they encourage reporting rather than opinion or interpretation.

Perhaps the most obvious limitation has to do with my reporting tied to course-catalog descriptions. Course-catalog descriptions can be out of date, and many people have told me that their catalog descriptions aren't fully followed anymore. When I've asked why it is that these people don't change the descriptions, sheepish answers typically focus on bureaucratic difficulties or political challenges. Writing faculty may be reluctant to negotiate course content with the wider academic community, to engage directly with those who wish for a different focus or emphasis in course content. Perennially, we face the challenge of wishing to focus more on higher-order concerns, while many in other disciplines, in the administration, or from the public at large wish we would focus more on lower-order concerns. I suspect it is this argument we are hoping to avoid when we are slow or unwilling to update our official curricula. I understand this impulse but would also speak against it: we have an obligation to argue for the curricula we believe in, certainly, but also to teach the curricula we have announced to our students through our catalogs and bulletins.

More broadly, although this study has 106 institutions included, it is not a study of these 106 institutions. That is, it would be incorrect to think that any of these 106 institutions' approaches to writing are portrayed individually or fully or that we really can get a comprehensive or even encapsulated view of any of these from this manuscript. Rather, this is a snapshot of US state comprehensive colleges and universities as a whole, with these 106 institutions serving as dots in the matrix of that snapshot.

Another limitation of this study is borne from the population I chose. Another sample—perhaps using all four-year colleges and universities in the United States—might have told another story, and perhaps a better one as well, though I think tables A.1–A.5 suggest that SCUs are not, on the whole, radically different from the larger population of four-year state universities at least. As discussed within the manuscript, each of the major researchers who have attempted to tell the national story as I have has used a different population to sample from, so comparisons are somewhat limited. In my decision to try to better investigate and see the world of the regional and comprehensive public state university, I skewed further away from the BA-granting university and top-research university, and certainly I have not at all considered the private four-year university or any two-year colleges. These are significant limitations, reflective of the need to focus the study's sample in order to make the project manageable.

DIRECTIONS IN WRITING STUDIES RESEARCH

It may surprise readers to learn that I am not calling for a great increase in use of statistics. Although I have employed statistics in this study, I believe they are only one tool of many to make discoveries about the world of writing instruction. Further, it is challenging for many of us to do statistical work well, and I encourage researchers to go no further than they are comfortable if well supported. Actually, a little statistics goes a long way: descriptive statistics are the place to start, and often end: correlation discoveries are often accidental or unrelated, and they always leave you with a chicken-and-egg problem. What I am passionate about is the limitations of the survey. I am hopeful future researchers will become convinced of what I believe was my most important methodological commitment, which was to resist the open survey call through

WPA or another listserv. I am persuaded that this is a careless and regrettable habit, akin to jumping on Facebook and asking your friends about their practices as shoppers. I exaggerate, but it's in service of my effort to try to persuade others to see how very limited such self-selective, non-random surveys are. Yet they continue to be a primary method for data gathering, regardless of the obvious skew of the resulting population and despite increasingly low percentages of respondents, as the historically organized table 2.1 makes clear.

Notes

1. For the top university study, Melinda Knight and I aimed for what we termed an *upward view*, toward top institutions, across region and type. More specifically, we derived our sample for this study from these 2010 lists: top national—ten schools; top public—twenty; top liberal arts—ten; top master's—five in each region (North, South, Midwest, and West); and top BA—three in each region ("America's Best Colleges"). We also selected schools from two other *US News* lists, "Top Historically Black" (the top five schools in the list) and the "writing in the disciplines schools" mentioned in the list of "academic programs to look for" (US News and World Reports 2010). Finally, on the assumption that views specifically from writing studies professional organizations matter, we included the US schools awarded the CCCC Writing Program Certificate of Excellence from 2004 to 2010. With these selection criteria, we produced a sample of 101 diverse, high-ranking national and regional institutions (many schools were on several lists), collecting data in August 2010 (Isaacs and Knight 2012, 2014).

2. All through my use of the Carnegie Classification of Institutions in Higher Education data, the Carnegie Foundation for the Advancement of Teaching was the sponsor of all the data. In October 2014, however, the Carnegie Foundation transferred responsibility for the data to Indiana University's Center for Postsecondary Research.

3. Andrew McDougall is an associate professor of mathematical science and director of the Statistical Consulting Center (SCP) at Montclair State University.

4. Carnegie data for the study sample was pulled on February 1, 2011; data pulled for the comparative data on all four-year public universities, with stated exclusions, was pulled on March 12, 2015. Likely the four intervening years changed the specific population of these lists, but it is very unlikely that the proportion of institutions in each category defined changed.

5. Thanks here goes to Julia Bleakney, my coding partner at the Dartmouth Summer Seminar for Composition Research, who was the first to attempt to use my coding sheets and whose feedback was very helpful to their revision.

APPENDIX B
Survey

Title: Survey of Writing Instruction, Support, and Administration at U.S. State Comprehensive Universities

For the purpose of this survey, please report on your institution's current status in terms of requirements, offerings, and conditions.

1. Your Institution's Name:

QUESTIONS ABOUT FIRST-YEAR COMPOSITION (FYC)

2. To satisfy a First-Year Composition (FYC) requirement, how many FYC courses (excluding basic composition) does your institution require?

   ❑ 0   ❑ 1   ❑ 2

3. Does your university require an exit exam for your First-Year Composition course or courses?

   ❑ Yes.   ❑ No.

   Comment (optional):

4. For the purpose of this survey, an "outcome statement" is a statement of knowledge, skills, and/or attitudes that students are expected to gain in a given course or set of courses that a program, department or university has adopted, and which is disseminated to both students and teaching faculty.

   Do you have an outcomes or equivalent statement for your FYC course(s)?

   ❑ Yes.   ❑ No.   ❑ I don't know.

5. If you have an outcomes statement, would it (or they) best be described as:

   ❑ The WPA Outcomes (adopted or adapted) statement
   ❑ A program- or department-developed statement
   ❑ A university-developed statement
   ❑ A state-developed statement
   ❑ Statements are really developed individually, by instructors
   ❑ COMMENT

DOI: 10.7330/9781607326397.c008

6. What is the current class size for your FYC course? (If your institution has more than one required course, consider the first required course in answering this question.)

7. By which of the following means are students able to receive FYC course credits, exemptions or substitutions?

    Check all that apply.
    - ❑ Specified Advanced Placement score (AP)
    - ❑ International Baccalaureate (IB)
    - ❑ Specified ACT score
    - ❑ Specified SAT Writing score
    - ❑ SAT Critical Reading score (formerly called the SAT Verbal)
    - ❑ Specified CLEP score
    - ❑ Portfolio of previously written work
    - ❑ In-house examination
    - ❑ Other:

8. As part of completing the FYC course(s), which of the following research activities are required?

    Check all that apply.
    - ❑ An essay which includes student-selected secondary sources
    - ❑ A research paper
    - ❑ Instruction in how to conduct library and/or external sources research
    - ❑ An annotated bibliography
    - ❑ Primary research (e.g., survey, interview, participation observation, etc.)
    - ❑ Another method for gathering information or doing research

QUESTIONS ABOUT BASIC (REMEDIAL) COMPOSITION

9. Does your institution offer a basic (or remedial) course(s) in composition?

    ❑ Yes.   ❑ No.   ❑ I am not sure.

    If you have answered no to question 9, please skip to question 13.

10. If your institution does offer a basic course(s) in composition, how does your institution determine students' course placement?

    Check all that apply.
    - ❑ SAT
    - ❑ ACT
    - ❑ COMPASS
    - ❑ ACCUPLACER

❑ Directed self-placement

❑ State-wide assessment: primarily based on student essay

❑ State-wide assessment: primarily based on objective examination (multiple choice, etc.)

❑ In-house examination: primarily based on student essay

❑ In-house examination: primarily based on objective examination (multiple choice, etc.)

❑ Other/Comment:

11. Does your university require an exit exam for your basic composition course or courses?

Select one.

❑ Yes.   ❑ No.

Comment (optional):

12. What is the current class size for your basic composition course? (If your institution has more than one basic composition course, consider the most frequently offered course in answering this question.)

QUESTIONS ABOUT ADMINISTRATIVE STRUCTURE

13. What is the institutional location—the fiscal and administrative home—of the First-Year Composition courses or program?

❑ English Department

❑ Humanities Department

❑ Writing Department

❑ Linguistics Department

❑ Education Department

❑ Independent program

❑ Other:

14. Is there a person designated as the primary program administrator for the First-Year Composition courses/program?

Select one.

❑ Yes.   ❑ No.

Comment (optional):

What is the title for that position:

15. What term best describes that person's position type?

❑ Tenure-Track Faculty

❑ Full-Time, Non-Tenure-Track Faculty or Staff

❑ Part-Time Non-Tenure-Track Faculty or Staff

❑ Graduate Student

❑ Other:

16. If the person designated as the program administrator is designated as faculty, what is the current—fall 2011—status of that person?

❑ Untenured, assistant professor

❑ Tenured, assistant professor

❑ Tenured, associate professor

❑ Tenured, full professor

❑ Distinguished professor

❑ Chair

❑ Other:

17. What are the positions of the people who teach First-Year Composition courses?

Check all that apply.

❑ Tenure-line faculty

❑ Full-time lecturers, indefinitely renewable

❑ Full-time lecturers, limited term

❑ Adjunct or part-time faculty

❑ Graduate student instructors

❑ Other:

18. The majority of the First-Year Composition courses are taught by people holding what position?

❑ Tenure-line faculty

❑ Full-time lecturer, indefinitely renewable

❑ Full-time lecturer, limited term

❑ Adjunct or part-time faculty

❑ Graduate student instructor

❑ Other:

NEW QUESTION:

In the FYC courses, how much individual control do instructors have on the syllabus. Check the box that best applies.

❑ Instructors use a department or program provided syllabus.

❑ Instructors are provided with guidelines for their syllabi, but are given some latitude.

❑ Instructors syllabi are subject to department or program approval

❑ Instructors develop their own syllabi.

19. Are instructors who teach FYC specifically trained in teaching writing at your university?

❑ Yes.   ❑ No.

If your instructors are provided with training, please explain what your institution provides to new and continuing faculty, and whether these opportunities are required or voluntary.

20. What kind of program assessment of your First-Year Composition courses/program is conducted?

    Check all that apply:

    ❑ No assessment conducted

    ❑ Informal review: discussion of program or courses by faculty

    ❑ Formal review: assessment of institutional data (e.g., grades, enrollment, student evaluations, peer observation reports)

    ❑ Formal review: assessment of perception data (e.g., student or faculty surveys of learning and instruction, focus groups)

    ❑ Formal review: assessment of qualitative data (e.g., review of student writing in light of outcomes or objectives)

    Other:

21. Additional General Education Courses in Writing: Beyond the FYC requirement, how many additional writing courses (e.g., a writing intensive course) or writing experiences (e.g., a graduation portfolio) does your institution require as part of students' general education?

    ❑ 0 ❑ 1 ❑ 2 ❑ 3 ❑ 4 ❑ 5 ❑ 6

    COMMENT:

22. Writing-in-the Disciplines: Is there an institution-wide requirement for writing courses or experiences within students' major courses of study? How many?

    ❑ 0 ❑ 1 ❑ 2 ❑ 3 ❑ 4

    COMMENT:

23. At your institution is there a major in writing, rhetoric, or related field?

    ❑ No.

    ❑ Yes. It is called:

24. At your institution are there any minors in writing, rhetoric, or related field?

    ❑ No.

    ❑ Yes. The name(s) of our minor(s) are:

25. Is there a writing center at your institution?

    ❑ Yes. ❑ No.

If you have answered no to question 25, please skip to question 27.

26. What is the institutional location—the fiscal and administrative home—of the writing center?

  ❑ English Department
  ❑ Academic Support/Resource/Learning Center
  ❑ Writing Department
  ❑ Independent Center
  ❑ Office of the Provost (or similar official)
  ❑ Other:

QUESTIONS ABOUT HONORS PROGRAMS AND COMPOSITION

27. Does your institution have an honors program?

  ❑ Yes.   ❑ No.   ❑ I am not sure.

  If no, the survey is complete. Thank you!

28. If you do have an honors program, does your institution provide a special or unique course or option for honors students to complete the FYC requirement?

  ❑ Yes.   ❑ No.   ❑ I am not sure.

29. If there is a special honors course or option for FYC, what is the course name or option?

If you'd like to comment additionally, or if one of the questions above requires elaboration, please comment here.

Thank you for completing this survey!

APPENDIX C
Coding Sheets

Dimension: Does the course description specify skills instruction?
Unit of Analysis: Course Description and/or Outcomes (depends on application)
Applied to: FYC 1, FYC 2, Sequence, BW

1 = has an emphasis on teaching/mastering specific lower-order skills; address of writing as fixed/defined.

0 = does not have an emphasis on teaching/mastering specific lower-order skills; address of writing as fixed/defined.

99 = no course

Dimension: Does the course description specify grammar instruction (or derivative)?
Unit of Analysis: Course Description and/or Outcomes (depends on application)
Applied to: FYC 1, FYC 2, Sequence, BW

1 = specifies grammar, grammatical, or word with similar root.

0 = does not specify grammar, grammatical, or word with similar root.

99 = no course

Dimension: Does the curriculum include research instruction?
Unit of Analysis: Course Description and/or Outcomes (depends on application)
Applied to: BW (for others, survey asks directly)

1 = evidence that research (research paper, research essay, activity of doing research) is required.

0 = no evidence that research is required.

99 = no course

Dimension: Does the curriculum include argumentation?
Unit of Analysis: Course Description and/or Outcomes (depends on application)

DOI: 10.7330/9781607326397.c009

Applied to: FYC 1, FYC 2, Sequence, BW

1 = there is evidence of instruction in argumentation through the use
of the word (or words with the same root): argument, persuade; language such as: take and support a position, provide evidence for one
side of a debate.

0 = no evidence of the above.

99 = no course

Dimension: Is there evidence of rhetorical instruction?

Unit of Analysis: Course Description and/or Outcomes (depends on
application)

Applied to: FYC 1, FYC 2, Sequence, BW

1 = indicates that writing is rhetorical, that it requires an awareness that
individuals make choices, that there isn't one set of procedures for
writing well in all situations; that writing is always situationally depen-
dent. Keywords include (but presence of which is not sufficient):
rhetoric, rhetorical, audience, purpose, invention, strategies, context.

0 = no indication that writing is rhetorical; rather, writing is a static activity, and that there is a way to write well, regardless of context.

99 = no course

Dimension: Are process writing methodologies evident?

Unit of Analysis: Course Description and/or Outcomes (depends on
application)

Applied to: FYC 1, FYC 2, Sequence, BW

1 = presence of process writing terms and approaches; that is, mention
of several of the following: deliberate attention to generating writing,
drafting writing, revising writing, editing writing (not only editing).

0 = no evidence of process writing terms of approaches.

99 = no course

Dimension: What is the topic identified?

Unit of Analysis: Course Description and/or Outcomes (depends on
application)

Applied to: FYC 1, FYC 2, Sequence, BW

1 = Literature-based; explicitly references the study and reading of
literature.

2 = Discipline-based; Will explicitly reference readings or topics that are
based in the disciplines, typically specified in particular sections.

3 = Announced, non-literary topic; may be an explicit topic or theme

for all sections (e.g., literary, African American culture, the subject of writing), or it may simply refer to topic or theme that will be chosen by individual instructors.

4 = Student Generated; Student interest, experience, or self-chosen topic is the subject or topic of the course or a significant majority of the course. Student aspect is explicitly mentioned.

5 = Research; Content is research, typically dominated by a culminating paper.

6 = Topic Non Specified; no discussion of topic or theme. Unspecified.

99 = no course

APPENDIX D
List of Variables

Variable source list for state comprehensive university study

	Source 1	Source 2	Source 3	Priority or reconciliation method	Comment
Institution name	AASCU list	Institution's website	Survey	Source 2	
State	AASCU list	Institution's website	Accrediting agency	No conflict	
Regional accrediting association	Accrediting agency's listing	Wikipedia		No conflict	
Basic Carnegie Classification	Carnegie Classification				
Carnegie size	Carnegie Classification				
Enrollment	Carnegie Classification				
Carnegie institutional selectivity	Carnegie Classification				
Carnegie grad class, condensed	Carnegie Classification				
Presence/ absence of FYC requirement	Catalog or bulletin	Gen ed policy doc	Survey	No conflict	
Carnegie 2010 enrollment profile	Carnegie Classification				
Carnegie special populations	Carnegie Classification				
Number of first-year composition courses required	Catalog or bulletin	Gen ed policy	Survey	No conflict	
Where is FYC located?	Survey	Catalog or bulletin	Institution website	no conflict	Sources 2 and 3 did not always reveal answers

continued on next page

DOI: 10.7330/9781607326397.c010

	Source 1	Source 2	Source 3	Priority or reconciliation method	Comment
How many additional general education writing requirements are there?	Survey	Catalog or bulletin	Gen ed policy doc	No conflict	
Is basic writing offered?	Catalog or bulletin	Survey	No conflict		
Is there a speaking requirement?	Catalog or bulletin	Gen ed policy			
Is there a writing center?	Catalog or bulletin	Survey	Institution website	No conflict	
Where is the WC located?	Survey	Institution website	Catalog or bulletin	No conflict	
Is there a WAC or WID program?	Survey	Catalog or bulletin	Institution website	Conflict; reported both, with primacy for catalog/bulletin and institution website	
Is writing required beyond the first year?	Survey	Catalog or bulletin	Gen ed policy doc	No conflict	
Robustness: How many writing courses or experiences?	Survey	Catalog or bulletin	Gen ed policy doc	No conflict	
Is there an undergraduate certificate in writing?	Catalog or bulletin	Survey		No conflict	
Undergraduate certificate name	Catalog or bulletin	Survey		No conflict	
Is there a writing emphasis/ concentration/ track or specialization within an English or other major?	Catalog or bulletin	Survey		Catalog given primacy	
Emphasis/name	Catalog or bulletin	Survey			
Is there a writing minor?	Catalog or bulletin	Survey		Catalog given primacy	
Minor name	Catalog or bulletin	Survey			
Is there a writing major?	Catalog or bulletin	Survey	.	Catalog given primacy	
Major name	Catalog or bulletin	Survey			

continued on next page

	Source 1	Source 2	Source 3	Priority or reconciliation method	Comment
Is there any undergradu-ate program in writing?					Compiled from previous variables
Is there a WPA?	Survey	Institution website		No conflict	
Writing program administrator title	Survey	Institution website		No conflict	
WPA title type	Analysis				
What type of WPA?	Analysis				
Is the WPA TT faculty?	Survey	Institution website	External searching on web—Linked in, etc.		Some sleuthing required!
What is position of the WPA or equivalent?	Survey	Institution website		No conflict	
Who teaches first-year com-position most?	Survey	Institution web-site: analysis of names of teach-ers in fall 11 reviewed against those indi-viduals' directory rank			Survey was almost always used on its own; sleuthing via source 2 in a few cases.
What is the class size?	Survey	Institution sched-ule for fall 11	Institution website		
Do tenure-line faculty teach FYC?	Survey	Institution web-site: analysis of names of teach-ers in fall 11 reviewed against those indi-viduals' directory rank			Survey was almost always used on its own; sleuthing via source 2 in a few cases.
Do full-time lecturers, renewable, teach FYC?	Survey	Institution web-site: analysis of names of teach-ers in fall 11 reviewed against those indi-viduals' directory rank			Survey was almost always used on its own; sleuthing via source 2 in a few cases.
Do full-time lecturers, lim-ited term, teach FYC?	Survey	Institution web-site: analysis of names of teach-ers in fall 11 reviewed against those indi-viduals' directory rank			Survey was almost always used on its own; sleuthing via source 2 in a few cases.

continued on next page

	Source 1	Source 2	Source 3	Priority or reconciliation method	Comment
Do adjunct or part-time faculty teach FYC?	Survey	Institution website: analysis of names of teachers in fall 11 reviewed against those individuals' directory rank			Survey was almost always used on its own; sleuthing via source 2 in a few cases.
Do graduate students teach FYC?	Survey	Institution website: analysis of names of teachers in fall 11 reviewed against those individuals' directory rank			Survey was almost always used on its own; sleuthing via source 2 in a few cases.
Do others teach FYC?	Survey	Institution website: analysis of names of teachers in fall 11 reviewed against those individuals' directory rank			Survey was almost always used on its own; sleuthing via source 2 in a few cases.
To what extent are the WPA Outcomes used?	Survey	Institutional website			
Have the WPA Outcomes been adopted or adapted?	Survey	Institutional website			
No assessment of FYC program or course(s) conducted	Survey				
Conduct assessment informally?	Survey				
Conduct assessment based on formal, institutional data?	Survey				
Conduct assessment based on formal, perception data?	Survey				
Conduct assessment based on formal, qualitative data?	Survey				
Conduct assessment through other means?	Survey	Institutional website			

continued on next page

	Source 1	Source 2	Source 3	Priority or reconciliation method	Comment
Is there an outcomes or equivalent statement?	Survey	Catalog	Institutional assessment reports	General education documents	
Are outcomes determined by individual instructors?	Survey				
Do outcomes exist on the program or dept. level?	Survey	Institutional website			
Do outcomes exist on the university level?	Survey	Institutional website			
Do outcomes exist on the state level?	Survey	Institutional website	State higher ed website		
Placement by SAT score(s)	Catalog	Survey		Catalog was relied upon	
Placement by ACT score(s)	Catalog	Survey		Catalog was relied upon	
Placement by COMPASS score	Catalog	Survey		Catalog was relied upon	
Placement by ACCUPLACER score	Catalog	Survey		Catalog was relied upon	
Placement by state-wide assessment	Catalog	Survey		Catalog was relied upon	
Placement by directed self-placement	Catalog	Survey		Survey was relied upon	
Statewide placement assessment is primarily essay	Catalog	Survey		Survey was relied upon	
Statewide placement assessment is primarily objective	Catalog	Survey		Survey was relied upon	
Placement by in-house assessment	Catalog	Survey		Survey was relied upon	
Placement by language or int'l. status	Catalog	Survey		Catalog was relied upon	
In-house placement assessment is primarily essay	Catalog	Survey		Survey was relied upon	

continued on next page

	Source 1	Source 2	Source 3	Priority or reconciliation method	Comment
In-house placement assessment is primarily objective	Catalog	Survey		Survey was relied upon	
Placement by other means	Survey				
Exemption by SAT writing	Catalog	Survey		Catalog was relied upon	
Exemption by SAT score(s)	Catalog	Survey		Catalog was relied upon	
Exemption by SAT critical reading	Catalog	Survey		Catalog was relied upon	
Exemption by ACT score(s)	Catalog	Survey		Catalog was relied upon	
Exemption by AP score	Catalog	Survey		Catalog was relied upon	
Exemption by IB score	Catalog	Survey		Catalog was relied upon	
Exemption by CLEP score	Catalog	Survey		Catalog was relied upon	
Exemption by portfolio of written work	Catalog	Survey		Catalog was relied upon	
Exemption by in-house assessment	Catalog	Survey		Catalog was relied upon	
Exemption by other means	Survey				
How much are syllabi standardized?	Survey				
Does FYC1 CD specify skills instruction?	Catalog				
Does FYC1 CD reference grammar instruction?	Catalog				
Does FYC1 CD or outcomes suggest process-writing instructional orientation?	Catalog	Institutional website			
Does FYC1 CD suggest instruction in the modes?	Catalog	Institutional website			

continued on next page

	Source 1	Source 2	Source 3	*Priority or reconciliation method*	*Comment*
Does FYC1 CD or outcomes reference argumentation?	Catalog	Institutional website			
FYC 1 class size	Catalog	Institutional website	Survey	Catalog and institutional website prioritized	
Does the institution have an honors program?	Catalog	Survey		Catalog prioritized	
Is there an honors option for FYC?	Catalog	Survey		Catalog prioritized	
FYC1 honors course title	Catalog				
FYC 1 course title	Catalog				
FYC 2 course title	Catalog				
What is the dominant instructional approach in course 1?	Catalog	Institutional website			
What is the dominant instructional approach in course 2?	Catalog	Institutional website			
Does FYC1 CD or outcomes suggest rhetorical instruction?	Catalog	Institutional website			
Does FYC2 CD or outcomes suggest rhetorical Instruction?	Catalog	Institutional website			
Does FYC2 CD specify skills instruction?	Catalog				
Does FYC2 CD reference grammar instruction?	Catalog				
What is the topic identified in FYC1 CD?	Catalog				
What is the topic identified in FYC2 CD?	Catalog				

continued on next page

	Source 1	Source 2	Source 3	Priority or reconciliation method	Comment
Does FYC2 CD or outcomes suggest process-writing instructional orientation?	Catalog	Institutional website			
Does FYC2 CD suggest instruction in the modes?	Catalog				
Does FYC1 CD or outcomes reference argumentation?	Catalog	Institutional website			
Does any of FYC sequence CD or outcomes suggest rhetorical instruction?	Catalog	Institutional website			
Does any of FYC sequence CD specify skills Instruction?	Catalog				
Does any of FYC sequence CD reference grammar?	Catalog				
Does any of FYC sequence CD or outcomes suggest process-writing instruction orientation?	Catalog	Institutional website			
Does the FYC curriculum include research instruction?	Catalog	Institutional website	Survey		
Does any of FYC sequence CD or outcomes reference argumentation?	Catalog	Institutional website			
Are modes taught in these courses?	Survey				
FYC2 honors course title	Catalog				
Is an exit exam required?	Survey				
Is there an FYC proficiency exam?	Survey				

continued on next page

	Source 1	Source 2	Source 3	Priority or reconciliation method	Comment
Basic writing course title	Catalog				
BW class size	Catalog	Institutional website	Survey	Catalog and institutional website prioritized	
Is there a required BW exit exam?	Survey				
Research: essay with secondary sources	Survey				
Research paper	Survey				
Research: instruction in research methods	Survey				
Research: annotated bibliography	Survey				
Research: primary research	Survey				
Research: other method	Survey				
Are FYC faculty trained to teach writing?	Survey				
Are FYC faculty required to attend a graduate course or practicum?	Survey				
Are FYC faculty required to attend a preteaching seminar?	Survey				
Are FYC faculty required to attend a grad course OR preteaching seminar?	Survey				
Are FYC faculty required to attend ongoing workshops?	Survey				

continued on next page

	Source 1	Source 2	Source 3	Priority or reconciliation method	Comment
Are FYC faculty required to attend other training activities?	Survey				
Are FYC faculty invited to attend a graduate course or practicum?	Survey				
Are FYC faculty invited to attend a preteaching seminar?	Survey				
Are FYC faculty invited to attend ongoing workshops?	Survey				
Are FYC faculty invited to attend other development opportunities?	Survey				
How many people presented at CCCC in 2010?	CCCC participation list from NCTE				
How many people presented at CCCC in 2011?	CCCC participation list from NCTE				
How many people presented at CCCC total?	CCCC participation list from NCTE				
Basic writing: does the CD include research instruction?	Catalog				
Basic writing: does the CD include argumentation instruction?	Catalog				
Basic writing: does the CD include rhetorical instruction?	Catalog				

continued on next page

	Source 1	Source 2	Source 3	Priority or reconciliation method	Comment
Basic writing: does the CD include writing process methodologies?	Catalog				
Basic writing: what is the identified topic of the course?	Catalog				
Basic writing: does the CD include evidence of reading instruction?	Catalog				
Basic writing: does the course description reference critical thinking?	Catalog				
Basic writing: does the CD specify grammar instruction?	Catalog				
Basic writing: does the CD reference instruction in "fundamentals"?	Catalog				
Basic writing: does the CD reference a tutorial component?	Catalog				
Basic writing: does BW course give credit toward the degree?	Catalog				

APPENDIX E
Sample List

University of South Alabama
Troy University
Alabama A&M University
Jacksonville State University
University of North Alabama
University of Alaska Anchorage
Northern Arizona University
University of Arkansas at Little Rock
Southern Arkansas University
University of Arkansas at Monticello
California State University, San
  Bernardino
California Polytechnic State
  University, San Luis Obispo
California Polytechnic State
  University, Pomona
California State University,
  Northridge
California State University, Long
  Beach
California State University,
  Monterey Bay
California State University,
  Stanislaus
University of Northern Colorado
Colorado Mesa University
University of Central Florida
New College of Florida
Georgia Southern University
Armstrong Atlantic State University
North Georgia College and State
  University
Georgia Southwestern State
  University
Fort Valley State University
Lewis-Clark State College

Illinois State University
Eastern Illinois University
Southern Illinois University,
  Carbondale
University of Illinois at Springfield
Ball State University
Indiana State University
Indiana University, South Bend
Indiana University, Northwest
Fort Hays State University
Grambling State University
University of Maine at Presque Isle
Salisbury University
Salem State University
Framingham State University
Westfield State University
Grand Valley State University
University of Michigan, Flint
Lake Superior State University
St. Cloud State University
Winona State University
Mississippi Valley State University
Mississippi University for Women
Missouri Western State University
Truman State University
Lincoln University
Montana Tech
University of Nebraska at Kearny
Chadron State College
Wayne State College
Nevada State College
Montclair State University
Thomas Edison State University
The College of New Jersey
Rowan University

DOI: 10.7330/9781607326397.c011

William Paterson University

CUNY Hunter College

SUNY Buffalo State

SUNY Purchase College

CUNY Medgar Evers College

SUNY at Fredonia

CUNY Lehman College

SUNY Empire State College

SUNY Cobleskill

East Carolina University

University of North Carolina Wilmington

North Carolina Central University

Fayetteville State University

Elizabeth City State University

Mayville State University

Dickinson State University

Southwestern Oklahoma State University

University of Science and Arts of Oklahoma

Southern Oregon University

Eastern Oregon University

Clarion University of Pennsylvania

California University of Pennsylvania

Lock Haven University of Pennsylvania

University of Pittsburgh, Greensburg

Cheyney University of Pennsylvania

University of South Carolina Upstate

South Carolina State University

The Citadel

Black Hills State University

Tennessee Technological University

University of Tennessee, Martin

Austin Peay State University

University of North Texas

University of Texas at Dallas

Texas A&M University, Corpus Christi

University of Houston, Clear Lake

Texas A&M International University

Sul Ross State University

James Madison University

George Mason University

Virginia State University

Eastern Washington University

Fairmont State University

University of Wisconsin, Parkside

University of Wisconsin, Platteville

REFERENCES

Abbott, Andrew Delano. 2004. *Methods of Discovery: Heuristics for the Social Sciences.* New York: W. W. Norton.

Addison, Joanne, and Sharon James McGee. 2010. "Writing in High School/Writing in College: Research Trends and Future Directions." *College Composition and Communication* 62 (1): 147–79.

Adler-Kassner, Linda. 2008. *The Activist WPA: Changing Stories about Writing and Writers.* Logan: Utah State University Press.

Adler-Kassner, Linda. 2012. "The Companies We Keep *or* the Companies We Would Like to Keep: Strategies and Tactics in Challenging Times." *WPA: Writing Program Administration* 36 (1): 119–40.

Adler-Kassner, Linda, and Peggy O'Neill. 2010. *Reframing Writing Assessment to Improve Teaching and Learning.* Logan: Utah State University Press.

Alabama Agricultural and Mechanical University. 2008. *Undergraduate Bulletin 2008–2011.* Normal, AL: Alabama Agricultural and Mechanical University.

American Association of State Colleges and Universities. 2010. *Advocacy, Leadership, and Service: AASCU in 2010.* Washington, DC: American Association of State Colleges and Universities.

American Association of State Colleges and Universities. 2014. *AASCU 2013: Influencing American Public Higher Education.* Washington, DC: American Association of State Colleges and Universities.

American Association of State Colleges and Universities. n.d. "Strategic Plan: Governing Ideas." Accessed January 27, 2012. AASCU.org.

American Association of University Professors (AAUP). 2013. *Trends in Faculty Employment Status, 1975–2011.* Washington, DC: AAUP.

American Historical Association. 2007. "Who Is Teaching in US College Classrooms? A Coalition on the Academic Workforce Study of Undergraduate Faculty (1999)." Accessed July 8, 2013. https://www.historians.org/caw/cawreport.htm.

Amorose, Tom. 2000. "WPA Work at the Small College: Re-imagining Power and Making the Small College Visible." *WPA: Writing Program Administration* 23 (3): 85–94.

Anderson, Judith H., and Christine R. Farris. 2007. *Integrating Literature and Writing Instruction.* New York: MLA.

Anson, Chris. 1988. "Toward a Multidimensional Model of Writing in the Academic Disciplines." In *Advances in Writing Research Vol 2: Writing in Academic Disciplines,* edited by David Joliffe, 1–33. Norwood, NJ: Ablex.

Aronson, Anne, and Craig Hansen. 2002. "A Field of Dreams." In *A Field of Dreams,* edited by Peggy O'Neill, Angela Crow, and Larry W. Burton, 50–61. Logan: Utah State University Press.

Association of Departments of English (ADE). 2009. "Ensuring the Quality of Undergraduate Programs in English and Foreign Languages: MLA Recommendations on Staffing." New York: MLA.

Association of Departments of English Ad Hoc Committee on Staffing. 2008. *Education in the Balance: A Report on the Academic Workforce in English.* New York: Modern Language Association and the Association of Department Chairs of English.

DOI: 10.7330/9781607326397.c012

Astin, Alexander W. 1993. *What Matters in College? Four Critical Years Revisited*. Jossey-Bass Higher and Adult Education Series. 1st ed. San Francisco, CA: Jossey-Bass.

Austin Peay State College. 2011. "2010–2011 Bulletin." www.apsu.edu/registrar/bulletins.

Austin Peay State College. n.d. "General Education Outcomes for Communication." Accessed May 24, 2012. www.apsu.edu/governance/general-education-outcomes -communication.

Balester, Valerie, and James C. McDonald. 2001. "A View of Status and Working Conditions: Relations between Writing Program and Writing Center Directors." *WPA: Writing Program Administration* 24 (3): 59–82.

Ball State University. 2011a. "English Department: ENG 103 Course Description." Accessed October 13, 2011. http://cms.bsu.edu/academics/collegesanddepartments/english /forcurrentstudents/writingprogram/courses/103.

Ball State University. 2011b. *Undergraduate Catalog 2011–2012*. Muncie, IA: Ball State University.

Balzhiser, Deborah, and Susan H. McLeod. 2010. "The Undergraduate Writing Major: What Is It? What Should It Be?" *College Composition and Communication* 61 (3): 415–33.

Barbett, Samuel, and Roslyn A. Korb. 1997. *Current Funds, Revenues, and Expenditures of Institutions of Higher Education: Fiscal Years 1987 through 1995*. Washington, DC: National Center for Educational Statistics.

Bartholomae, David. 1989. "Freshman English, Composition and CCCC." *College Composition and Communication* 40 (1): 38–50. http://dx.doi.org/10.2307/358179.

Bartholomae, David. 2000. "Composition, 1900–2000." *PMLA* 115 (7): 1950–54. http://dx .doi.org/10.2307/463613.

Bartholomae, David. 2011. "Highlights from the ADE Survey of Staffing Patterns in English." *Pedagogy* 11 (1): 7–32. http://dx.doi.org/10.1215/15314200-2010-012.

Barton, Andrew, and Christiane Donahue. 2009. "Multiple Assessments of a First-Year Seminar Pilot." *JGE: Journal of General Education* 58 (4): 259–78. http://dx.doi.org /10.1353/jge.0.0051.

Bazerman, Charles. 1995. "Response: Curricular Responsibilities and Professional Definition." In *Reconceiving Writing, Rethinking Writing Instruction*, edited by Joseph Petraglia, 249–60. New York: Routledge.

Bazerman, Charles, and Paul Prior, eds. 2009. *What Writing Does and How It Does It*. New York: Routledge.

Beard, David. 2010. "Dancing with Our Siblings: The Unlikely Case for a Rhetoric Major." In *What We Are Becoming*, edited by Joseph Gibaldi and Thomas A. Moriarty, 130–50. Logan: Logan State University Press.

Bedard, Kelly, and Peter Kuhn. 2008. "Where Class Size Really Matters: Class Size and Student Ratings of Instructor Effectiveness." *Economics of Education Review* 27 (3): 253–65. http://dx.doi.org/10.1016/j.econedurev.2006.08.007.

Behm, Nicholas, Greg Glau, Deborah Holdstein, Duane Roen, and Edward M. White, eds. 2012. *The WPA Outcomes Statement: A Decade Later*. Anderson, SC: Parlor.

Bergeron, Katherine. 2009. "The Free Elective Curriculum." Paper presented at the Collegium/College/Kolegium: College and Academic Community in the European and American Tradition conference, University of Warsaw, May.

Bergmann, Linda S., and Edith M. Baker. 2006. *Composition and/or Literature*. Urbana, IL: NCTE.

Birks, Melanie, and Jane Mills. 2015. *Grounded Theory: A Practical Guide*. 2nd ed. Washington, DC: SAGE.

Bishop, Wendy. 1997. *Teaching Lives: Essays and Stories*. Logan: Utah State University Press.

Bishop, Wendy. 1999. "Places to Stand: The Reflective Writer-Teacher-Writer in Composition." *College Composition and Communication* 51 (1): 9–31. http://dx.doi.org/10.2307 /358957.

Bishop, Wendy. 2003. "Suddenly Sexy: Creative Nonfiction Rear-Ends Composition." *College English* 65 (3): 257. http://dx.doi.org/10.2307/3594257.

Blakesley, David. 2002. "Directed Self-Placement in the University." *WPA: Writing Program Administration* 25 (3): 9–40.

Bloom, Lynn Z. 1998. *Composition Studies as a Creative Art: Teaching, Writing, Scholarship, Administration.* Logan: Utah State University Press.

Bousquet, Marc. 2002. "Composition as Management Science: Toward a University without a WPA." *JAC* 22 (3): 493–525.

Bousquet, Marc. 2008. *How the University Works: Higher Education and the Low-Wage Nation, Cultural Front.* New York: New York University Press.

Brandt, Deborah. 2014. *The Rise of Writing: Redefining Mass Literacy.* London: Cambridge University Press.

Brown, Johanna Atwood. 2002. "The Peer Who Isn't a Peer: Authority and the Graduate Student Administrator." In *The Writing Program Administrator's Resource: A Guide to Reflective Institutional Practice,* edited by Stuart Brown, Theresa Enos, and Catherine Chaput, 120–25. Mahwah, NJ: Lawrence Erlbaum.

Bruffee, Kenneth. 1978. "Editorial." *WPA: Writing Program Administration* 1 (1): 6–12.

Buffalo State College. 2011. *Buffalo State College Undergraduate Catalog 2011–2012.* Buffalo, NY: Buffalo State College.

Burhans, Clinton S. 1983. "The Teaching of Writing and the Knowledge Gap." *College English* 45 (7): 639–56. http://dx.doi.org/10.2307/377174.

Calhoon-Dillahunt, Carolyn. 2011. "Writing Programs without Administrators: Frameworks for Successful Writing Programs in the Two-Year College." *WPA: Writing Program Administration* 35 (1): 118–34.

California Polytechnic State University. 2011. *2011–2013 Catalog.* San Luis Obispo: California Polytechnic State University.

Campbell, Lee, and Debra Jacobs. 2010. "Toward a Description of Undergraduate Writing Majors." In *What We Are Becoming,* edited by Greg A. Giberson and Thomas A. Moriarty, 277–86. Logan: Utah State University Press.

Carnegie Foundation. 2011. "Carnegie Classifications." Accessed November 2011. http://www.carnegiefoundation.org/classifications/index.asp?key=805.

Carpini, Dominic Delli. 2007. "Re-Writing the Humanities: The Writing Major's Effect upon Undergraduate Studies in English Departments." *Composition Studies* 35 (1): 15–36.

Chapman, David, Jeanette Harris, and Christine Hult. 1995. "Agents for Change: Undergraduate Writing Programs in Departments of English." *Rhetoric Review* 13 (2): 421–34. http://dx.doi.org/10.1080/07350199509359196.

Charlton, Jonikka, and Shirley K. Rose. 2009. "Twenty More Years in the WPA's Progress." *WPA: Writing Program Administration* 32 (1–2): 114–45.

Coalition on the Academic Workforce. 2012. "A Portrait of Part-Time Faculty Members: A Summary of Findings on Part-time Faculty Respondents to the Coalition on the Academic Workforce Survey of Contingent Faculty Members and Instructors." http://www.academicworkforce.org/survey.html

College Board. 2013. "Trends in College Pricing 2013." https://trends.collegeboard.org/sites/default/files/college-pricing-2013-full-report.pdf.

Colomb, Gregory G. 2010. "Franchising the Future." *College Composition and Communication* 62 (1): 11–30.

Conference on College Composition and Communication. 2010. CCCC Annual Convention 2010 Database of Accepted Individuals. Urbana, IL: NCTE.

Conference on College Composition and Communication. 2011. CCCC Annual Convention 2011 Database of Accepted Individuals. Urbana, IL: NCTE.

Conference on College Composition and Communication. 2015. "Principles for the Postsecondary Teaching of Writing." http://www.ncte.org/cccc/resources/positions/postsecondarywriting. Urbana, IL: NCTE.

Connors, Robert J., and Andrea A. Lunsford. 1993. "Teachers' Rhetorical Comments on Student Papers." *College Composition and Communication* 44 (2): 200–23. http://dx.doi.org/10.2307/358839.

Cooper, Charles R. 1983. "Procedures for Describing Written Texts." In *Research on Writing: Principles and Methods*, edited by Peter Mosenthal, Lynne Tamor, and Sean A. Walmsley, 287–313. New York: Longman.

Council of Writing Program Administrators. 2008. "WPA Outcomes Statement for First-Year Composition." https://www.in.gov/che/files/WPA_Outcomes_Statement_for_First -Year_Composition.pdf.

Council of Writing Program Administrators. 2014. "WPA Outcomes Statement for First-Year Composition." http://wpacouncil.org/positions/outcomes.html.

Council of Writing Program Administrators, National Council of Teachers of English, and National Writing Project. 2011. "Framework for Success in Postsecondary Writing." http://wpacouncil.org/files/framework-for-success-postsecondary-writing.pdf.

Crowley, Sharon. 1995. "Composition's Ethic of Service, the Universal Requirement, and the Discourse of Student Need." *Journal of Advanced Composition* 15 (2): 227–39.

Crowley, Sharon. 1998. *Composition in the University: Historical and Polemical Essay*. Pittsburgh Series in Composition, Literacy, and Culture. Pittsburgh, PA: Pittsburgh University Press.

Cushman, Ellen. 2003. "Vertical Writing Programs in Departments of Rhetoric and Writing." In *Composition Studies in the New Millenium: Rereading the Past, Rewriting the Future*, edited by Lynn Z. Bloom, Donald A. Daiker, and Edward M. White, 75–89. Carbondale: Southern Illinois University Press.

Dadas, Caroline. 2013. "Reaching the Profession: The Locations of the Rhetoric and Composition Job Market." *College Composition and Communication* 65 (1): 67–89.

Desser, Daphne, and Darin Payne. 2002. "Writing Program Administration Internships." In *The Writing Program Administrator's Resource: A Guide to Reflective Institutional Practice*, edited by Stuart Brown, Theresa Enos, and Catherine Chaput, 88–100. Mahwah, NJ: Lawrence Erlbaum.

Diamond, Suzanne. 1999. "What's in a Title? Reflections on a Survey of Writing Center Directors." *Writing Lab Newsletter* 24 (1): 1–7.

Doheny-Farina, Stephen, and Lee Odell. 1985. "Ethnographic Research on Writing: Assumptions and Methodology." In *Writing in Nonacademic Settings*, edited by Lee Odell and Dixie Goswami, 503–35. New York: Guilford.

Downs, Douglas, and Elizabeth Wardle. 2007. "Teaching about Writing, Righting Misconceptions: (Re)envisioning 'First-Year Composition' as 'Introduction to Writing Studies.'" *College Composition and Communication* 58 (4): 552–84.

Dryer, Dylan B. 2013. "Scaling Writing Ability: A Corpus-Driven Inquiry." *Written Communication* 30 (1): 3–35. http://dx.doi.org/10.1177/0741088312466992.

East Carolina University. 2005. "Goals of the Liberal Arts Foundations Curriculum." Accessed May 5, 2012. http://www.ecu.edu/cs-acad/fsonline/as/liberalartsfoundation.cfm.

East Carolina University. 2011. "Writing Intensive Requirement." Accessed April 28. www .ecu.edu.

Eastern Illinois University. 2011. *Undergraduate Catalog 2011–2012*. Charleston: Eastern Illinois University.

Ebest, Sally Barr. 2005. *Changing the Way We Teach: Writing and Resistance in the Training of Teaching Assistants*. Carbondale: Southern Illinois University Press.

Elbow, Peter. 1973. *Writing without Teachers*. New York: Oxford University Press.

Elbow, Peter. 1990. "Foreword: About Personal Expressive Academic Writing." *Pre-Text: A Journal of Rhetorical Theory* 11 (1–2):7–20.

Elbow, Peter. 1995. "Being a Writer vs. Being an Academic: A Conflict in Goals." *College Composition and Communication* 46 (1): 72. http://dx.doi.org/10.2307/358871.

Elizabeth City State University. 2008. *Elizabeth City State University Undergraduate Catalog*. Elizabeth City, NC: Elizabeth City State University.

Elliot, Norbert, Vladimir Briller, and Kamal Joshi. 2007. "Portfolio Assessment Quantification and Community." *Journal of Writing Assessment* 3 (1): 5–30.

Elliot, Norbert, Perry Deess, Alex Rudniy, and Kamal Joshi. 2012. "Placement of Students into First-Year Writing Courses." *Research in the Teaching of English* 46 (3): 285–313.

Enos, Theresa, Shane Borrowman, and Jillian Skeffington, eds. 2008. *The Promise and Perils of Writing Program Administration.* West Lafayette, IN: Parlor.

Ericsson, Patricia Louise Freitag. 2003. "Beyond the Laments, Beyond the Boundaries: Communicating about Composition." PhD diss., Michigan Technological University.

Ervin, Christopher. 2002. "The Writing Centers Research Project Survey Results, AY 2000–2001." *The Writing Lab Newsletter* 27 (1): 1–4.

Estrem, Heidi. 2007. "Growing Pains: The Writing Major in Composition and Rhetoric." *Composition Studies* 35 (1): 11–14.

Estrem, Heidi, and Shelley E. Reid. 2012. "Writing Pedagogy Education: Instructor Development in Composition Studies." In *Exploring Composition Studies*, edited by Kelly Ritter and Paul Kei Matsuda, 223–39. Logan: Utah State University Press.

Farris, Christine. 2013. "The Managerial Unconscious in the History of Composition Studies/What We Are Becoming: Developments in Undergraduate Writing Majors." *College Composition and Communication* 65 (1): 209–16.

Fleming, David. 1998. "Rhetoric as a Course of Study." *College English* 61 (2): 169–91. http://dx.doi.org/10.2307/378878.

Foley, Colleen, and Kate Huber, eds. 2009. "The Intersection of Literature and Composition." Special issue, *Lore* (Spring).

Fontaine, Sheryl. 1998. "Revising Administrative Models and Questioning the Value of Appointing Graduate Student WPAs." In *Foregrounding Ethical Awareness in Composition and English Studies*, edited by Sheryl I. Fontaine and Susan M. Hunter, 83–92. Portsmouth, NH: Boynton/Cook.

Fort Valley State University. 2011. "Course Catalog Fall 2011." Accessed May 20.

Fralix, Brandon, Jill Gladstein, Dara Regaignon, and Jennifer Wells. 2015. "The WPA Census Project." Accessed January 3, 2015. wpacensus.swarthmore.edu.

Framingham State University. 2011. *Undergraduate Catalog 2011–2012.* Framingham, MA: Framingham State University.

Fulkerson, Richard. 2001. "Of Pre- and Post-Process: Reviews and Ruminations." *Composition Studies* 29 (2): 93–119.

Fulkerson, Richard. 2005. "Composition at the Turn of the Twenty-First Century." *College Composition and Communication* 56 (4): 654–87.

Geisler, Cheryl. 2004. *Analyzing Streams of Language.* New York: Pearson.

Geisler, Cheryl. 2011. "Methods Lecture." Dartmouth Summer Seminar for Composition Research, Hanover, NH, August 3.

General Education Committee at California State University, Northridge. 2005. "General Education: Undergraduate Learning Goals and Student Learning Outcomes." Northridge: California State University, Northridge.

George, Diana, ed. 1999. *Kitchen Cooks, Plate Twirlers and Troubadours: Writing Program Administrators Tell their Stories.* CrossCurrents Series. Portsmouth, NH: Boynton/Cook.

George Mason University. 2011. "University General Education-George Mason University." Accessed May 29, 2012. catalog.gmu.edu/preview_program.php?catoid=17&poid=7266.

Georgia Southern University. 2011. *Georgia Southern University Undergraduate Catalog 2011–2012.* Statesboro: Georgia Southern University.

Georgia Southwestern State University. 2004a. "Department of English: Course Outline: ENGL 1101: Composition I." Accessed March 28, 2011. http://gsw.edu/Academics/Schools-and-Departments/College-of-Art-and-Science/Departments/Department-of-English-and-Modern-Languages/Core-Classes/index.

Georgia Southwestern State University. 2004b. "Department of English: Course Outline: ENGL 1102 Composition II." Accessed March 25, 2011. http://gsw.edu/Academics

/Schools-and-Departments/College-of-Art-and-Science/Departments/Department-of
-English-and-Modern-Languages/Core-Classes/index.

Georgia Southwestern State University. 2011. *The Undergraduate Bulletin 2011–2012.* Americus: Georgia Southwestern State University.

Gerber, John C. 1950. "The Conference on College Composition and Communication." *College Composition and Communication* 1 (1): 12.

Gere, Anne Ruggles. 2009. *Initial Report on Survey of CCCC Members.* Urbana, IL: NCTE.

Gere, Anne Ruggles, Laura Aull, Timothy Green, and Anne Porter. 2010. "Assessing the Validity of Directed Self-Placement at a Large University." *Assessing Writing* 15 (3): 154–76. http://dx.doi.org/10.1016/j.asw.2010.08.003.

Gibaldi, Joseph, and James V. Mirollo. 1981. *The Teaching Apprentice Program in Language and Literature, Options for Teaching.* New York: MLA.

Giberson, Greg A., and Thomas A. Moriarty. 2010. *What We Are Becoming: Developments in Undergraduate Writing Majors.* Logan: Utah State University Press.

Gladstein, Jill, Lisa Lebduska, and Dara Rossman Regaignon. 2009. "Consortia as Sites of Inquiry: Steps Toward a National Portrait of Writing Program Administration." *WPA: Writing Program Administration* 32 (3): 13–36.

Gladstein, Jill, and Dara Rossman Regaignon. 2012. *Writing Program Administration at Small Liberal Arts Colleges.* Anderson, SC: Parlor.

Glaser, Barney G., and Anselm Strauss. 1967. *The Discovery of Grounded Theory. Strategies for Qualitative Research.* Chicago, IL: Aldine.

Glau, Gregory R. 2007. "Stretch at 10: A Progress Report on Arizona State University's Stretch Program." *Journal of Basic Writing* 26 (2): 30–48.

Glenn, Cheryl. 2000. "The Last Good Job in America." *Forum: Newsletter of the Non-tenure Track Faculty Special Interest Group* 4 (1): A12–A15.

Glenn, Cheryl. 2008. "Representing Ourselves." *College Composition and Communication* 60 (2): 420–39.

Goen-Salter, Sugie. 2008. "Critiquing the Need to Eliminate Remediation: Lessons from San Francisco State." *Journal of Basic Writing* 27 (2): 81–105.

Goggin, Maureen Daly, and Susan Kay Miller. 2000. "What Is New about the 'New Abolitionists': Continuities and Discontinuities in the Great Debate." *Composition Studies* 28 (2): 85.

Grand Valley State University. 2011. *Grand Valley State University Catalog 2011.* Allendale, MI: Grand Valley State University.

Greene, Nicole Pepinster, and Patricia J. McAlexander. 2008. *Basic Writing in America: The History of Nine College Programs.* Cresskill, NJ: Hampton.

Griffin, Jo Ann, Daniel Keller, Iswari P. Pandey, Anne-Marie Pedersen, and Carolyn Skinner. 2006. "Local Practices, National Consequences: Surveying and (Re) Constructing Writing Center Identities." *Writing Center Journal* 26 (2): 3–21.

Hairston, Maxine. 1982. "The Winds of Change: Thomas Kuhn and the Revolution in the Teaching of Writing." *College Composition and Communication* 33 (1): 76–88. http://dx.doi.org/10.2307/357846.

Hairston, Maxine. 1985. "Breaking Our Bonds and Reaffirming Our Connections." *College Composition and Communication* 36 (3): 272–82. http://dx.doi.org/10.2307/357971.

Hanstedt, Paul, and Tom Amorose. 2004. "The Idea of the Small School: Beginning a Discussion about Composition at Small Colleges and Universities." *Composition Studies* 32 (2): 13–29.

Harrington, Susanmarie. 2005. "Learning to Ride the Waves: Making Decisions about Placement Testing." *WPA: Writing Program Administration* 28 (3): 9–29.

Harrington, Susanmarie, Keith Rhodes, Ruth Overman Fischer, and Rita Malenczyk, eds. 2005. *The Outcomes Book: Debate and Consensus after the WPA Outcomes Statement.* Logan: Utah State University Press.

Harris, Joseph. 2000. "Meet the New Boss, Same as the Old Boss: Class Consciousness in Composition." *College Composition and Communication* 52 (1): 43–68. http://dx.doi.org /10.2307/358543.

Harris, Joseph. 2006. "Deja Vu All Over Again." *College Composition and Communication* 57 (3): 535–42.

Hartzog, Carol. 1986a. *Composition and the Academy: A Study of AAU Writing Program Administration.* New York: MLA.

Hartzog, Carol. 1986b. "Freshman English 1984: Politics and Administrative Process." *WPA: Writing Program Administration* 8 (1–2): 7–15.

Haswell, Richard, and Susan Wyche-Smith. 1994. "Adventuring into Writing Assessment." *College Composition and Communication* 45 (2): 220. http://dx.doi.org/10.2307/359007.

Haswell, Richard H. 2005. "NCTE/CCCC's Recent War on Scholarship." *Written Communication* 22 (2): 198–223. http://dx.doi.org/10.1177/0741088305275367.

Haswell, Richard H. 2010. "Hieroglyphic World: A Review of Five Background Readers for Novice Writing Teachers." *WPA: Writing Program Administration* 33 (3): 104–15.

Healy, Dave. 1995. "Writing Center Directors: An Emerging Portrait of the Profession." *WPA: Writing Program Administration* 18 (3): 26–43.

Hebb, Judith. 2005. "Reenvisioning WPAs in Small Colleges as 'Writing People Advocates.'" *WPA: Writing Program Administration* 29 (1/2): 97–110.

Heckathorn, Amy. 2004. "Moving toward a Group Identity: WPA Professionalization from the 1940s to the 1970s." In *Historical Studies in Writing Program Administration: Individuals, Communities, and the Formation of a Discipline*, edited by Barbara L'Eplattenier and Lisa Mastrangelo, 191–220. West Lafayette, IN: Parlor.

Helmbrecht, Brenda M., and Connie Kendall. 2007. "Graduate Students Hearing Voices: (Mis)Recognition and (Re)Definition of the jWPA Identity." In *Untenured Faculty as Writing Program Administrators: Institutional Practices and Politics*, edited by Debra Frank Dew and Alice Horning, 172–88. West Lafayette, IN: Parlor.

Henderson, Bruce B. 2007. *Teaching at the People's University: An Introduction to the State Comprehensive University.* Bolton, MA: Anker.

Herrington, Anne J. 1989. "The First Twenty Years of Research in the Teaching of English and the Growth of a Research Community in Composition Studies." *Research in the Teaching of English* 23 (2): 117–38.

Herrington, Anne J. 1993. "Reflections on Empirical Research: Examining Some Ties between Theory and Action." In *Theory and Practice in the Teaching of Writing: Rethinking the Discipline*, edited by Lee Odell, 40–70. Carbondale: Southern Illinois Press.

Herrington, Anne J., and Marcia Curtis. 2000. *Persons in Process: Four Stories of Writing and Personal Development in College.* Urbana, IL: NCTE.

Hesse, Doug. 1993. "Portfolios and Public Discourse: Beyond the Academic/Personal Writing Polarity." *Journal of Teaching Writing* 12 (1): 1–12.

Hesse, Doug. 2003. "The Place of Creative Nonfiction." *College English* 65 (3): 237. http://dx .doi.org/10.2307/3594255.

Hesse, Doug. 2005. "2005 CCCC Chair's Address: Who Owns Writing?" *College Composition and Communication* 57 (2): 335–57.

Hesse, Doug. 2009. "Imagining a Place for Creative Nonfiction." *English Journal* 99 (2): 18–24.

Hood, Carra Leah. 2010. "Ways of Research: The Status of the Traditional Research Paper Assignment in First-year Writing/Composition Courses." *Composition Forum* (22).

Horner, Bruce. 2009. "Redefining Work and Value for Writing Program Administration." In *The Writing Program Interrupted: Making Space for Critical Discourse*, edited by Donna Strickland and Jeanne Gunner, 72–85. Portsmouth, NH: Boynton/Cook.

Horning, Alice. 2007. "The Definitive Article on Class Size." *WPA: Writing Program Administration* 31 (1–2): 11–34.

References

213

Howard, Rebecca Moore. 1993. "Power Revisited; Or, How We Became a Department." *WPA: Writing Program Administration* 16 (3): 37–49.
Howard, Rebecca Moore. 2000. "Assumptions and Applications of Student Self-Assessment." In *Self- Assessment and Development in Writing: A Collaborative Inquiry*, edited by Jane Bowman Smith and Kathleen Blake Yancey, 35–58. Cresskill, NJ: Hampton.
Howard, Rebecca Moore. 2007. "Curricular Activism: The Writing Major as Counterdiscourse." *Composition Studies* 35 (1): 41–52.
Huckin, Thomas. 1992. "Context-Sensitive Text Analysis." In *Methods and Methodologies in Composition Research*, edited by Gesa Kirsh and Patricia Sullivan, 84–104. Urbana: Southern Illinois University Press.
Huckin, Thomas. 2009. "Content Analysis: What Texts Talk About." In *What Writing Does and How It Does It*, edited by Charles Bazerman and Paul Prior, 13–32. New York: Routledge.
Hult, Christine, David Joliffe, Kathleen Kelly, Dana Mead, and Charles Schuster. 1992. "The Portland Resolution." *WPA: Writing Program Administration* 16 (1–2): 88–94.
Huot, Brian. 1996. "Toward a New Theory of Writing Assessment." *College Composition and Communication* 47 (4): 549. http://dx.doi.org/10.2307/358601.
Huot, Brian, Peggy O'Neill, and Cindy Moore. 2010. "A Usable Past for Writing Assessment." *College English* 72 (5): 495–517.
Hurley, Daniel J., Thomas L. Harnisch, and Barnak Nassirian. 2014. "A Proposed Federal Matching Program to Stop the Privatization of Public Higher Education." *Policy Matters: A Higher Education Policy Brief.* Washington, DC: American Association of State Colleges and Universities.
Ianetta, Melissa. 2010. "Disciplinarity, Divorce, and the Displacement of Labor Issues: Rereading Histories of Composition and Literature." *College Composition and Communication* 62 (1): 53–72.
Indiana State University. 2014. "Department of English: Welcome." Accessed November 25, 2014. www.indstate.edu/English.
Inoue, Asao. 2015. *Anti-Racism Assessment Ecologies: Teaching and Assessing Writing for a Socially Just Future.* Anderson, SC: Parlor.
Inoue, Asao, and Mya Poe. 2014. *Race and Writing Assessment.* New York: Peter Lang.
Irwin, L. Lennie. 2009. "The Activist WPA in Action: A Profile of the First-Year Writing Program at Eastern Michigan University." *Composition Forum* 20 (Summer). Accessed January 8, 2013.
Isaacs, Emily J. 2008. "After the Fall: Rebuilding a Writing Center." *Writing Lab Newsletter* 33 (3): 5–8.
Isaacs, Emily J. 2009. "Teaching General Education Writing: Is There a Place for Literature?" *Pedagogy* 9 (1): 97–120. http://dx.doi.org/10.1215/15314200-2008-019.
Isaacs, Emily J., and Catherine Keohane. 2012. "Writing Placement That Supports Teaching and Learning." *WPA: Writing Program Administration* 35 (2): 55–84.
Isaacs, Emily J., and Melinda Knight. 2012. "Assessing the Impact of the Outcomes Statement." In *The WPA Outcomes Statement: A Decade Later*, edited by Nicholas Behm, Greg Glau, Deborah Holdstein, Duane Roen, and Edward White, 378–402. West Lafayette, IN: Parlor.
Isaacs, Emily J., and Melinda Knight. 2014. "A Bird's Eye View of Writing Centers: Infrastructure, Scope, and Programmatic Issues, Reported Practices." *WPA: Writing Program Administration* 37 (3): 36–67.
Isaacs, Emily J., and Sean A. Molloy. 2010. "SATs for Writing Placement: A Critique and Counterproposal." *College English* 72 (5): 518–38.
Jakuri, Stephen Davenport, and W. J. Williamson. 1999. "How to Be a Wishy-Washy Graduate Student WPA, or Undefined but Overdetermined." In *Kitchen Cooks, Plate Twirlers, and Troubadors: Writing Program Administrators Tell Their Stories*, edited by Diane George, 105–19. Portsmouth, NH: Heinemann.

Johanek, Cindy. 2000. *Composing Research: A Contextualist Paradigm for Rhetoric and Composition*. Logan: Utah State University Press.

Johnson, Iryna Y. 2010. "Class Size and Student Performance at a Public Research University: A Cross-Classified Model." *Research in Higher Education* 51 (8): 701–23. http://dx.doi.org/10.1007/s11162-010-9179-y.

Jordan, John E. 1965. "What Are We Doing to Train College Teachers of English." *College English* 27 (2): 109–13. http://dx.doi.org/10.2307/373181.

Kalbfleisch, Elizabeth. 2016. "*Imitatio* Reconsidered: Notes Toward a Reading Pedagogy for the Writing Classroom." *Pedagogy* 16 (1): 35–59. http://dx.doi.org/10.1215/15314200-3158605.

Kelly-Riley, Diane, and Norbert Elliot. 2014. "The WPA Outcomes Statement, Validation, and the Pursuit of Localism." *Assessing Writing* 21:89–103. http://dx.doi.org/10.1016/j.asw.2014.03.004.

Kinney, Kelly. 2009. "Fellowship for the Ring: A Defense of Critical Administration in the Corporate University." *WPA: Writing Program Administration* 32 (3): 37–48.

Kitzhaber, Albert R. 1962. "Freshman English: A Prognosis." *College English* 23 (6): 476–83. http://dx.doi.org/10.2307/373210.

Kitzhaber, Albert R. 1963. *Themes, Theories, and Therapy, The Teaching of Writing in College. The Report of the Dartmouth Study of Student Writing*. New York: Carnegie Foundation.

Lake Superior State University. 2011. *2011–2012 Catalog*. Sault Ste. Marie, MI: Lake Superior State University.

Lamos, Steve. 2011. "Credentialing College Writing Teachers: WPAs and Labor Reform." *WPA: Writing Program Administration* 35 (1): 45–72.

Larson, Richard L. 1982. "The 'Research Paper' in the Writing Course: A Non-Form of Writing." *College English* 44 (8): 811–16. http://dx.doi.org/10.2307/377337.

Larson, Richard L. 1994. *Curricula in College Writing Programs: Much Diversity, Little Assessment*. New York: Ford Foundation.

Lauer, Janice M. 2010. Foreword to *What We Are Becoming*, edited by Greg A. Giberson and Thomas A. Moriarty, vii–viii. Logan: Utah State University.

LeCompte, Margaret Diane, and Judith Goetz. 1993. *Ethnography and Qualitative Design in Educational Research*. Waltham, MA: Academic.

Lerner, Neal. 2000. "Confessions of a First-Time Writing Center Director." *Writing Center Journal* 21 (1): 19.

Lerner, Neal. 2009. *The Idea of a Writing Laboratory*. Carbondale: Southern Illinois University Press.

Lewis-Clark State College. 2011. *2011–2012 Catalog*. Lewiston, ID: Lewis-Clark State College.

CompFAQs. 2017. "List of Schools Using DSP." Accessed September 29, 2017. http://compfaqs.org/DSP/SchoolList.

Lock Haven University of Pennsylvania. 2011. *Relationship Among Course, Program, and University Student Learning Outcomes for ENGL100 Composition*. Lock Haven: Lock Haven University of Pennsylvania.

Long, Mark C., Jennifer H. Holberg, and Marcy M. Taylor. 1996. "Beyond Apprenticeships: Graduate Students, Professional Development Programs and the Future(s) of English Studies." *WPA: Writing Program Administration* 20 (1–2): 67–78.

Lowe, Kelly. 2007. "Against the Writing Major." *Composition Studies* 35 (1): 97–98.

Lowe, Kelly, and William J. Macauley. 2010. "'Between the Idea and the Reality . . . Falls the Shadow': The Promise and Peril of a Small College Writing Major." In *What We Are Becoming*, edited by Greg A. Giberson and Thomas A. Moriarty, 81–97. Logan: Utah State University Press.

Lundsteen, Sara W., Alvina Treut Burrows, Robert C. Calfee, James T. Fleming, and Eileen Tway. 1976. *Help for the Teacher of Written Composition: New Directions in Research*. Urbana, IL: ERIC Clearinghouse on Reading and Communication Skills.

Lunsford, Andrea A., and Karen J. Lunsford. 2008. *"Mistakes Are a Fact of Life"*: *A National Comparative Study.* College Composition and Communication 59 (4): 782–806.

Lunsford, Andrea A., and John J. Ruszkiewicz. 1998. *Everything's an Argument.* 1st ed. New York: St Martin's.

Mackiewicz, Jo, and Isabelle Thompson. 2013. "Motivational Scaffolding, Politeness, and Writing Center Tutoring." *Writing Center Journal* 33 (1): 38–73.

Mackiewicz, Jo, and Isabelle Thompson. 2014. "Instruction, Cognitive Scaffolding, and Motivational Scaffolding in Writing Center Tutoring." *Composition Studies* 42 (1): 54–78.

Marshall, Catherine, and Gretchen Rossman. 1989. *Designing Qualitative Research.* Newbury Park, CA: SAGE.

Mauriello, Nicholas, William J. Macauley, and Robert T. Koch. 2011. *Before and after the Tutorial: Writing Centers and Institutional Relationships.* Cresskill, NJ: Hampton.

McKee, Heidi A., and Dànielle Nicole DeVoss, eds. 2007. *Digital Writing Research: Technologies, Methodologies, and Ethical Issues.* Cresskill, NJ: Hampton.

McKee, Heidi, and James E. Porter. 2008. "The Ethics of Digital Writing Research: A Rhetorical Approach." *College Composition and Communication* 59 (4): 711–49.

McLendon, Michael K., James C. Hearn, Christine G. Mokher. 2009. "Partisans, Professionals, and Power: The Role of Political Factors in State Higher Education Funding." *Journal of Higher Education* 80 (6): 686–713. http://dx.doi.org/10.1353/jhe .0.0075.

McLeod, Susan H. 2000. "Writing Across the Curriculum: An Introduction." In *Writing Across the Curriculum: A Guide to Developing Programs*, edited by Susan McLeod and Margot Soven, 1–8. Fort Collins, CO: WAC Clearinghouse Landmark Publications in Writing Studies. First published in 1992 by SAGE, Newbury Park, CA.

McLeod, Susan H., ed. 2002. *Strengthening Programs for Writing across the Curriculum.* Fort Collins, CO: WAC Clearinghouse Landmark Publications in Writing Studies. First published in 1988 by Jossey-Bass, San Francisco, CA.

McLeod, Susan H. 2006. "'Breaking Our Bonds and Reaffirming Our Connections' Twenty Years Later." *College Composition and Communication* 57 (3): 523–34.

McLeod, Susan H. 2007. *Writing Program Administration.* Anderson, NC: Parlor.

McLeod, Susan H. 2010. Afterword to *What We Are Becoming*, edited by Greg A. Giberson and Thomas A. Moriarty, 287–89. Logan: Utah State University Press.

Mejia, Jaime Armin. 2006. "Response to Richard Fulkerson's 'Composition at the Turn of the Twenty-First Century.'" *College Composition and Communication* 57 (4): 738–51.

Melzer, Dan. 2009. "Writing Assignments across the Curriculum: A National Study of College Writing." *College Composition and Communication* 61 (2): W240–W261.

Melzer, Dan. 2014. *Assignments across the Curriculum: A National Study of College Writing.* Logan: Utah State University Press.

Mendenhall, Annie. 2013. "The Historical Problem of Vertical Coherence: Writing, Research, and Legitimacy in Early 20th Century Rhetoric and Composition." *Composition Studies* 41 (1): 84–100.

Mississippi University for Women. 2011. "2011–2012 Undergraduate Bulletin." Accessed May 22, 2012. catalog.muw.acalog.com.

Missouri Western State University. 2012. "Department of English, Foreign Languages, and Journalism: ENG108: College Writing with Research Goals and Objectives." Accessed April 7, 2012. www.missouriwestern.edu/eflj/eng108.asp.

Mitchell, Michael, Vincent Palacios, and Michael Leachman. 2014. *States Are Still Funding Higher Education below Pre-Recession Levels.* Washington, DC: Center on Budget and Policy Priorities.

Moghtader, Michael, Alanna Cotch, and Kristen Hague. 2001. "The First-Year Composition Requirement Revisited: A Survey." *College Composition and Communication* 52 (3): 455–67. http://dx.doi.org/10.2307/358628.

Monks, James, Robert Schmidt, and the Cornell Higher Education Research Institute. 2010. *The Impact of Class Size and Number of Students on Outcomes in Higher Education.* Ithaca, NY: Cornell Higher Education Research Institute.

Moore, Cindy, Peggy O'Neill, and Angela Crow. 2016. "Assessing for Learning in an Age for Comparability." In *Reclaiming Accountability: Improving Writing Programming through Accreditation and Large-Scale Assessments,* edited by Wendy Sherer, Tracey Anne Morse, Michele F. Eble, and William P. Banks, 17–35. Logan: Utah State University Press. http://dx.doi.org/10.7330/9781607324355.c001.

Mortensen, Thomas G. 2012. "State Funding: A Race to the Bottom." *Presidency* (Winter): 26–29.

Murphy, Michael. 2000. "New Faculty for a New University: Toward a Full-Time Teaching-Intensive Faculty Track in Composition." *College Composition and Communication* 52 (1): 14–42. http://dx.doi.org/10.2307/358542.

Murray, Donald. 1968. *A Writer Teaches Writing: A Practical Method of Teaching Composition.* Boston, MA: Houghton Mifflin.

National Center for Education Statistics. 1993. *Table 343: Current-Fund Expenditures per Full-Time-Equivalent Student in Institutions of Higher Education, by Control and Type of Institution and Purpose of Expenditures: 1992–93.* Washington, DC: US Department of Education, National Center for Educational Statistics.

National Center for Education Statistics. 1995. *Table 336: Educational and General Expenditures of Public 4-Year Colleges, by Purpose: 1976–77 to 1992–93.* Washington, DC: National Center for Educational Research, Department of Education.

National Center for Education Statistics. 2010. "Table 198: Total Fall Enrollment in Degree-Granting Institutions by Control and Type of Institution: 1963 through 2009." In *Digest of Education Statistics.* Washington, DC: US Department of Education, National Center for Educational Statistics.

National Center for Education Statistics. 2011. "Table 281: Fall Enrollment, Degrees Conferred, and Expenditures in Degree-Granting Historically Black Colleges and Universities, by Institution: 2010, 2011, and 2010–11." Washington, DC: Department of Education.

National Center for Education Statistics. 2012a. *Digest of Educational Statistics: 2012.* Washington, DC: Department of Education, National Center for Education Statistics.

National Center for Education Statistics. 2012b. *Table 285: Total and Full-Time-Equivalent (FTE) Staff and FTE Student/FTE Staff Ratios in Postsecondary Institutions Participating in Title IV Programs, by Degree-Granting Status, Control of Institution, and Primary Occupation: Fall 1991, Fall 2001, and Fall 2011.* Washington, DC: US Department of Education, National Center for Educational Statistics.

National Center for Education Statistics. 2013. *Table 334.10: Expenditures of Public Degree-Granting Post Secondary Institutions, by Purpose of Expenditure and Level of Instruction: 2005–06 through 2011–12.* Washington, DC: US Department of Education, National Center for Educational Statistics.

National Center for Educational Statistics. 2010. "Table 248: Enrollment and Degrees Conferred in Degree-Granting Institutions that Serve Large Proportions of Hispanic Undergraduate Students, by selected Characteristics and Institution: Fall 2009 and 2008–09." In *Edited by National Center for Education Statistics.* Washington, DC: Department of Education.

National Council of Teachers of English. 1985. "Teaching Composition: A Position Statement." Urbana, IL: NCTE.

National Council of Teachers of English. 2009. "Writing Majors at a Glance." Urbana, IL: NCTE.

National Council of Teachers of English. 2016. "Professional Knowledge for the Teaching of Writing." Urbana, IL: NCTE.

Nelson, Bonnie. 1968. "College Programs in Freshman Composition." *ADE Bulletin* 18 (September): 22–32. http://dx.doi.org/10.1632/ade.18.22.

New College of Florida. 2011. "About Us." Accessed July 27, 2011. https://www.ncf.edu /about/.

New College of Florida. 2012. "New College of Florida—Our Academic Program." Accessed July 26, 2012. www.ncf.edu/our-academic-program.

North, Stephen M. 2011. "On the Place of Writing in Higher Education (and Why It Doesn't Include Composition)." In *The Changing of Knowledge in Composition: Contemporary Perspectives*, edited by Lance Massey and Richard C. Gebhardt, 194–210. Logan: Utah State University Press.

North Carolina Central University. 2011. *Bulletin of North Carolina Central University: University Undergraduate Catalog 2011–2013*. Durham: North Carolina Central University.

North Georgia College and State University. 2011. "Academic Catalog 2011–2012." Accessed May 18, 2012. http://catalog-ngcsu.ung.edu/2011-12%20Undergraduate%20 Catalog/index.htm.

Nugent, Jim. 2013. "A Survey of US Certificate Programs in Technical Communication." *Programmatic Perspectives* 5 (1): 58–85.

O'Neill, Peggy, Linda Adler-Kassner, Cathy Fleischer, and Anne-Marie Hall. 2012. "Creating the Framework for Success in Postsecondary Writing." *College English* 74 (6): 520–33.

O'Neill, Peggy, Angela Crow, and Larry W. Burton. 2002. *A Field of Dreams: Independent Writing Programs and the Future of Composition Studies.* Logan: Utah State University Press.

O'Neill, Peggy, Cindy Moore, and Brian Huot. 2009. *A Guide to College Writing Assessment.* Logan: Utah State University Press.

Odom, Stephanie Marie. 2013. "Literature in First-Year Composition: A Mixed Methods Analysis." PhD diss., University of Texas.

Olson, Gary A., and Evelyn Ashton-Jones. 1988. "Writing Center Directors: The Search for Professional Status." *WPA: Writing Program Administration* 12 (1–2): 9.

Otte, George, and Rebecca Williams Mlynarczyk. 2010. *Basic Writing.* West Lafayette, IN: Parlor.

Parker, William Riley. 1967. "Where Do English Departments Come From?" *ADE Bulletin* 28 (5): 8–18. http://dx.doi.org/10.1632/ade.11.8.

Parsad, Basmat, and Laurie Lewis. 2003. "Remedial Education at Degree-Granting Postsecondary Institutions in Fall 2000." Washington, DC: US Department of Education, National Center for Educational Statistics.

Pearsall, Thomas E., and Thomas L. Warren. 1996. "The Council for Programs in Technical and Scientific Communication: A Retrospective." *Journal of Technical Writing and Communication* 25 (2): 139–46.

Peckham, Irvin. 2009. "Online Placement in First-Year Writing." *College Composition and Communication* 60 (3): 517–40.

Peterson, Linda H. 1987. "The WPA's Progress: A Survey, Story and Commentary on the Career Patterns of Writing Program Administrators." *WPA: Writing Program Administration* 10 (3): 11–18.

Phelps, Louise Wetherbee, and John M. Ackerman. 2010. "Making the Case for Disciplinarity in Rhetoric, Composition, and Writing Studies: The Visibility Project." *College Composition and Communication* 62 (1): 180–215.

Poe, Mya, Norbert Elliot, John Aloysius Cogan, and Tito G. Nurudeen. 2014. "The Legal and the Local: Using Disparate Impact Analysis to Understand the Consequences of Writing Assessment." *College Composition and Communication* 65 (4): 588–611.

Purcell-Gates, Victoria, Kristen H. Perry, and Adriana Briseno. 2011. "Analyzing Literacy Practice: Grounded Theory to Model." *Research in the Teaching of English* 45 (4): 439–58.

Pytlik, Betty Parsons, and Sarah Liggett. 2002. *Preparing College Teachers of Writing: Histories, Theories, Programs, Practices.* New York: Oxford University Press.

Raymond, Richard C. 2010. "Re-placing Lit in Comp II: Pragmatic/Humanistic Benefits." *Teaching English in the Two-Year College* 37 (4): 384–96.

Riley, Terrance. 1994. "The Unpromising Future of Writing Centers." *Writing Center Journal* 15 (1): 14.

Roozen, Kevin, and Karen J. Lunsford. 2012. "'One Story of Many to Be Told': Following Empirical Studies of College and Adult Writing through 100 Years of NCTE Journals." *Research in the Teaching of English* 46 (2): 193–209.

Rose, Mike. 2012. "Rethinking Remedial Education and the Academic-Vocational Divide." *Mind, Culture, and Activity* 19 (1): 1–16. http://dx.doi.org/10.1080/10749039.2011.6 32053.

Rose, Shirley K., and Irwin Weiser, eds. 1999. *The Writing Program Administrator as Researcher: Inquiry in Action and Reflection.* Portsmouth, NH: Boynton/Cook.

Royer, Daniel J., and Roger Gilles. 1998. "Directed Self-Placement: An Attitude of Orientation." *College Composition and Communication* 50 (1): 54–70. http://dx.doi.org /10.2307/358352.

Royer, Daniel J., and Roger Gilles. 2002. "The Origins of the Department of Academic, Creative, and Professional Writing at Grand Valley State University." In *A Field of Dreams*, edited by Peggy O'Neill, Angela Crow, and Larry W. Burton, 21–37. Logan: Utah State University Press.

Royer, Daniel J., and Roger Gilles, eds. 2003. *Directed Self-Placement Principles and Practices.* Cresskill, NJ: Hampton.

Ruecker, Todd. 2011. "Reimagining 'English 1311: Expository English Composition' as 'Introduction to Rhetoric and Writing Studies.'" *Composition Studies* 39 (1): 87–111.

Russell, David R. 1988. "Romantics on Writing: Liberal Culture and the Abolition of Composition Courses." *Rhetoric Review* 6 (2): 132–48. http://dx.doi.org/10.1080/07350198 809359159.

Russell, David R. 1990. "Writing across the Curriculum in Historical Perspective: Toward a Social Interpretation." *College English* 52 (1): 52–73. http://dx.doi.org/10.2307/377412.

Russell, David R. 1995. "Activity Theory and Its Implications for Writing Instruction." In *Reconceiving Writing, Rethinking Writing Instruction*, edited by Joseph Petraglia, 51–78. Mahwah, NJ: Lawrence Erlbaum.

Russell, David R. 2002. *Writing in the Academic Disciplines, 1870–1990: A Curricular History.* 2nd ed. Normal: Southern Illinois University Press.

Saldana, Johnny. 2012. *The Coding Manual for Qualitative Research Analysis.* 2nd ed. New York: SAGE.

Sams, Henry W., C. V. Wicker, Jerome W. Archer, et al. 1950. "Administration of the Composition Course: The Report of Workshop No. 13." *College Composition and Communication* 1 (2): 40–42. http://dx.doi.org/10.2307/355620.

Sasser, Earl L. 1952. "Some Aspects of Freshman English." *College Composition and Communication* 3 (3): 12–14. http://dx.doi.org/10.2307/354564.

Schell, Eileen E., and Patricia L. Stock, eds. 2001. *Moving a Mountain: Transforming the Role of Contingent Faculty in Composition Studies and Higher Education.* Urbana, IL: NCTE.

Schilb, John. 1994. "Getting Disciplined?" *Rhetoric Review* 12 (2): 398–405. http://dx.doi.org /10.1080/07350199409389045.

Schumaker, Arthur W. 1982. "How Can a Major in Composition Be Established?" *JAC* 2 (1–2): 139–46.

Scott, Tony. 2007. "The Cart, the Horse, and the Road They Are Driving Down: Thinking Ecologically about a New Writing Major." *Composition Studies* 35 (1): 81–93.

Scott, Tony. 2009. "How We Do What We Do: Facing the Contradictory Political Economies of Writing Programs." In *Writing Program Interrupted: Making Space for Critical Discourse*, edited by Donna Strickland and Jeanne Gunner, 41–55. Portsmouth, NH: Boynton/ Cook.

Shamoon, Linda K., Rebecca Moore Howard, Sandra Jameson, and Robert A. Schwegler, eds. 2000. *Coming of Age: The Advanced Writing Curriculum, CrossCurrents.* Portsmouth, NH: Boynton/Cook.

Shamoon, Linda, and Celest Martin. 2007. "Which Part of the Elephant Is This? Questioning Creative Non-Fiction in the Writing Major." *Composition Studies* 35 (1): 53–54.

Shuck, Emerson C. 1955. "Administration of the Freshman English Program." *College Composition and Communication* 6 (4): 205–10. http://dx.doi.org/10.2307/355535.

Sideris, Jeremy Brian. 2004. "First-Year Composition Course Descriptions and Writing Program Pedagogy: A Taxonomy." PhD diss., New Mexico State University.

Skeffington, Jillian, Shane Borrowman, and Theresa Enos. 2008. "Living in the Spaces between: Profiling the Writing Program Administrator." In *The Promise and Peril of Writing Program Administration,* edited by Theresa Enos and Shane Borrowman, 5–20. West Lafayette, IN: Parlor.

Sledd, James. 2001. "Disciplinarity and Exploitation: Compositionists as Good Professionals." *Workplace: A Journal of Academic Labor* 4 (1).

Smagorinsky, Peter. 2008. "The Method Section as Conceptual Epicenter in Constructing Social Science Research Reports." *Written Communication* 25 (3): 389–411. http://dx.doi.org/10.1177/0741088308317815.

Smith, Ron. 1974. "The Composition Requirement Today: A Report on a Nationwide Survey of Four-Year Colleges and Universities." *College Composition and Communication* 25 (2): 138–48. http://dx.doi.org/10.2307/357162.

Southern Arkansas University. 2011. Undergraduate Catalog 2011–2012. Magnolia: Southern Arkansas University.

Southern Oregon University. 2011. 2011–12 Catalog. Ashland: Southern Oregon University.

Southern Oregon University. 2011–2012. "University Studies Requirements Guide." Accessed June 2016. https://inside.sou.edu/houses/requirementguide.html.

State Higher Education Executive Officers. 2014. *State Higher Education Finance FY2013.* Boulder, CO: State Higher Education Policy Center.

Steinmann, Martin. 1978. "What's the Real Crisis?" *Profession* 78:9–12.

Tade, George, Gary Tate, and Jim Corder. 1975. "For Sale, Lease, or Rent: A Curriculum for an Undergraduate Program in Rhetoric." *College Composition and Communication* 26 (1): 20–24. http://dx.doi.org/10.2307/356794.

Taylor, Hill. 2007. "Black Spaces: Examining the Writing Major at an Urban HBCU." *Composition Studies* 35 (1): 99–112.

Taylor, Rebecca. 2004. "Preparing WPAs for the Small College Context." *Composition Forum* 32 (2):53–74.

Taylor, Warner. 1929. "A National Survey of Conditions in Freshman English." *Bureau of Educational Research Bulletin* (11):1–44.

Thaiss, Chris, and Tara Porter. 2010. "The State of WAC/WID in 2010: Methods and Results of the U.S. Survey of the International WAC/WID Mapping Project." *College Composition and Communication* 61 (3): 534–70.

Thomas Edison State University. 2011a. *2011–2012 College Catalog.* Trenton, NJ: Thomas Edison State University.

Thomas Edison State University. 2011b. "Syllabus for ENC–101." Accessed April 15, 2011. http://www2.tesc.edu/syllabus/current/ENC-102/syllabus_ENC-102.html.

Thomas Edison State University. 2011c. "Syllabus for ENC–102." Accessed April 15, 2011. http://www2.tesc.edu/syllabus/current/ENC-102/syllabus_ENC-102.html.

Thompson, Isabelle. 2006. "Writing Center Assessment: Why and a Little How." *Writing Center Journal* 26 (1): 33–61.

Thompson, Isabelle. 2009. "Scaffolding in the Writing Center: A Microanalysis of an Experienced Tutor's Verbal and Nonverbal Tutoring Strategies." *Written Communication* 26 (4): 417–53. http://dx.doi.org/10.1177/0741088309342364.

Thompson, Isabelle, and Jo Mackiewicz. 2013. "Questioning in Writing Center Conferences." *Writing Center Journal* 33 (2): 37–70.

Thompson, Isabelle, Alyson Whyte, David Shannon, Amanda Muse, Kristen Miller, Milla Chappell, and Abby Whigham. 2009. "Examining Our Lore: A Survey of Students' and Tutors' Satisfaction with Writing Center Conferences." *Writing Center Journal* 29 (1): 78–105.

Tinberg, Howard, and Patricia Sullivan, eds. 2006. *What Is "College" Writing?* Urbana, IL: NCTE.

Tobin, Lad. 1994. "Introduction: How the Writing Process Was Born—And Other Conversion Narratives." In *Taking Stock: The Writing Process Movement in the '90s*, edited by Lad Tobin and Thomas Newkirk, 1–14. Portsmouth, NH: Boynton/Cook-Heinemann.

Trimbur, John. 1999. "The Problem of Freshman English (Only): Toward Programs of Study in Writing." *WPA: Writing Program Administration* 22 (3): 9–30.

Trimmer, Joseph F. 1987. "Basic Skills, Basic Writing, Basic Research." *Journal of Basic Writing* 6 (1): 3–9.

Tromble, Kate. 2008. *The Higher Education Opportunity Act I: New Reporting and Disclosure Requirements for Colleges and Universities.* NACUA Notes.

Troy University. 2011. "Troy University: A Future of Opportunities." Accessed May 17, 2012. https://www.troy.edu/studentsupportservices/index.html.

University of Arkansas at Little Rock. 2011. *Undergraduate Catalog 2011–2012.* Little Rock: University of Arkansas at Little Rock.

University of Arkansas at Monticello. 2011. *University of Arkansas 2011–13 Catalog.* Monticello: University of Arkansas.

University of Central Florida. 2011. *2011–2012 Undergraduate Catalog.* Orlando: University of Central Florida.

University of Central Florida. 2012a. "Department of Writing and Rhetoric in the College of Arts and Humanities: ENC1101 Course Description." Accessed April 4, 2012. https://www.ucf.edu.

University of Central Florida. 2012b. "Writing and Rhetoric Department: ENC1101 Course Description." Accessed April 4, 2012. https://www.ucf.edu.

University of Michigan–Flint. 2011. "Courses." *In 2011–2012 Catalog.* [Archived Catalog]. Flint: University of Michigan–Flint.

University of Nebraska at Kearney. 2011. *2011–2012 Undergraduate Catalog.* Kearney: University of Nebraska at Kearney.

University of Northern Colorado. 2011. "First-Year Composition Program: About the First-Year English Program." http://www.unco.edu/english/first_year_writing.html.

University of Texas at Dallas. 2011. "2011 Undergraduate Catalog." www.utdallas.edu /student/catalog/undergrad11.

US News and World Reports. 2010. "America's Best Colleges 2010." *US News and World Reports.* https://www.usnews.com/topics/series/america_s_best_colleges_2010.

Vaughn, William. 2004. "I Was an Adjunct Administrator." In *Tenured Bosses and Disposable Teachers: Writing Instruction in the Managed University*, edited by Marc Bousquet, Tony Scott, and Leo Parascondola, 165–70. Carbondale: Southern Illinois University Press.

Wardle, Elizabeth. 2009. "'Mutt Genres' and the Goal of FYC: Can We Help Students Write the Genres of the University?" *College Composition and Communication* 60 (4): 765–89.

Wardle, Elizabeth, and Douglas Downs. 2010. *Writing about Writing: A College Reader.* New York: Bedford/St Martin's.

Weerts, David J., and Justin M. Ronca. 2012. "Understanding Differences in State Support for Higher Education across States, Sectors, and Institutions: A Longitudinal Study." *Journal of Higher Education* 83 (2): 155–85. http://dx.doi.org/10.1353/jhe.2012.0012.

Weisser, Christian, and Laurie Grobman. 2012. "Undergraduate Writing Majors and the Rhetoric of Professionalism." *Composition Studies* 40 (1): 39–59.

White, Edward M. 2008. "Testing In and Testing Out." *WPA: Writing Program Administration* 32 (1/2): 129–42.

White, Edward M., Norbert Elliot, and Irvin Peckham. 2015. *Very Like a Whale: The Evaluation of Writing Instruction*. Logan: Utah State University Press.

White, Edward M., and Leon L. Thomas. 1981. "Racial Minorities and Writing Skills Assessment in the California State University and Colleges." *College English* 43 (3): 276–83.

Wilcox, Thomas W. 1968. "The Study of Undergraduate English Programs: Some Preliminary Findings." *College English* 29 (6): 440–49. http://dx.doi.org/10.2307/374372.

Wilcox, Thomas W. 1969. "More Findings from the National Survey of Undergraduate Programs in English." *ADE Bulletin* 20 (January): 27–28. http://dx.doi.org/10.1632/ade.20.27.

Wilcox, Thomas W. 1972. "The Varieties of Freshman English." *College English* 33 (6): 686–701. http://dx.doi.org/10.2307/374799.

Wilcox, Thomas W. 1973. *Anatomy of College English*. San Francisco, CA: Jossey.

William Paterson University. 2010. *University Core Curriculum Programs SLOS*. Wayne, NJ: William Paterson University.

Witte, Stephen P., Roger D. Cherry, and Paul R. Meyer. 1982. *The Goals of Freshman Writing Programs as Perceived by a National Sample of College and University Writing Program Directors and Teachers*. Technical Report No. 5. Austin: University of Texas.

Witte, Stephen P., Paul R. Meyer, and Thomas P. Miller. 1982. *A National Survey of College and University Writing Teachers*. Technical Report No. 4.

Witte, Stephen P., Paul R. Meyer, Thomas P. Miller, and Lester Faigley. 1981. *A National Survey of College and University Writing Program Directors*. Technical Report Number 2. Austin: University of Texas.

Yancey, Kathleen Blake. 2004. "Made Not Only in Words: Composition in a New Key." *College Composition and Communication* 56 (2): 297–328. http://dx.doi.org/10.2307/4140651.

Young, Richard E. 1978. "Paradigms and Problems: Needed Research on Rhetorical Invention." In *Research on Composing: Points of Departure*, edited by Charles Cooper and Lee Odell, 29–47. Urbana: Southern Illinois University Press.

ABOUT THE AUTHOR

EMILY J. ISAACS is an associate dean for academic affairs at Montclair State University and a professor specializing in writing pedagogy, assessment, and programming in higher education. Her articles have appeared in *Pedagogy, College English, Writing Program Administration, Writing Center Journal,* and *Journal of Teaching Writing,* and she has coedited and contributed to several books, including *Public Works: Student Writing as Public Text* and *Intersections: A Thematic Reader for Writers.*

INDEX

Peterson, Linda, 24, 25
Pfister, John, 170
placement, 20, 163, 164; in basic writing classes, 75–79
placement tests, 19, 45, 79
Poe, Mya, 77, 164
Porter, Tara, 8; on writing across curriculum, 127, 131–32
Portland Resolution (1992), 51–52, 58
"Principles for the Postsecondary Teaching of Writing" (CCCC), 34, 159
process writing, 161; instruction in, 108–13; language of, 113–14
professional and technical communications departments, 153
professors, WPAs as, 57
provost's office, 49
public higher education, 23, 43(n6); funding, 14, 37–40, 42(n5); spending patterns, 40–41
public record, data available in, 9–10

Reframing Writing Assessment (Adler-Kassner and O'Neill), 34
Regaignon, Dara, 52
regional public universities. *See* state comprehensive universities
requirements, 97; FYC as, 86–94; writing, 127–33, 139; writing-intensive, 137–38
research, 17(n6); changing methodologies in, 26–27; instruction in, 99–102, 104–5, 154; personal biases in, 11–12; reportorial vs. rhetorical approaches, 29–30
Research in the Teaching of English (*RTE*) (Herrington), 22–23, 26
research methods: changing, 26–27; coding, 190–92; data analysis, 178–79; data collection, 174–78; institutions studied, 204–5; limitations to, 181–83; sample selection, 170–73; statistics in, 179–80; survey, 184–89; variables in, 173–74, 193–203
research practices, in FYC, 99–102
rhetoric, 47; writing as, 120–21
rhetoric major, 144
Ronca, Justin, 39
Roozen, Kevin, 26
Rose, Mike, 72
Rose, Shirley, 28
Rowan University, 154
Royer, Daniel, 77
RTE. See *Research in the Teaching of English*
Russell, David R., 126–27
Ruszkiewicz, John, 108

SACS. *See* Southern Association of Colleges and Schools
Salem State University, 81
sampling, 27; in Kitzhaber study, 20–21; selection in, 170–73
Sasser, Earl, 20, 42(n1)
SAT, 75, 76
Savage, Gerald J., 147
Schmidt, Robert, 72
school size, 20
scientific writing, 146–47
Scott, Tony, 58; on writing majors, 148–49
SCUs. *See* state comprehensive universities
self-assessment, in writing studies, 164–65
Shamoon, Linda, 46, 144
SHEEOs. *See* State Higher Education Executive Officers
Shirley, Susan, 127
Shuck, Emerson, 20, 53, 68, 78, 103–4
Shumaker, Arthur, on composition majors, 144–45
skills: grammatical, 114–17; writing as, 113–14
Sledd, James, 62
Smagorinsky, Peter, 26
Smith, Ron, 9, 23, 87, 90
South Carolina State University, 81
South Dakota, 97
Southern Association of Colleges and Schools (SACS), 92
Southern Oregon University, 104; communications classes, 88–89
speech classes, 88–89
spending, public higher education, 40–41
staff, staffing, first-year composition classes, 19, 41–42, 45; WPAs and, 56–58
Standard American English, 160
standardization, of syllabi, 67–68
state comprehensive universities (SCUs), 3, 15; as category, 4–5; writing programs at, 15–17, 151–58
State Higher Education Executive Officers (SHEEOs), 14; funding analyses, 38–39
State Objective test, 75
states, 74, 93, 97; higher education funding, 37–39
statistics, use of, 170, 179–81
status, 70; of WPAs, 54–58
status studies, 27–28
Stewart, Donald, 151
Stretch program, 71
student development, writing centers, 139–40
student life, learning centers, 142–43
students: African American and Hispanic, 77–78; writing instruction survey, 28–29

"WPA Outcomes Statement for First-Year Composition" (Council of Writing Program Administrators), 34
WPAs. *See* writing program administrators
"WPA's Progress, The" (Peterson), 25
writing, 11, 22, 27, 33, 45; as discipline, 125, 159–60; in disciplines, 132–33; as mastering of skills, 113–14; as process, 108–13, 161; requirements, 127–32; research, 104–5; as rhetoric, 120–21; and speech classes, 88–89; surveys on, 28–29; teaching, 107–8; teaching about, 103–4; technical and scientific, 146–47
writing across the curriculum (WAC) programs, 29, 125, 157, 158; growth of, 126–27; requirements, 127–30, 137–38, 139; schools with, 134–37
writing centers, 15, 28, 158; administrative placement of, 139–43, 177–78
writing clinics, 22
writing concentration, 151
writing departments, 143, 153–54
writing-intensive (WI) courses, 87; required, 137–38, 139
Writing in the Academic Disciplines, 1870–1990: A Curricular History (Russell), 126–27
writing in the disciplines (WID), 15, 131–33; and directed self-placement, 136–37
writing laboratories, 22

writing majors, 158, 160–61; debates over, 147–51; proponents of, 143–47; schools with, 151–57
writing-process movement, 161–62
writing program administrators (WPAs), 3, 25, 33, 45, 75, 85, 101, 167; and institutional size, 52–53; and instructional approach, 121–23; Portland Resolution and, 51–52; role of, 53–54; status of, 28, 54–58; on training and development, 65–66, 163
Writing Program Excellence certification, 166–67
writing programs, 3–4; administration of, 11, 27, 49; advocacy for, 165–66; calls for unity in, 32–34; debates over, 147–51; departmental placement of, 177–78; maintaining and supporting, 72–75; major studies of, 35–37 (tables); professionalization of, 51–52; surveys of, 24–29. *See also* vertical writing programs; writing program administrators
writing robustness, 137
writing studies, 13, 14, 15, 125, 126, 159–61; advocacy for, 165–66; changes in, 32–33; impacts of, 85–86; research directions, 182–83; self-assessment, 164–65
Wyoming, 39
Wyoming resolution (1987), 52

Yancey, Kathleen Blake, 31
York College, 149